MW00609084

THE DEEP WELL TAPES

Marc Bregman

with
Susan Marie Scavo
and Ellen Keene

Copyright © 2006 by Marc Bregman

We would like to thank the following for permission to use poetry and artwork:
Karla Van Vliet, Cat, Patsy Fortney, Ellen Keene, Kristin Kehler, Christa Lancaster, Laura Ruth and Denise Wilder

Backcover photo by Hannes Otter

All rights reserved.

Printed in the United States of America.
No part of this book may be used or reproduced in any manner whatsoever
without written permission. For information, contact
North of Eden Press, 26 Loomis Street, Montpelier, VT 05602

www.northofeden.com

Dedication

This book is dedicated to my loving wife, Dianne:

For the three decades of love and support
without which I may have wandered far from the teacher's call.

THE DEEP WELL TAPES

TABLE OF CONTENTS

List of Illustrations

Poems by Karla Van Vliet

THE DEEP WELL TAPES

The Headwaters

Spring rising from the deepness
I have dug out. To my lips I bring

what tastes of iron, womb's flood.
I am born here out of near dusk

my breaking over tumbled rock,
cry or song, the brook from my mouth.

It is enough that I soak the ground
boundaries over flowed, what will grow

from my abundance: forest
with its damp moss, trout lily.

Little yellow star to light my way.

Karla Van Vliet

Essence

One of the central goals of Archetypal Dreamwork is to create the capacity in an individual to feel and experience his or her unique essence. Essence is an individual's particular capacity to feel God's love in a direct and personal way, living in the underlying truth of God's existence. This state of being allows an individual to be in conversation with the Divine through an intimate relationship with God.

A person in essence has the heart that can know God. Through the psyche, the potential exists in all of us to have an open doorway to another dimension - God's dimension, the Archetypal Realm. Dreams are a portal to God - as portals, they reveal how God sees each person.

A therapist, one who works with clients and their dreams, can only dare to know what God is showing a client through a dream by standing solidly in his/her own connection to essence.

This book is not about ideas, concepts or beliefs, however helpful they might be. It is not about a technique to pick up and use, nor is it possible to learn to do this kind of work alone or with others merely by reading about it. Essence is the key that unlocks the door of understanding and it can only be "understood" when felt.

Feeling Essence: Just the Beginning

When a person is in essence, Archetypes can relate with her in real and profound ways through her dreams. Archetypes, usually the Animus and Anima, love with infinite patience and terrifying potency. The client can feel that love and even carry it into her waking life. If the client is not yet deeply rooted in her essence, then this feeling may dissipate into memory, concept or idea within a few days. But over time, moving through dream after dream, if the client has a commitment to her process and a willingness to surrender, the death of the ego self allows the experience to grow and deepen. One day, the client will realize she is more often in her essence than not.

When in essence, the center of gravity shifts from the ego/mind/worldly self to the psyche/heart/inner self which allows the client to stay in connection to the Divine. In that connection, needs come from God rather than from the world - external things become less relevant the more a person feels supported from within. Even in the face of hardship and tragedy, a person can stay connected to and supported by the deep love.

The client grounded in essence does not get caught up in making things work according to her own plans or to her struggles to survive, be secure, safe, in control. She can be in the world but not of it.

Being conscious of God, however, does not mean the client is a perfect person or all-knowing. It actually does not mean anything at all. It is simply something felt and experienced - feeling the Divine and the workings of the heart. This is the starting point for the relationship with God. Getting to essence is just the beginning, not the end result. It is one of the goals of the work and on an individual level it means people change a great deal, in ways that are unique to them.

The Dreamwork: Highly Individualized for Each Individual

The very nature of the dreamwork is highly individual because no two clients are alike and no two clients follow the same set of steps, though there may be similarities along the way. The goal is certainly the same: every client is bound for essence and being in essence is an experience that will feel relatively similar to everyone. But the journey leading to the goal is as unique as every individual. Each client's issues are different and the psyche will speak in ways that are meaningful for that specific individual. Therefore, therapists approach each client and each dream from a place of openness and not-knowing in order to allow the individualness of that person to emerge.

For example, being a so-called "good" person can get in the way of what the Archetypes are trying to show a client. This work is not based in values or goodness as a guiding principle. Doing good, loving things in the world is not necessarily helpful in the dreamwork; it depends on how it feels to the client. If what the client is doing in the world creates disconnection, if it perpetuates his isolation from the Divine, then it is a barrier to the Archetypes. Psychological goodness can be such a barrier when it has nothing to do with spiritual connection. The Archetype cannot get in there.

A specific example - a man who was a Christian minister came to the dreamwork because his wife, who was doing the dreamwork, requested he do so. He loved Christ, was happy with his flourishing ministry, and was doing "good" work with people. Then he had this dream:

Dream:
  I am carrying a statue of Christ in four feet of water.

The client was carrying Christ, not being carried by Christ. Through this dream, he was able to see that he felt burdened and overwhelmed by the weight of this statue. The dream allowed him to explore a part of his ego self that he did not want to admit. He thought God wanted him to just accept the burden and that being responsible to God was the way to be with Him. The client's relationship to the Animus, who in this case came as a statue of Christ instead of a living being, was not intimate. Instead, the client was in control, carrying Christ instead of being in a different relationship with him.

To enter into relationship with the Divine in this work, one must be as a child. For an adult who has learned to survive in the world, perhaps even by doing good and right things, it is impossible to be in an intimate relationship with the Animus.

Although the mind naturally wants to generalize in order to apply knowledge, it is a dangerous tendency. Images, people, feelings in dreams cannot be listed and itemized and given generic meanings because each piece of a dream relates to other aspects in ways that are deeply unique and individual to the specific client. To make general assumptions can actually be destructive. For example, while anger is a very intense feeling when it comes up in dreams, a general assumption cannot be made about it. It cannot be assumed anger is always "good" or always "bad." For one person, anger could be poison but another person may need to go through deep anger as a part of his process.

The Responsibility of the Therapist

The job of the therapist is to focus on the material in the client's dreams, to discover what the people, places and things in each dream mean specifically to the client, not to anyone else. The therapist does not assume to know how the Archetypes act in someone else's dreams based on her own relationship and experience with the Archetypes. The goal is to respond to and interpret what is happening in the psyche of each unique individual. It is not the goal to take a dream and create intellectual concepts to cram down the client's throat.

To assume anything at all is to make generalizations such as "this" means "that" for everyone. This creates the danger of getting lost and becoming tricked into blindness by the pathology. Because of this, generalizations are avoided by the therapist through getting associations from the client.

Gathering associations from the client about dreams means playing detective. Associations are what the client feels, thinks or believes about a person, place, image, event or feeling in a dream. The associations are highly unique to each client and they help the therapist and the client decipher the meaning of the dream. One person's association will be wildly different than another person's association, even when working with a similar image.

Of course, an individual psyche will also use the language and symbolism of the collective psyche in dreams, symbolism based on the mythology of our Western civilization. This mythology, however, is only used as a general guideline because, again, the psyche will use a specific symbol for the feeling and meaning it carries for the individual.

An important aspect of working with dreams, especially in the early stages, is that often what seems "bad" to the client, and maybe even to the therapist, is actually good and what seems "good" is actually bad. Things may not always be as they appear in dreams because the client may be fundamentally tricked and in a blind spot. The dreams in this situation will reflect the upside-down reality of the client.

And while there are some symbols that are almost always "bad" or "good," even those are not a hundred percent true in every case. Owls, for example, are almost universally considered evil in the psyche. They are creatures of the night which has to do with the underworld and demons in the generalized perspective. But for at least one client, owls had a more childlike association. He had worked as a young man in a raptor recovery clinic and he felt a heart connection to owls. For this client, the dream presented owls in order to help him access his feelings for them based on his experience, not some generalized universal meaning.

In this process of listening to the specificity of the dream, the therapist's job is to understand and even to feel what a client is experiencing in a dream in order to discern the message of the dream. But this is tricky because what is happening in a dream is often different than what the client believes is happening, especially in a client new to the dreamwork.

For example, in a dream, a woman believed her husband killed another woman, but there was no gun and no body. The husband in the dream could not be convicted of anything because there was no evidence. The dream is addressing some other issue. The therapist will work to discover associations, perhaps by asking questions about the client's relationship with her husband, to begin to uncover the real message of the dream for the client.

The therapist must carefully separate out the truth in the dream from what the client believes is happening. This is particularly crucial for clients in the early stages of the dreamwork because what the client believes is often false. Working to find the associations, feelings and relationships in the dreams help the therapist break any bias of the client to find what the dream is actually trying to say.

Dreams and Religion

A lot of pathology takes place in the outer world in the name of God and many people have religious wounds, real and imagined. Sometimes people get offended in their work based on their religious upbringing or lack thereof. Some people also have profound religious beliefs. The job of the therapist is to focus on the material in a client's dream, not any outside understanding or religious group. The Animus may come as a bartender, Jesus, a neighbor, Bruce Springsteen, Buddha, a famous actor, Jehovah - whatever He chooses based on what He wants to show the client. How the Animus appears in a dream is not meant as a proselytization of a religious belief. Instead, it presents an underlying issue unique to the client that the Animus is trying to illustrate.

In Hands

This is the way it goes:
bird rising through rain,
the sigh of wind-bent grass.

Look, here, your touch,
on my reaching hand.

This too, can be love:
rain falling, the earth
catching it like an open palm.

Karla Van Vliet

Fundamental Aspects of the Three Stages of Archetypal Dreamwork

Stage One

The dreamwork has three stages in which both the focus of the work and the behavior of the pathology are relatively specific. These stages are guidelines only - they may overlap with each other, they may circle around or they may proceed in a relatively linear fashion, depending on the client. Examining each stage, however, is useful in laying out the basic structure of this work.

Stage One

The focus of Stage One dreamwork is to discover pathology. The client learns how to recognize and see, in depth, how pathology works in his life. This is an enormous task because the will of pathology is to shut the client down and limit any possibility of the experience of true self. The focus of pathology is to keep the client asleep, confused, emotionally reactive, unaware of true feelings, lost from God.

Most Stage One clients do not know that anything like pathology even exists. Most people come to the first session for help, support and understanding. Therapists can provide some of this support, but the process of the work is not to look for points of agreements with a person's perception of himself. Instead, in this stage, the challenge is to look for points where the person is in disagreement - with himself, with the Divine, with God's perception of the person as shown in his dreams.

In this moment in history, most people struggle to understand their difficulties based on childhood experience and/or trauma - looking for the proverbial smoking gun to provide a key to understanding dysfunction. While this is valid, it also leads to searching outside the self for the cause or causes of suffering. The real source, however, is not outside, but inside. Pathology is not only within each person, but the person is also an unwitting participant. Pathology, which is not of essence nor is it even part of the self, eclipses consciousness without the person even being aware of it. It can only exist in this lack of awareness, the blind spots.

In the process of Stage One, a client will not know how to change behavior patterns. He may go through blaming a spouse, a parent, himself. He may have few issues in his past to work through or many, such as trauma; he may have been victim or victimizer. No matter what the client faces in his personal history, however, all clients must learn that pathology has entered their psyches and is in control. It has a will, hooks and does not want to be seen.

It is difficult for anyone to accept that negative forces exist inside their psyches. The heart of Stage One work is the client coming to terms with the reality that he is facing a force inside that knows how to take advantage of and manipulate events of his life, but that is in fact a separate agent. Before change can happen, a client must learn how to see pathology, to understand how it controls his experience of reality and what he believes about reality. Pathology controls through behavior and reactions that play off these experiences and beliefs about reality.

The great challenge, again, is that pathology does not want to be seen. When a Stage One client begins to expose his pathology, he will often feel responsible and blame himself. Pathology will feed this telling him it is his fault, that he is indeed responsible, convincing the client that he is the pathology so that he will become identified with it. In this struggle, the client may feel "bad" and/or defensive, may slip into thinking that the therapist is wrong. All of this is simply part of the process of the pathology trying to remain hidden.

Feelings versus Emotions

Part of identifying pathology is seeing how it controls through emotions, thoughts and ideas. In this work, there is a great difference between emotions and feelings. Feelings are how a person truly responds and receives - they come from and are about essence, about what God created in a person's psyche. Emotions, on the other hand, are a mutation of feelings. It is easy to confuse emotions with feelings because any feeling can be an emotion and vice versa: love, anger, shame, joy, passion, fear, hurt, vulnerability, etc. But emotions are how a person protects herself from what she does not want to feel. A person uses emotion to bury feelings like hurt, fear, anger, or even passion, with the belief she needs to do so in order to survive in the world. So, instead of relying on feelings from the true self, a person relies on emotions for guidance.

What further complicates this issue is that emotions can lead to justification of both good and bad behavior. Emotions and the behaviors they engender can be seen as good in the worldly perspective - they may help someone become a great artist, writer or physicist or they may even help a person find God on a spiritual journey. Emotions, of course, can also lead to dark, destructive, violent behavior. But no matter what the outward manifestation of emotions, they are directly in the way of a relationship with God because they block transformation.

Emotions, more or less, bring a person into an external relationship with the outside world and are in service to the survival of the psyche in the world. Even though emotions can help one be in the world (for good or ill), they cannot be transformed. This work is about transformation and Alchemy. Alchemy is a process that requires feeling not emotion. Emotion is a defensive mutation away from feeling that causes an essential quality or ability to reflect the consciousness of the soul to be lost. Alchemy is strictly a part of Stage Two work, but it is important to understand how emotions block Alchemy while feelings allow it.

The consciousness of a soul is buried deep in the bowels of feelings, but those feelings are not completely evolved consciousness. They need to continue to evolve regardless of the stage or degree of evolution present in the soul. In this way, they have the capacity to open a corridor of transformation that leads the essential consciousness to other higher forms of knowing and awareness. Feelings are really the essential self with all its current and past accumulated consciousness. The essential feeling self of a person can vary greatly from her emotional persona.

To shift the center of gravity from emotional life (persona) to feeling life (essence) requires Alchemy. Alchemy demands feelings to be felt as the core to transformation. This transformation leads to the death of the emotional life - the process of Dying to Self. The psychological death of the old self, the emotional self, includes the death of the pathology that controls via the emotional life.

The overarching issue of process (or Archetype) versus pathology is a spiritual one. Pathology is not an aspect of the psyche that has lost its way; it is instead a force, its own agent of control that takes advantage of the lost psyche in order to perpetuate separation from God. Once a person connects with and experiences essential feelings, she has come under the aegis of the Archetype, which is God's agent, and the pathology can no longer manipulate her through the emotion. So, while the difference between emotions and feelings is a psychological dynamic, it has profound spiritual implications.

Tracking Pathology

The tracking of the pathology in all stages occurs through the dreams. Stage One dreams show through different ways, but with great detail, how a client is caught in the pathology. One dream can show a behavior that mirrors the existence of pathology while another dream shows a malaise of belief or an experience of consciousness that is not true. When people take their reality for granted, which is how most people function, the pathology has a distinct advantage because there is no way to contrast a current belief with Archetypal belief. In places in the psyche where there is a lack of consciousness, called blind spots, the pathology hides and calls the shots. A blind spot is simply a repressed feeling, a hole in the psyche. Every hole carries a feeling to be explored and felt. And every feeling leads a client closer to Alchemy and transformation.

Feelings are process: part of the true self. Emotions are pathology: not of the true self. For example, when fear is a core feeling, it often mutates into the emotion of shame. Shame is an avoidance of the experience of that core fear and pain, creating a "safe refuge" from feeling. To create something gives a sense of control, which gives the illusion of safety, and the pathology is right there whispering with encouragement. If a blind spot is a hole in the psyche through which Alchemy can enter, it is also the place where pathology can enter. Through the mutation, when a feeling is not felt, pathology can get inside and take control. But pathology cannot control through a true feeling for this is where God's presence is known.

In a dream, everything is a reflection of a feeling or an emotion and every dream is full of clues as to which is which. Typically, in the dreams of a Stage One client, everything is upside down. Bad things appear good, good things appear bad and there are many deceptions in the dream. Things are not what they seem in Stage One because the client is already tricked by the pathology. The work is to find the trickery, the blind spots, the emotional mutation. Once emotions and feelings are differentiated, a client can learn how he is being manipulated by pathology.

The purpose of this differentiation is not just to discover the pathology and learn about it, but, more important, to begin to separate from it. Even just a crack of awareness between the client and his pathology is a huge turning point. At this point, the client will have a dream in which he sees the pathology personified as separate from himself where previously he was identified with pathology, behaving as pathology, in dream after dream. To separate from the pathology represents a real breakthrough. For example - after dreaming over and over again about being an angry and aggressive man, a client dreams about an encounter with an angry, aggressive man and recognizes him as a demon. The client has worked to own that part of his behavior is driven by mutated emotions - anger and aggression - and ultimately pathology. This dream shows that the client has accepted the reality that he is separate from the pathology.

Breaking through to see the separation of self and pathology is moving into Stage Two work - the work of transformation and Alchemy.

Turning Things Upside Down

Often early in the work, things perceived as good in a dream are often not so good and things perceived as bad are actually good. A client's assumptions about what is good and bad, right and wrong, can be challenged in a dream where the reverse is true. The Animus, in His trickster role, may come in a way that fools the client into confronting her assumptions. If a client does not want a relationship with the Animus, the Animus may come as evil and dark in order to show the client the extent of her projection. If the client projects her own failings onto the Animus, then He may come as a terrible or dangerous man to embody how the client feels threatened when confronting that place in her self.

When the Animus comes in this way, it shows that the client is at war with Him in a fundamental way that needs to change. In coming as the epitome of that projection, the Animus is provoking the client to see her projections in order to facilitate that change.

When a client is at war with an Archetype, she is caught in a type of horizontal thinking. Horizontal thinking includes any intellectual thought that is not related to a deep core feeling or to issues that have been discovered and plumbed in the true self. These kinds of thoughts are usually pathological - but not necessarily because they are right or wrong. They may even be right. The issue is how emotions, not feelings, surround the thinking or the belief.

Of course, sometimes a dark man in a dream is dark - not every man in a dream is the Animus. On the flip side, sometimes there are men in dreams who seem loving and beautiful, who seem to be the Animus but are not. While there is a great deal of confusion about the Animus, who He is depends fundamentally on the individual. Each client's relationship with the Animus depends on her emotional state in relationship to the male principle. Every man in a dream is not the Animus - it is the therapist's job to help the client discern the difference.

Scrubbing
by Laura Ruth

Dream:
> I am in a house at the foot of a beautiful mountain. I am scrubbing the floor, I have to clean now. I hardly notice the family. The family that lives there - a man, a woman, a girl and a boy - is starving.

From Laura:

I just remember how potent this was. To discover that I was putting all my energy into cleaning while the family was starving and the mountain was waiting. I felt there was a man who wanted me to go to the mountain but I had to clean first.

The Cat Dreams
by Ellen Keene

Dreams:

I am standing beside a highway. My cat Merlin is loose and I am afraid he will run off. I am in a boat on the water and Merlin is sleeping on my lap. I feel safe in the boat. I want to protect Merlin from the water. I do not want to let go of him.

I see a tapeworm and blood on the floor near my cat. I am throwing up the same tapeworms and blood. I feel gross.

I am holding Merlin while two angry teenagers are trying to distract him with mice. They are bugging me.

From Ellen:

This drawing is an early attempt to come to terms with the existence of pathology in myself. This was very difficult for me because every time I was confronted with pathology, I felt responsible for it which triggered my nihilism and self-hate all over again.

In one dream, I am clinging to my cat rather than letting go and jumping out of the boat and into the water. My work here is to see the truth of my condition rather than to trying to change it. I am not given the homework of jumping into the water even though Marc tells me that breathing water is part of the initiation to come. Through the drawing I am working to see what I am holding onto. I think it is my beloved cat Merlin and I am trying to digest that he is pathology. He is in dream after dream of my first stage journey and I am beginning to question my attachment to him.

In Prison
by Ellen Keene

Dream:

I am in a prison. A man is chasing me, shooting me with a big shotgun. I am running for dear life, terrified.

From Ellen:

In this drawing I am working with the homework: to turn and face the man and let him shoot me. I am extremely terrified. I would rather run. This is my first attempt to face my terror head on. Though I run in the dream, I practice responding differently in my homework.

These dreams give clear examples of Stage One dreams where the dreamers do not understand the kind of pathological realities they live in. They are accepting things at face value only. Consequently, they have no understanding of the damage that is being done to them.

In the first dream, Laura sees her Divine self, but is powerless to do anything about it. She is almost content to go back and continue that life. The attachment of a person to her pathological life is what makes Stage One work so difficult. The person can be aware of something damning, but is convinced that this is the only way to behave, the only way to live. Even with the awareness of a different choice, there is no choice. Every opportunity that the Archetypes create is thwarted.

It is as if the person can do nothing else but what she is doing, which is to continue the nose dive. The only solution is the wrong solution. At this stage in the work, it does not matter why, for it is too early to be concerned with the underlying issues. It is enough to know that the behavior is a symptom. A person is faced with looking at herself in way that she does not see herself. The value of the work in Stage One lies in revealing to the person the insipid way in which she lives. For Laura, she may have concluded that cleaning may have been perceived as taking care of others in some wonderful way, instead of seeing how it leaves the family in the dream starving.

For Ellen, the pathology is being revealed in all the ways the demon hides as her beloved cat, which is not really so beloved. She is shown that she is attached to something that is causing her harm.

Worrying about the cat is a projection of her own fear onto the cat which is what the demon as the cat wants. For example, she feels safe in the boat with the cat because she is attached to the cat in order to feel safe. The tapeworm part of the dream shows that the cat is a parasite and that the parasite is in Ellie. Stage One clients are often very attached to the very thing that is parasitically living inside of them.

The best aggressive act of the pathology is to hide from the person that it is there, in the same way that a parasite hides from its host. For Ellie, the parasite pathology is hiding as her cat. The tapeworm lives secretly inside while it grows stronger and stronger without the host even knowing it is there. Most people are good people - if they know that something dark is inside, they would want it out. The pathology must hide, it must not be seen in order to continue its hold on the person.

When under the power of the parasite, a person makes wrong choices. In Ellie's second dream, the Animus wants to shoot her. Of course He wants to shoot her because He wants to kill the parasite that is inside of her, the parasite that is not her. Because she is connected to pathology, because she does not understand that the pathology is not her, she runs for her life thinking she will be killed. The pathology's fear of being shot, fear of dying, becomes the client's fear of being shot, fear of dying. But the act of shooting does not kill the person - the person is to live. Part of the blind spot makes a person believe the pathology and even care for it, the way that Ellie cares for the cat in her cat sequence dreams. Anything that may dislodge her from her base of being with the pathology is seen as a threat. The defense mechanism of the pathology, the parasite, becomes part of the host. What the parasite avoids, the host avoids. When the parasite gets scared, the host gets scared. Not alchemical fear, but the fear of the cure. When Ellie flees in the dream, she is running away from the Animus instead of feeling joyful that the medicine has arrived.

The pathology's greatest treachery is that the person's reaction perpetuates its life in the person. The reaction actually feeds the parasite. The very things that a person uses as survival skills are the very things that actually keep the parasitical pathology alive and well. The desire for survival, as with Ellie running from the Animus, is not the person's survival but the desire of the pathology to survive. For when a person is already dead and lost in its grips, the only thing that can be felt is what the pathology feels. Unraveling this blind spot is the goal of Stage One Work.

The Role of the Therapist

It is part of the therapist's job to help the client discern the Archetypal imperative. To differentiate between what is "good" and what is not in a dream is to know the difference between what is feeling and what is emotion for that particular individual. An emotion is part of a pattern that repeats - either in a destructive manner or in a constructive manner. In either case, the emotion is replicated in the client's life and controls him. The client may even believe that best decisions come from this emotional bias, but it is an emotional bias that never changes.

By contrast, feelings always change. Feelings change because they are part of what can be transformed. Feelings are the raw materials of the soul: fear can become essence, inadequacy can become love, vulnerability can become power, anger can become clarity. Feelings provoke deeper dreams because as feelings emerge, a client's ability to transform becomes more possible. Awareness moves more vertically into Archetypal feeling and into the inner life of the subconscious while emotions work in the opposite way. Emotions move more horizontally: anger mutates into rage and nihilism, tenderness mutates into seduction, inadequacy mutates into worthlessness, etc. Emotions cannot transform - they only beget the same belief in a different variety. A client in emotions remains trapped in the horizontal mental way of thinking.

The therapist has clues in discerning what is feeling and what is emotion in a client - through dreams, the client's experiences and even the client's natal astrology chart. Understanding an emotion and being able to contrast it with the deeper feeling helps the client recognize how he is being manipulated by the pathology. Understanding the specific behavior that the emotion engenders helps the client see how the pathology is reflected into the world. From there the client can begin to withdraw his projection from the world and others, and can have a basis for the ownership of his failure to discern the truth about himself. The truth that the Archetypes have brought to the person's awareness.

A word about astrology: The astrological birth chart is an important tool for discerning whether something in a dream is process/feeling or pathology/emotion and can be especially helpful in Stage One when a therapist is just getting to know the client. How the dreamwork specifically works with a client's birth chart will be explored elsewhere.

Walking Along the Shore

The ocean is a thin line from here,
a deceiving distance.
I'm surprised, when I reach out
to brush his face, that my fingers
don't touch skin and lashes,
but scatter clouds and knock down
mountains. The moon came up
full and laden, yellow-white
in the blue dust of eastern sky.
I thought I saw his face
in the water there with mine.
Half crazy, they might have said, or more,
as they watched me wander over sand,
arms spread wide to the deceptive, wind.

Karla Van Vliet

Psyche and Projection

Psyche

The psyche is the vessel that holds the imagination, soul, dreams, feelings, and even the pathology for every person. As the container that holds everything in a person, both positive and negative, it is also the container for the dreamwork journey. It is like an inner room where the theater of transformation can take place.

Psyche, however, is not just a portal - it is also the part of the self that becomes a consort to the Archetypal world. As consort, the psyche becomes imbued with the qualities of that world. It is not enough to simply knock on heaven's door. Preparation and initiation are required to develop the capacity of consciousness to resonate with that world.

Sometimes people have dreams where they are given the gift of entering into the Archetypal Realm before they are fully prepared and they wander around with no idea what it all means. Encountering the miraculous without the capacity to experience it is a reminder of the estrangement of the soul from the Archetypal Realm. It is also a reminder of where the journey leads. Part of the development of the psyche is the preparation for, or in some cases the remembering of, the soul's reality. This preparation/remembering leads to experiencing it and, in this experiencing, a person begins to be in relationship with the Divine.

Psyche is not the same thing as persona, which is a covering of the psyche. Most people have very little knowledge of psyche, of the dimension of the inner life.

Development of Projection

For most people, the essential feeling component is experienced at birth when the soul is fresh from unity and connection with God. A child then projects this experience of Divine being onto his or her mother and father, who are, of course, only human. In addition, a child's feeling component and essential knowingness of God's love are rarely nurtured by the world. Even though there are children who experience a disquieting feeling that something is not right, most children cannot adapt to a world without God. The child self dies and is lost to the psyche. The emerging ego may ignore the loss and not be aware of the problem or it may be aware of this loss on some level and try to do something about it throughout life. Those who are aware possess an underlying desire or unstated passion to find what was lost.

As the child grows, it continues to develop away from the child self that remembers essence and the Archetypal world. Through the "helpful hands" of the pathology, the child adapts itself into adulthood in a manner that can be functional or dysfunctional, depending on the person. This self, which learns to live without the child self connected with the Archetypal world, must die in the psyche if the person desires to find the part of the self capable of knowing God. This death of the "self" is necessary even though it may be the only self the person has known since the loss of the connected child self. The dreamwork provides a structure for this difficult process of disintegrating the ego as well as effectively working to reinstate the connected child self.

Projection, a defense mechanism, develops as part of the process of a person separating from her child self and God. In projection, the neurotic and incomplete inner life is projected into the outer world. Because the outer world, rather than the inner world, becomes the place where a person can experience her conflicts, desires, hopes and dreams, the person is often disappointed. Projection can also lead to the deception that a person is actually living the life she is capable of living. Through projection, the neurotic psyche survives because it covers the reality that there is no real inner life.

What Makes One

One day I opened myself like a jewelry box:
a small ballerina began to dance.

I painted my bathroom green: a cool jungle
in the desert of my home.

Between one mountain range and another:
this great loneliness of separation.

Why do you insist the black lines I scribble
are secrets: as if I would not tell you.

I wonder the distance to the nearest border:
escape involves crossing it, so does salvation.

Chinese plum trees blossom in winter:
red petals like blood against your white white skin.

Once the man I slept beside was struck
by lightning: but it was I who burned him.

Small blue eggs break open:
song emerges from what must release.

Pedro had eyes for a woman with hips,
he could not see me: I did not yet exist.

Far off, beyond the tree lined fields, the yips
of coyotes: yearning melds with night.

If I had words, this is what I would have said:
I am just a little girl, don't hurt me.

The moon rose over the hill:
some things larger than we understand.

Dreams come each night like rain:
images to be hung on a tree like laundry.

He said, I can no longer be here:
words that should have come from my own lips.

It was simple, without her, I did not know myself:
to love was to be no longer.

The tealeaves read I would break many hearts:
not one more than my own.

Karla Van Vliet

FUNDAMENTAL ASPECTS OF THE THREE STAGES OF ARCHETYPAL DREAMWORK

Stage Two

By the time a client is moving out of late Stage One and into early Stage Two, he has begun to both separate from the pathology and to understand that he is not the pathogen. Part of this process is accepting that there is nothing he can "do" about pathology because it is stronger than him. He cannot change it nor can he defeat it. But identifying pathology, how it functions in him and recognizing when he is lost are the crucial tools necessary for the next step of Stage Two work.

Being human means living in relationship. Everyone is in an inner relationship - either with the Divine or with pathology. Learning to see the relationship with pathology and how it works is crucial preparatory work for Alchemy. Alchemy does defeat pathology. It also serves as the building block for the relationship with the Divine.

The primary issue for early Stage Two work is coming into relationship with the Archetypal world. Besides learning about pathology, the early Stage Two client has also begun to acknowledge the reality of the inner life and the Archetypal world. He can move from the emphasis of developing an awareness of the pathology to developing an awareness of the Divine. Getting rid of pathology just to be rid of it does not actually accomplish anything. If a person does not move out of pathology into connection with the Divine, he just moves into a different relationship with pathology in another form.

Clients also begin to work with the difference between sensitivity and vulnerability. Sensitivity, as defined here, is an emotion often confused with feeling. It is the projection of seemingly deep feeling into the world and the idea that the needs which result are just and right. When in sensitivity, a person is often convinced that his emotions are feelings and, since one of the definitions of sensitivity is responsiveness to external stimuli, he is looking for some kind of outer world response. In this way, sensitivity is really a reactive mechanism.

Vulnerability, on the other hand, is a state of absolute inner acceptance of feeling. When in vulnerability, a person can accept his true feelings regardless of any outside triggers or need for response. Being in a state of deep vulnerability means not being concerned with outside stimulus, but is instead deeply self-referential. Through this acceptance and understanding of feelings - through vulnerability - a client is slowly prepared for Stage Two work.

At this stage, the dreams begin to shift away from the Stage One priority of confronting the false self to some thread of inner desire of the client to be other than what he has been. This is both part of the process of becoming aware of the child self or the soul self and it also introduces the problem of free will. The work becomes less about something controlling the client and more about making choices as presented in the dreams themselves. For example, if a client dreams about a cliff where he feels both the desire to jump and the complete terror of falling, he can choose not to jump off a cliff or to jump even though he is terrified. In this example, openness to that terror allows movement into vulnerability and deeper consciousness while not choosing is choosing against the deeper vulnerability.

Accepting the vulnerability, in this example through fear, is an act of inheriting a new part of the self that is necessary for Alchemy. This vulnerability allows for the beginning of accepting the love of the Animus. The feeling that brings the client into vulnerability, whether it is fear or grief or joy, is what transmutes into essence and the capacity to receive love.

It is not enough to say yes to just the Animus, though it is important. The yes must be both for the Animus and to the feelings associated with the yes. Accepting the feelings is saying yes to being in relationship with the Archetypes, to being an active participant in the relationship. Feeling the feeling associated with the vulnerability - the fear in the cliff example - is how to say yes and is Alchemy in action.

The emerging relationship with the Archetypes means that the old self is perpetually under attack. While the transition to the Archetypal world does eventually become seamless as the old self dissolves, any emerging connection with the Divine often involves a painful process of disintegration. Learning to accept the love of the Animus and to feel the feelings that arise means the death of some part of the ego self. This too is part of the choosing. Stage One clients, of course, can and often do have strong visitations of the Divine in their dream life. These dreams strengthen them for the Dying to Self to come. By the time they are in Stage Two, that death has already started to occur.

In core Stage Two work, the disintegration of the old self has allowed the relationship with the Animus to become established. The relationship becomes more direct even if it is not yet profound. This is different than Stage One dreams, where the Animus often behaves in an indirect way or like a trickster. In Stage One dreams, the Archetype may even mirror some aspect of the client's false self to catch the client off-guard, with the intention of giving the client an experience to see and feel something that is still unconscious. Since the pathology is in control and the client does not know it in Stage One work, the Animus will use anything to spark learning. The Animus' independent desire is to create the opportunity for change. He is the Penetrator, the Transformer. With each piece of work, the Animus reveals the truth of the essential self and the feeling life of the client. Ultimately, the Archetype wants a relationship with each person, a rich relationship with levels and layers of meaning.

By the time a client is moving into Stage Two work, the Animus has brought him into a place where he can be taught more directly. He is becoming a vessel, an autonomous self which has separated from pathology. Within that vessel, feelings - not emotions - arise that create the threads for future Alchemy to occur. It is the absolute acceptance of the new feeling threads in relationship to the Archetypes, a deep sense of vulnerability, which creates the basis for Alchemy to occur.

Fear and Alchemy

Fear is a primary part of the alchemical process. A layer of fear with an impersonal quality is embedded in all consciousness, regardless of the personal issue or experience. Typically, this kind of fear is part of the alchemical process and will be transformed into a core feeling. The core feeling then becomes the basis for higher consciousness experiences such as the experience of essence and the beginning of a deeper relationship with the Archetypes as developed by future dreams.

This impersonal fear, which is innate in every person, can become tainted through trauma in childhood. When past memories or unconscious echoes of the traumatic experiences or events become attached to the fear, then this fear leads to the trauma, not to core feeling.

The damage to a person's psyche caused by trauma needs to be accepted. While feelings around trauma may seem an unfortunate detour to naturally occurring feelings such as fear or intimacy or vulnerability, they are feelings that the client needs to feel. Learning to accept feelings is an important, key part of the work. It is even possible that trauma itself can actually aid the journey to be in relationship to the Archetypal connection by focusing the personal feelings repressed in the trauma. In other words, the Archetype can often use trauma to its advantage.

There is a cultural assumption that spiritual gain is less possible for people with trauma, but this work has proven that the opposite is true. If the client and the therapist have the courage to face into the feelings and not be deterred by them, there can be remarkable growth. The client must learn to fundamentally accept and feel the feelings, and to avoid the emotions that may have mutated from the repression of the feelings around the trauma. Thus, the most concentrated form of the wound can become the basis for vulnerability and for the possibility of a deep relationship with the Divine to emerge.

The damage to a person's psyche caused by trauma needs Archetypal intervention. In such cases, since the fear is attached to the trauma, the Archetype may use a different feeling besides fear for Alchemy. In Alchemy, when a person is working through a feeling, that feeling can be the raw material out of which other feelings evolve. For example, if a person does not have trauma and is alchemizing through the feeling of fear, the fear will lead to other feelings. One feeling evolves into another feeling and another feeling if given a chance. The feeling of anger, for example, comes like a storm and passes, evolving into another feeling, the same way the sun emerges after the storm passes. In contrast, emotions do not change or do anything because they are a mutation of the feelings - the way to avoid the feelings. They repress the feelings and the feelings then fester.

An example: a client experiences a relationship with his father in a dream where he feels fundamentally unworthy and reactive, but on a deeper level, the client really feels vulnerable and scared of the father the way a five-year-old child might feel. He feels vulnerable and scared for no other reason than the father is big. This feeling is "inadequacy" - specifically being "in" the "adequacy" of the father. The client is experiencing a five-year-old desire to be loved and supported by the father, to be under his wing, to be in the father's adequacy. (This is true about father love only because love from the mother is more primal - generally being "in the adequacy" of the mother does not occur.)

There is a distinction to be made between the feeling of inadequacy versus the emotion of unworthiness. The client initially feels unworthy and reactive in relation to the father. Unworthiness, here, is a form of shame which makes a client believe he is unworthy. If a therapist encounters such an emotion, she must look to the dream to find a deeper connection to a feeling. Such unworthiness can never lead to healing because it hides or covers up the feeling of inadequacy, which lies on a deeper level. The dream is asking the client to encounter the father from a very young perspective, that of a five-year-old. Most likely, the client has spent his entire life avoiding such a raw, vulnerable place, creating some kind of ego self instead in order to survive in the world. This ego self identity must die in order to open up the deep soul self to the Archetypal father. The dying can accommodate a more youthful experience of encountering the father as the five-year-old in the father's adequacy.

In subsequent dreams, the client may begin to experience love from the Divine Father, a love he had never previously known. Such love on an Archetypal scale has little to do with love often experienced in the world. At the very least, feeling this love will enhance the client's understanding of love so that many priorities about self-perception and what he wants to do may change.

The Process of Transformation versus the Process of Alchemy

Like sensitivity and vulnerability, there is a significant difference between transformation and Alchemy. Stage One clients often experience psychological growth and even new spiritual awareness. They may even consciously integrate their new insights. But this growth does not involve any damage to the ego self.

The next step after growing awareness is through the process of transformation. Transformation is when the client begins to become aware of feeling. It is deeper than Stage One work, but it can also occur without the separation of emotion and feelings. Transformation covers many experiences, but they are experiences in which the ego remains intact. Transformation literally means 'to change the shape or form of,' and in this case it applies to the ego. The form is changed and perhaps strengthened, but it does not die.

Many spiritual paths work to the point of transformation, but transformation is really just a baby step, a necessary one, toward Alchemy. The process of transforming the ego, of strengthening it, is often necessary in the process of the death of the ego. It is important for a person to be strong enough to face the death of the false self. To have a thread of connection to feeling and the Archetypes.

Alchemy, on the other hand requires a death of the ego self so that the new consciousness can emerge. In the original medieval definition, it was the attempt to transmute base materials into gold through a chemical process. Archetypal Alchemy is similar to this - it is the transmutation of the basic material of feelings into deep inner, spiritual change. To the gold of being in relationship with the Divine through feelings. Enlightenment is not awareness of the Divine, it is being in relationship through a feeling experience with the Divine.

In order to be open to Alchemy, awareness of feeling in the process of transformation is necessary in order to access the feelings. Transformation is preparation for Alchemy, for the feelings that emerge are the basic material used in the process of Alchemy.

The Process of Alchemy

Alchemy brings a person into a deeper self which allows for a deeper relationship with the Archetypes. Most people do not have awareness of their soul self. The nexus of the vessel may be the size of a thimble or like a sieve or even nonexistent. The soul self is the vessel that can receive and hold God's love. To be able to do this, the soul self needs to be a substantial vessel. Alchemy works to create and strengthen this vessel.

Alchemy is a process in which inner chemistry is changed on a very deep spiritual level through a specific geometric formula based on inner relationships. The formula:

The 2 becomes 3 becomes 4 becomes 2.

The Two

The first part of the formula is the two - a dyadic relationship. A dyadic relationship in dreams often places the client, in his current state of being, in an oppositional relationship with another element. The other element can be an Archetype, like the Animus or Anima, or a feeling, or even pathology since pathology is externalized in Stage Two:

Client Now	————————	Archetype
Client Now	————————	A Feeling
Client Now	————————	Pathology

The dyadic relationship is always the client in his current state of being and the other. The client's current state of being - "client now" - is not the core of his true self, but where he is in the moment. The dyadic relationship embodies how the client is disconnected from self and challenges him to see and experience the separation.

It is very much like the process of restoring an old house. The process usually requires tearing down the parts of the structure that are no longer sound while keeping the parts that are healthy. Before the new can be built, it is necessary to see and understand the current state of the building.

Creating an oppositional relationship gives the client the opportunity to witness where he is in the state of disconnection from his soul self and the Archetypes. It is a way to show what is no longer sound in the psyche.

For example, a client may have a dream that reflects a dyad with the Anima in which he experiences a newfound relationship with the mother through an Archetypal mother. This dyad allows the client to experience a true relationship, but he is still in his current state of being.

Learning what is not real in the self is the first step of the reclamation process of getting rid of what is not real and discovering what is real. By setting up dyadic, oppositional relationships, the client can begin to separate old and wrong ideas so he can create space for true feelings and ideas that used to be present that he may or may not remember. It can also create the opportunity to birth/rebirth feelings he never had.

This beginning dyadic relationship is not the same as the complete dyadic relationship at the end of the alchemical formula - 2 becomes 3 becomes 4 becomes 2 - because a death of self is not yet a part of the relationship. The initial dyad shows the oppositional relationship and thus begins the alchemical formula. This level can span Stage One and Stage Two work.

The Two Becomes Three

The next step in the alchemical process is when a third point is revealed resulting in the dyadic relationship changing to triangulation - the Two becomes Three. The third point represents something new coming into the client's consciousness, usually the new feeling that has been distilled from separating it from emotion. In a sense, this creates another dyad which is then placed into relationship with the first dyad.

The emergence of a third point in a dream is a positive reflection of the self that results from an Archetypal aspect reflected in a previous dyadic relationship. Once the dyadic relationship is established, acknowledged and felt, the new aspect arises allowing for the dyadic relationship to evolve.

In the case of the dyadic relationship between the "client now" and the Archetypal Anima Mother, when the client feels a bonding with the Archetypal Mother that he may have never felt with his biological mother, he may then have a dream with an abandoned child. That abandoned child is the emergence of the third point. Usually, the client will have a cluster of dreams around the abandoned child that illustrate and explore the feelings associated with the separation of the child and the mother.

This third point of the abandoned child acknowledges the client's wound which produced the separation from his child self. The development of this third point allows the Alchemy to work with feelings in both directions - the feelings associated with the abandoned child and the feelings of bonding with the Archetypal Mother. The client can receive the love and support of the Archetypal Mother at the same time he feels the abandonment of the lost child.

Experiencing the feelings of the abandoned child, as difficult as they are, allows the client to move back in time to when the wound occurred. Then, through the support of the Archetypal Mother, he can feel the anguish of the loss of the mother's love that created the separation. As the client goes deeper into the past, deeper into reclaiming the feelings, the anguish becomes the capacity for redemption. Meaning, in this example, the ability to fully receive the love from the Mother. Of course, the accepting of love can be from any Archetypal figure such as the Mother, the Father, the Anima, the Animus, etc. The reemergence of the child and the beginning of the capacity to rebond with the Mother, in this case the Archetypal Mother, can only happen by going back through the trauma. At the root of the trauma, the true child self is fully resplendent, perfect and alive as before the trauma/separation happened.

At this point, the triangulation occurs when the "client now" can become the child he used to be with the Archetypal Mother. Once triangulation occurs and has been processed, the next step of the alchemical process begins to emerge.

Pregnancy and Children as the Third Point

When the third point is an unborn child, an infant or a baby, the child often represents a new consciousness of the self being born into the psyche. For women who dream of pregnancy, it is the opportunity for new life, a newly birthed form of the self that is gestating within the client that is emerging - not as a mother but as the child.

The Three Becomes Four

Once the client begins to triangulate with and become associated with the third point, the scar of the old self which is part of the "client now" begins to emerge or perhaps has already emerged in the client's consciousness as not part of his true self. It is this part of the self, the part of the client that represents him as he has become, that needs to die. The death of this self, the ego self, in the triangulated relationship is the fourth point - the Three becomes Four.

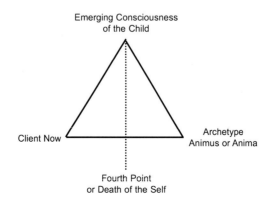

The part of the self that needs to die is not necessarily good or bad, it is just not real. The Archetypes cannot be in relationship with a reformulated self or a transformed self, only with the true soul self. In other words, the Archetypes cannot be in relationship with the "client now," only with the client's emerging essence.

When the old self dies, the "client now" who did not have awareness or feelings of the child self is "cut-off" from the relationship with the Archetype and triangulation is complete. In our example, once the client becomes more associated with the child instead of his old ego self, a dream will come that illustrates the death of that ego self. It will often come as the death of a pathological figure.

One cannot die to self, the self that is enthralled to pathology, if still identified with it. The battleground for this work is not ideas, but consciousness which is fluid and cannot be controlled. Dying to Self is a necessary part of deepening and awakening spiritual consciousness. In the process of transformation, clients will sometimes mistakenly think they are God or the Animus or the Anima as well as thinking they are the demon. But the key to this work is in the relationship to the Archetype. And of course, nothing actually dies in the psyche - the pathological self simply becomes less of a factor because the client now can see through it.

With the death of the old self, the client fully becomes the child in relationship to the Archetype. He is in a new experience of self with a reference point to a deeper self that has no connection with the pathology.

The Four Becomes Two

Once the death of the old self has occurred, then Four become Two. The process has returned to a dyadic relationship, but the client in his current state of being is now able to integrate this new lost part of his soul self which then allows him to be in a new relationship with the Archetype - in our example, the Anima.

Emerging Consciousness ———————— Animus or Anima

In this newfound relationship, the client is now able to receive new learning and new life because the ability to have a relationship with the Archetype is now free to happen. The client comes to a one-on-one relationship with the Archetype from a deeper place.

The Archetypes are Working on Me
by Laura Ruth

Three Dreams:

> I am at a house. I am a boy with a disk, like a painting, with signs of the constellations on it, red. There are other people there. I am very very pleased with my disk. The feeling is joy.

> I am your son. I am the son of the big animal - the bear. I am feeling that this just is.

> Three nights in a row dreaming of me and two others in water, like a pool. I am a baby and the other two are grown up - a man and a woman. They are tossing me in the water, rolling me, and I am fluid like I have no bones, being rolled and turned in the water, back and forth between them. Tumbling. It is ecstatic and sensual - pure experience of movement and being united with the fluidity of movement without bones.

From Laura:

> Homework was around the juicy sensuality, the Archetypes working me in the container, and the boy with the disk referring back to several bear dreams of the fall/winter. And not to be hiding God's love that He gave me, or hide my genius. To accept the good stuff - that there is no such thing as humility of spirit. To take on the joy of the boy, the sensuality of the baby being tumbled.

The boy, the boy, the boy. All three of these dreams are about the boy. The third dream is about the birth of the boy, of Laura being the boy and feeling life without neurosis, without doubt about who she is. In the first dream, the boy, who is Laura, is very pleased with himself. He is autonomous - the *I am that I am* that had been missing in Laura. Without the boy, she gave to others without her self, she was with the gods but not potent. But now - the boy, the boy, the boy.

In the bear dream, the boy is the son of the bear. The bear who is potency, energy, aliveness, passion that becomes compassion. And Laura is the son, obedient and vital, surrendered and assertive, with the other but also with self. This is the classic way the son is with the true Father. It is the nature of the Father to support the son's potency and it is the nature of the boy to love his Father. It is the individuated self - the boy, the boy, the boy. The boy is not someone to relate to, not someone to be in relationship with as with being in relationship with the Divine. The boy, the boy, the boy - is Laura.

The Continuing Cycle of Transformation-Alchemy-Transformation-Alchemy

The process of Alchemy through triangulation occurs every time a client is asked to die to a deeper part of the self in order to have a deeper relationship with an Archetype.

Alchemy, however, is not a process that occurs once. It is part of the ongoing cycle of deepening the relationship with the soul self which can then deepen the relationship with the Archetypes.

When a client moves through real change, his feelings get stronger. Alchemy is the process through which the feeling life deepens and strengthens. After a cycle of Alchemy, once a client becomes more soul connected, from that new place the relationship with the Archetypes can continue to develop. This developing relationship is the result of the Alchemy, but it is not Alchemy. Instead, it is entering into another level of transformation. Entering into another level of transformation prepares the client for the next level of Alchemy. Alchemy then prepares the client for more transformation. The continuing cycle of transformation and Alchemy together forms the fundamental core of this work. Alchemy creates the vessel for God to be received and then the transformational relationship unfolds which leads to more Alchemy and the ability to receive God even more.

Mutuality

Moving through the process of transformation and Alchemy, however, is not the final step. The real learning of this work, the gold after the process of Alchemy, is learning to walk with God from the deep core of true essence. In this walk, the client moves into a relationship which is based on mutuality, where both entities are active participants, each receiving the other.

In mutuality, the soul and the psyche of the client are congruent with God's knowledge of client's soul self. From this place, a person can serve God at the same time as manifesting his true self, so that the inner experience manifests to outer experience.

In Stage Three work, the client has moved to a place where there is less pathology because he is deeper in his soul self. From here, he can move into discovering his true calling. A calling is manifesting the connection with the Divine in the inner growth process to the outer world from a place of connection to the Divine. Of course, the client is still ignorant, for ignorance is the state of human experience. The client will always be the student to the Archetypes, needing to learn more. Even when the obstruction of the pathology is lessened, he still has work to do - it just becomes a different kind of work.

Manifesting a calling is simply allowing what is natural to who the person is, that is his core essence, to manifest in the outer world. The soul self of each person was created for that very thing - his own personal thing whatever it happens to be. The calling is both the very thing that the client wants to do and the very thing that God wants him to do.

Manifesting a calling for a client means doing what God created him to do and doing it from his relationship with the Divine based on mutuality. The idea of "having to obey God" is not mutuality from this standpoint because it is based on the will of another even if it is the will of the Divine. Mutuality is not defined as "obeying God's will." It is being the person that God created. This is why the word *be* is at the heart of *obey* - it is the core meaning of the word. The client manifests who he is from a place of passion which comes from his true self.

Mutuality is the relationship that occurs through the true self of the individual and the Archetypal form in which the Archetypes choose to relate to the individual. This dynamic relationship that develops is clearly presented in the dreams and varies greatly from client to client.

As It Is

There are two ways to live in the world
I have made: walk the fields collecting

dashes of color in my sweaty fist, or dig, dig
the hole I will bury the hunched back of my body in.

Which would you choose, kind sir? The flowers sit
in a vase on the counter, and now in the new darkness,

through the opened window, peepers.

Karla Van Vliet

THE DYADIC JOURNEY
AN OVERVIEW

Dyads as Part of the Process of Alchemy

Alchemy is a process in which inner chemistry is changed on a very deep spiritual level through a specific geometric formula based on inner relationships. The formula again:

The 2 becomes 3 becomes 4 becomes 2

The beginning of the formula and the process of Alchemy is the two which manifests as dyads in dreams. A dyad is the pairing of two things where a relationship is suggested. Dreams often create dyadic relationships as part of the process of reclaiming a feeling from its emotional polar opposite. As such, a dyadic relationship is used to attempt to pinpoint a particular aspect of an individual's psyche as revealed by a particular dream.

There are many possible combinations. For example, two points of a dyad could be the "client now" versus a feeling, or the "client now" versus pathology. The "client now" refers to where the client is in his or her process - often, especially in the beginning, it is the client in his or her disconnected self.

In the early stages of the dreamwork, setting up a dyad is an essential tool in the process of comparing and contrasting: the good guy versus the bad guy, the feeling versus the emotion, process versus pathology.

The mechanism of a dyad as shown in a dream or a series of dreams reflects the current condition of the client. By having the client reflect or contrast one side of the dyad with the other as manifested in daily life using the dream imagery, the underlying issues become clearer and are brought into awareness. When a dyad is created, it is a working hypothesis that can achieve a result by the process of seeing and recognizing. It is important to remember that dyads are not created by the therapist - they cannot be determined and decided upon using the mind. Instead, they come directly from the client's dreams.

While dyads are the first steps of the alchemical process, there are also intermediary steps within the realm of dyads. While the structure of the dyad is established using the client and something else, a dyad is really working to contrast a feeling and an emotion.

There are two kinds of dyads - static and transformational. A static dyad has no chance for the "emotion" element to change into the "feeling" element because the emotion is not a direct mutation of the feeling. Transformational dyads are created when the emotion side of the dyad is a mutation of the feeling side. As such, when the feeling part of the dyad emerges, the emotion side dissipates.

The process of the dyadic journey is that most clients work first with static dyads. The static dyad work, which can be many layered, leads to the transformational dyads where real change can occur. This work, in turn, leads to alchemical triangulation.

Static Dyads versus Transformational Dyads

Static Dyads

The first step for most clients is working with static dyads. A static dyad is created when an emotion is not a direct mutation of a feeling. The client can see and feel the difference between the two opposites, but will not be able to move through that feeling in an alchemical sense. A static dyad offers no opportunity for feeling, therefore change is not yet possible.

Static dyads are most common in Stage One work. They represent the most difficult form of understanding because they do not actually offer any key or clue to the resolution or reconciliation of a psychological or spiritual problem. Instead, they are meant to confuse and disorient the client as they work at breaking the false self reality from which the client lives. Part of the process of Stage One dyad work is to break existing static dyads so that the client can go deeper into the work of transformational dyads.

The key to working with a static dyad is for the client to simply notice the existence of the relationship. The breakdown of the static relationship needs only awareness of how the two sides manifest as behavior in the world. Just knowing and bringing this into awareness is enough to break the spell. The key to moving past the static dyads into transformational dyads, however, is the willingness of the client to go deeper to feel the deeper feelings when the opportunity is presented.

Since a client cannot move into Alchemy through a static dyad, there are no dream motifs associated with them. Instead, static dyads usually work through a parable story that shows a particular complexity in the client's psyche that he simply needs to witness and bring into awareness. The actual pieces of that complexity do not create a way to break pathology.

Static dyads simply give the client the awareness that she is in a maze with no way out. They help the client to see and understand the lies and the lies on top of the lies that she may believe and even experience.

Dream:
> I am with two former teachers at a party by the ocean. I am worried about how they feel about me now that I am no longer doing the work they trained me to do as they expect me to do it. Then suddenly, I am with a man on a boat on land. Impossibly, he makes the boat sail. It feels exhilarating and freeing.

In this dream, the dyad is the emotion of worry the client feels that she will always fail or disappoint others on one side, with the feeling of exhilaration with the Animus on the other. If the client was given the assignment to be in the freedom versus being in her worry, she would be unable to do it. As a static dyad, there is no way for the worry and uncertainty to change into the exhilaration and freedom. The dream sets up a dyad to simply illustrate the split between the two, a chasm wide and deep with no way to the other side.

The illustration allows the client to become aware of how worried and unworthy she feels against the backdrop of being with the Animus. Since she has never felt this exhilaration in her life up to this point, the contrast helps her to become aware of the constancy of her worry and uncertainty. It is likely that she is unaware of this state of being, taking it for granted, instead, as part of the natural course of living. The challenge of Stage One work is for these kinds of beliefs to be challenged and confronted, but not to be changed. The client must become fully aware of her current state of being

- it is impossible to address an issue if the client does not even know that it exists.

In the overview of the psyche, static dyads begin the process of Alchemy by working down from the conscious ego and bringing the true condition of the subconscious into awareness.

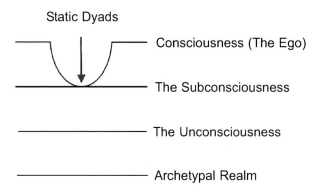

Static Dyads

Consciousness (The Ego)

The Subconsciousness

The Unconsciousness

Archetypal Realm

Once the subconscious dyads are seen and consciousness is opened enough to begin to release feelings, transformational dyads begin to emerge in the dream process. Depending on the individual, this process can take a few sessions or many years.

In working with static dyads, there is little room for error, for if the therapist becomes lost with the client in a static dyad, the client could be lost indefinitely with no real change. The behavior of the client may change in the outer world, but the insipid inner condition will remain the same.

Transformational Dyads

Once a static dyad is reconciled and understood to be a form of consciousness that offers no opportunity for change, the dreams will begin to offer transformational dyads as the client is able to feel deeper into himself. Transformational dyads, by their nature, create a way to break through the client's pathology. When an emotion comes from a repressed feeling and the feeling emerges, then the emotion dies. The polar opposite directly affects the other end of the dyad so that when the two things come together, something actually happens.

Since transformational dyads offer the opportunity for feeling, they are connected to and determined by deeper aspects of the self that often manifest in dreams as children, animals and acute feelings, usually presented in dream motifs. For example, the dyad of fear versus control may be presented in motifs such as the client going over a waterfall or being devoured by a bear or needing to stop and face what is chasing him. If the client can work with the dyad through the motif, then the motif can extend to something else - to what happens when the client goes over the waterfall, is devoured, stops and faces what is chasing him. Examples of transformational dyads are pain versus nihilism, inadequacy versus shame or unworthiness, and fear versus control or security.

In the overview of the psyche, transformational dyads continue the process of Alchemy by working down from the subconscious that was exposed by the static dyads and bringing the true condition of the unconscious into awareness.

Transformational Dyads

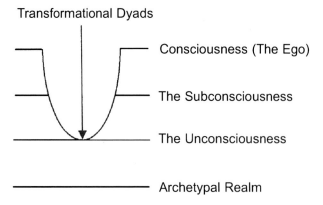

- Consciousness (The Ego)
- The Subconsciousness
- The Unconsciousness
- Archetypal Realm

In a transformational dyad, the two components are more aligned and mostly similar, sharing an approximation of experience. Once a transformational dyad is established and felt, and the feeling aspect of the dyad begins to dissolve the emotion, the process of triangulation can begin to emerge.

Dyads and Triangulation

The dyads change as they are worked - working one static dyad opens up another one which when worked opens another and another and another until they become deep enough for transformational dyads to emerge. Once transformational dyads begin to manifest in dreams, the Alchemy of triangulation can be created, for triangulation is basically two transformational dyads working together.

Alchemical Triangulation

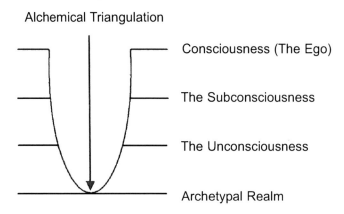

- Consciousness (The Ego)
- The Subconsciousness
- The Unconsciousness
- Archetypal Realm

Triangulation further deepens the process of delving into the psyche by opening up awareness of the Archetypal Realm.

When the Archetypal Realm begins to open for a client, the possibility of deep change, growth, connection and relationship with the Divine also opens.

The Process of Dyads and Triangulation and the Stages of the Work

The dyads take the client deeper into the psyche. Through the learning presented by dyadic relationships based on dreams, the client's awareness is able to change. Each awareness builds another awareness. Unfortunately, the awareness most clients begin with about their true self is incorrect. Part of the work of the static dyads is to help the client unlearn what she believes - what and how she thinks about the self, how she behaves and why, the way she feels about anything, even the way she experiences life.

Everything that eludes the client must be revealed within the backdrop of an awakening awareness of the reality and journey that is waiting just underneath the surface. Once that revealing process is completed, the client will find she is in the Archetypal Realm, resplendent with opportunities and experiences - the place where miracles abound. In the Archetypal Realm, nothing is beyond the client's reach and every obstacle is an opportunity for change and growth. It is only the client's own resistance and personal history that says she cannot move forth.

Transformational dyads are the lifeblood of the dreamwork, but not easily obtainable. The client must not only have awareness, but also a willingness and desire to move beyond the known aspects of her psychological world. Transformational dyads offer an opportunity only if the client is willing to take advantage of them. Free will is the wildcard factor. Change has a psychotic element to it, leading the client into lands and experiences that open the self to feelings and relationships that are usually new. Sometimes these relationships, although filled with love and power, are horrific to the client. She may react by attempting to scramble back to the old self or try to instigate a way to do her work without leaving the ego self behind. These are great challenges of the work because transformational dyads lead the client to the alchemical process in which some of the self will die. The loss of those false selfs is terrifying and requires great inner and outer preparation. Transformational dyads along with static dyads work for this preparation. When the client is ready, the Alchemy will begin.

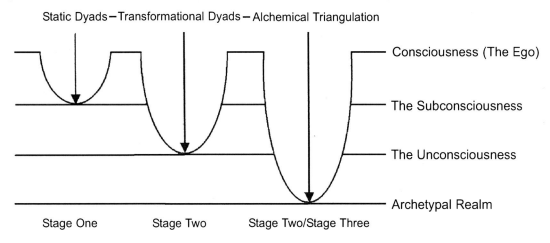

Static Dyads – Transformational Dyads – Alchemical Triangulation

Consciousness (The Ego)

The Subconsciousness

The Unconsciousness

Archetypal Realm

Stage One   Stage Two   Stage Two/Stage Three

In most cases, the alchemical process is not just a Dying to Self but a deeper emergence of relationship where the newfound ego imbued with new relationship and the capacity to feel profound experiences within the psyche is able to become part of the relationships offered. This is mutuality. No longer is the Animus the trickster. He can become an ally to the client - sharing, touching, loving, embracing the client which allows the client in turn to live that life inwardly with a profound desire to live it outwardly as well.

The next step beyond Alchemy is fulfilling a calling specific to the client. Again, a calling is not a duty or a service or a kindness or a value or a judgment. Rather, it is the passionate essence of the soul's desire to manifest its being in the world in the same way the Divine desires for the soul to manifest. Many are called but few are chosen - to be chosen, a client must have this relationship. Serving without the relationship with the Archetypes is not a fulfillment of a calling. It may be a marvelous way to spend a life, but without relationship with the Archetypes, there is no mutuality where the soul self can be free to feel, express and live.

Becoming the World

Then orange light broke over the valley.
Like words, set so long in the territory of the mouth.

Light made sound. Lips seared. I stood.

One must bear the throat's breath, the shiver of leaves
made strange by meaning.

Karla Van Vliet

THE DYADIC JOURNEY
AN EXPLORATION

Feeling versus Emotion

Reclaiming a feeling from its emotional polar opposite through dyadic work is the way to reconnect with the soul self or child self. For clients with deep hurts or trauma, there is usually an inordinate amount of repressed feeling to reclaim. The process of psychological healing for the deeply wounded involves journeying back to experience the feelings that created the wounds. Of course, even people whose wounds are not necessarily associated with traumatic events have repressed feelings. In all cases, repressed feelings need to be acknowledged and reclaimed.

Whatever the specific path to the soul self might be for individual clients, it always leads through feelings. When the true child self emerges in a dream, it is the client's task to feel whatever that child feels in the dream. For example, a client may have a dream in which the child self feels anger. The client may need to feel that anger to reach or work through hurt in order to get to the child self, but the anger or even the hurt is not the final experience. Feelings are steps downward and inward on the way to becoming the child self.

Stage One work focuses, in part, on withdrawing the projection of feeling into the world because projecting unfelt feeling creates and sustains pathological emotion. When a client withdraws projection, the underlying feeling self can emerge, and that emergence is like a breached dam. These feelings are the raw material which allow for the beginning of the alchemical process to transform the psyche. Emotions are not raw material. They are useless to the alchemical process and have to be rigorously separated from the feelings underneath.

Dreams attempt to triangulate feelings that emerge from underneath emotions in a way that allows for Alchemy to occur.

A deep cavity of feeling is often packed with emotions surrounding the feelings. This "packing" is where the contamination or the mutation of feeling into emotion occurs. Since it creates confusion and serves as a way to avoid feeling for the client, it can also cause confusion and avoidance on the part of the therapist as well. In some cases, a client may finally experience a feeling only to have it immediately mutate back into its dyadic emotional counterpart. Learning to stay with the feeling is essential because the client's inability to separate feeling from emotion in his own experience perpetuates the pathology. Thus the dyadic work is a fundamental part of the dreamwork process.

Moving away from the experience of an emotion and into the experience of the feeling underneath is really the secret of this work. In dyads, the work is always to distinguish between an emotion that behaves like a feeling and a feeling that is a feeling.

Paper, Rock, Scissors

In the realm of feelings and emotions, there are inherent rules that make some emotions stronger than some feelings and some feelings stronger than some emotions - just like the game of paper, rock, scissors. When an emotion is stronger than the feeling, then a static dyad is created because the emotion blocks the chance for feeling to emerge. When the feeling side of the dyad is stronger than the emotion, then the dyad is transformational.

For example, fear is more powerful than guilt or shame, so that when a dyad of fear versus guilt is created by a dream, then it is a transformational dyad with the chance for the guilt to be dissolved by the fear. However, guilt is stronger than passion. As such, passion does not offer a way for the guilt to transform and guilt acts as a block to the passion, creating a static dyad.

Fear Dyads

The most powerful of all feelings in the process of Alchemy is fear. As such, whether it is process fear or pathological fear, it trumps all other feelings, always creating a transformational dyad.

All alchemical work involves fear and fear raises the issue of trauma. Any time there is a trauma, the client's fear is real. Trauma changes things because it comes from a real source, a real event that that has to be reconciled. Many people have repressed fear that relates to trauma around memories and events that severely wounded and scarred the psyche. There is a difference between fear that is associated with traumatic events and Archetypal fear that relates to change and moving into a new realm of consciousness.

Archetypal fear is a spiritual opening, a doorway, into Alchemy and into the unknown. Because the mechanism of this kind of fear alchemizes to love, it is an essential element of the alchemical transformational process. Fear is essence in disguise, a gateway to the soul self. Archetypal fear arises in a person's confrontation with God or as the person comes to terms with her own ego death or as she opens up to her creative soul self which can be terrifying.

It is a strange concept to feel terror in the face of spiritual and creative growth, but it is also common experience. For most people, to be different than their self perceptions can be overwhelming. Jung postulated that the process of the ego breaking down to the point where it no longer recognizes itself is a psychotic, therefore terrifying, experience. Through the dreamwork, however, this is exactly the experience necessary to free the self of the suffering it inflicts on itself. Fear, then, is the greatest ally. When the concepts of self and the relationship between that self and the world are changing or about to be changed, the step into the unknown creates a vacuum in which fear naturally arises.

Exploding Mountain
by Ellen Keene

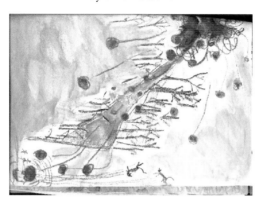

Dream:

> An initiation is taking place on a hill. The earth moves and spews dirt and debris and I am scared. I try to cover my companion. Other people are hit. The force of it throws cats into the air.

From Ellie:

> I had been seeing Marc for ten months when I had this dream. I was just learning to shift my attention from habitually looking outside myself to looking inward. I had no relationship with my inner life because I focused on the outer world for my sense of self. This was a set up that only reinforced my feelings of worthlessness. I was filled with anger. I barely functioned, unaware of how my crippling shame and self-hate polluted everything I attempted. I did this drawing as a way of working with my homework which was: go to the exploding mountain and the initiation will come. This homework awakened deep longing, hope, possibility and fear in me. The promise of this mysterious initiation touched a place inside where I was convinced of my utter worthlessness and it challenged that assumption.

Unworthiness and shame are the hallmarks of the pathology's attempt to repress fear. The fear of something large and spiritually empowering can cause an implosion or an explosion, which are basically the same thing. They are both really implosions in the psyche. The exploding mountain is the release of the energy and excitement that Ellie can only feel as fear. It would be many years before she could claim the prize of the energy. At the time, it was a breakthrough to challenge her to look at her anger and her shame in ways she had never seen.

The opportunity to move through Archetypal fear is presented in dreams in many ways: falling or jumping off a cliff, facing the Animus who appears to be bearing down in a destructive way, confronting a wild animal, drowning or needing to breathe water. All these dream experiences are invitations to move through Archetypal fear. Many in the psychological community are confused by such encounters because the assumption is that the fear is based on some actual event, that there must be a "smoking gun." Instead, it is an invitation for the person to be born into the true self.

When a person has trauma, the feelings related to trauma can be helpful not only in the healing process of the psyche but also in the spiritual reconciliation with the child self. The dreams have a consciousness of intent as a part of Divine will and the Archetypes will guide that process. If the person is not ready, she simply will not have the dreams. The fear repressed around the feelings related to trauma simply makes it more difficult to experience the Archetypal fear of opening up to change and to the Divine.

But, repressed trauma dreams can be mixed with underlying spiritual feelings; for example, the fear of abuse and its counterpart, the fear of the Divine. These two fears appear to have nothing in common, but they are both fear. Fear always indicates something hidden in the psyche - whether is a memory that reveals feelings, however difficult, or the memory of the spiritual self long forgotten. It actually does not matter what is forgotten. Fear is the clue that there is something to be found, something to be discovered, that something has been lost.

There have been writings that have suggested that traumatic feelings do not allow for a spiritual reconciliation with the self. The view is that the traumatized feelings that emerge are related to an attachment dysfunction from childhood that has to be resolved before deeper feelings can emerge and be used for an alchemical process. However, it may actually be possible to use those difficult traumatic experiences to cause an emergence of the soul self. Again, although this process is more challenging for a profoundly wounded person, trauma is not necessarily a barrier to alchemical experience. The dreams guide the process and the therapist to courageously go down those difficult feeling corridors with the client.

Dream:

> My brother, who sexualized me when I was a child, is lying on the bed with a big seductive smile. I do not feel sure he is my brother, but I am completely terrified. I leave the bed in horror.

In this dream, the repressed memory of the client's brother is manifesting in the dream as fear with the Beloved lover, the Animus. The lover is the Animus. He smiles to her in a loving way, but she is still trapped in the memory of her brother. When she was asked to return to the bed as her homework from the dream, she refused, believing she could not face her fear with the Animus until things were resolved with her brother.

In fact, she may have issues and fears with men regardless of the unconscious memory. Fear of men is a common experience for most clients, regardless of childhood experiences. It is also innate to be scared of the Animus because He is so potent and His presence challenges the self to emerge. This challenge triggers resistance in the client based on her particular patterns of self-deception and dubious personality development. The Animus challenges the client, every client, to be utterly and starkly honest.

The choice appears to be to feel the fear and awe of the Divine or to stay with the fear from old memories of the past. But, perhaps the two can come together and serve the same end which is the discovery of what is lost. In this way, fear becomes an awakening agent, for a client is just as afraid of traumatic memories of the past as she is of the Divine. Although it initially seems absurd to be afraid of that which loves us unconditionally, the deepest levels of spiritual relationship and mutuality with the Animus requires an individual to face nothing less then death - the death of the false self. For the Animus sees through all the lies and half truths, leaving the individual to tremble in His seeing, even in the idea of His seeing.

In an individual without trauma, the pathological and feeling material are both in the subconscious and are projected into the world. These issues are not necessarily trauma because there is no defining wound that creates enough of a fear to be repressed. Only when fear is repressed is there trauma in the psyche. The issue with a person with little or no trauma is that the material can be more easily obtained and drawn back into the ego.

In the case of trauma, however, the repression of the fear is so deep that it actually interrelates with Archetypal issues or material.

Sometimes, a therapist may have fears that a difficult dream which opens up traumatic areas will cause damage to the client or that the client will feel suicidal. To the therapist with these fears, this kind of moving through dreams can be frightening and overwhelming. But a client with deep trauma can be transformed and healed in a radical and dramatic way. God's power in this area is surprising. The dreams have a consciousness of intent as a part of Divine will. If a client is unable to take the difficult passage in the psyche through the trauma, then she will not have dreams about the trauma.

When the therapist feels afraid of the process of a client, it could be that the therapist has other work to do in her own process that relates to the work she is doing with the client. The challenge for the therapist with every client is to feel into her own personal experience. If a therapist can do this, then she can descend down the labyrinth with her clients and explore realities in difficult realms. If the therapist is unwilling to feel through her own difficult feelings, then she may have an unconscious desire that aborts the process.

For some deeply wounded clients, there may be years of preparation for such a journey. The client will be strengthened for the passage through trauma by continuous dream experiences of love and empowerment as well as looking at pathological tendencies and trends. Such experiences are not alchemical because the psyche is not yet able to transform due to the feeling material lost in the trauma. Many Stage One clients have extraordinary spiritual experiences which a therapist can mistake as alchemical when they are actually related to strengthening the ego self. Sometimes the person is empowered while the pathological behavior and patterns continue unabated. Such invigoration allows the person to be ready to confront the traumatic event and or to go through a Dying to Self experience with the necessary strength.

Inadequacy Dyads

Not all passages to Dying to Self involve direct confrontation with fear and the flashing knife. Inadequacy is a feeling component opposing unworthiness and can be another passage of change. Here, inadequacy means to be "in the adequacy of the other" - much as a five-year-old boy might feel when he looks to his father. In the adequacy of his father, he does not have to be anything other than a young boy. Vulnerable, small and dependent. At the emotional polar opposite, unworthiness and shame allows a person to define his self without the need to face the father and feel inadequate. He can decide what to do to make himself more worthy and to not be dependent.

Inadequacy requires dependency and a sense of worth outside the self from the Divine. Not co-dependency on another person, but in deep relationship with the Archetypal Father. This relationship with the Archetypal Father requires an individual to have a sense of his child self apart from the world, where he can simply stand in an innocent way and ask for love.

But the asking also means that the person must develop the capacity to receive the love. Receiving is very difficult. While the attention is nice, it is difficult to take in, especially when there is resistance. But a five-year-old boy is without barriers and shame. It is impossible for him to prove himself worthy or to react to the father and rebel. Not yet. The boy has nothing but the desire to be loved and accepted. This moment of pure desire for love and acceptance is the inadequacy or being in the adequacy of the father.

A mother's love informs a child who he is in a deep way and can be more unconditional and primal. But a child does not know the father in this way. Inadequacy is palpable, a rawness and uncertainty that many children experience with their fathers and many adults experience with authority. It is the uncertainty in the moment before the child realizes that the father loves him without him needing to do anything. Before the child realizes the father simply loves him for being. It is a rare experience to encounter in the world, but it is the language of the unconscious.

The emotion of shame serves the individual by keeping him from feeling the incredible rawness and vulnerability of inadequacy and blocks the feelings of the child self. The child self does not feel shame. With the emotion of shame, the original child self vulnerability atrophies or mutates. The opportunity to stand in openness and innocence before the Father and ask for his love is lost.

The child carries the dysfunction in relation to the father into adulthood. To go back through the dysfunction as an adult is to acknowledge the shame as pathological. Once this is acknowledged, the dreams will give the client the key to feeling the vulnerability of inadequacy with the Father and receiving His validation. For example:

Dream:
>   I see a man who I know is my father, though not my biological father, reach out his
>   hand to me. I feel ashamed.

This dream shows the motif of receiving the love of the Father. The client feels shame in the face of the love and support, but if he reached out to take the hand of the Father, the shame could transform into the feeling of inadequacy of being in the Father's care.

Experiencing rawness and need with the Father is often excruciating, depending on the client's experience with his biological father. Often for men, when they stay in that feeling of rawness and need, the inadequacy of the child mutates into shame. From here, it can mutate in different directions - maybe then into independence and then into being accomplished in some field. Or, it can go the other way where the person becomes self-destructive, perhaps becoming an alcoholic. No matter where the mutation takes the client, he is not going to want to return to feeling inadequate because he has become a self-made man. Undoing all the reactions, getting to the shame and getting underneath the shame is part of the long process of Stage One work.

Reclaiming the feeling of inadequacy takes the individual to feeling his boy and then becoming the boy. And that is all it takes. In alchemical triangulation, once the client becomes the child self, then he can be with the Father.

A client can be with the Father without working through the child but it is not necessarily a transformational relationship. For example, a client may feel satisfied that he has a good relationship with the Father without the child self, but it may not be satisfying to the psyche. While the client may say, "But I like my relationship to the Father," it may be very similar to the question, "Why will the Animus not come the way I want him to come?" Opening up to being the boy or girl in relationship to the Father, no matter how it looks, allows the client to be drawn deeper into his feelings. Going deeper may lead into difficult feelings, even trauma feelings, but the client will be led by the Archetype. And in the going deeper, the client feels differently and can reform his relationship with the Archetype. The reformed relationship is often in a dyadic relationship.

Triangulation is a series of changes that brings the client deeper into his feeling self as it kills part of the ego. After the transformation, the client returns to a dyadic relationship with the Archetype, but the relationship is deeper. It is a stepping down. The client relates to the Father in one way and then connects to the child self in a different way by going through the feeling, which in this example is inadequacy. Then the dyadic relationship is reestablished, but at a different level. Each time a client steps down deeper, down into the child soul self, he triangulates through another feeling and more ego dies.

Traditional psychology does not require a person to become the child in and of itself, only to know the child is there. From this place, most people project an idea of the child onto the child self and then try to reclaim it by relating to it. This is not alchemical work. Alchemical work requires a death of the ego self in order for the person to become the child self because there is some material in the psyche which requires this becoming.

Becoming the child is one of the aspects the client works on becoming. Other aspects, however, the client does not become. With the Archetypes, the client becomes in relationship to them. The distinction is important. The aspects that the client becomes, like the child self, are parts of the client's soul self and it involves becoming more his essence. The Archetypal aspects in a client's psyche are of God and the client evolves into a Divine relationship. The client never "becomes" the Animus or the Father. These are two distinct processes.

When a client becomes the child soul self, he may be able to be in a peer relationship with the Anima or Animus. Similarly, to feel the inadequacy with the Father is a way of receiving love from the Father. The client does not become the Father, but is the child feeling or even not feeling the love of the Father.

The relationship with the Father, once established by the boy in the inadequacy, creates the opportunity for a connection that reinforces the existence of the boy. The boy cannot exist without the Father. The Father, however, can exist without the boy because God exists even if the client blames Him for not existing. Without the boy, the client has no way of knowing God. Without the child self, the client has no way to know support from God. The dyadic journey from shame and unworthiness to inadequacy is a way back to having an understanding of God's presence.

Being loved by the Father opens the door to a deeper Father - the Uranian Father or the spiritual Father. The feelings associated with the Uranian Father and the boy are reflected more in terms of the relationship that the boy later develops with the Animus.

Once the relationship with the earthly father is worked through, then the father can become the spiritual Father. The connection to the Father as love is spiritual by definition. Of course, some biological fathers are loving and, in that sense, have an Archetypal quality to them. If a male client had such a father, then that template should already be set in the psyche. It can be used or touched on as the client does his work even though he may not have lived feeling his father's love. If the love was there then it may be easy for the client to reclaim it. It is a mistake to assume every father is a problem. Some sons do have loving fathers and the psyche can use the client's memory and connection to manifest a foundation for relationship with the spiritual father or the Uranian Father.

Relating to the Uranian Father forms a bridge for the individual to the Animus. The spiritual Father can only be a temporary connection because the client needs a teacher with whom to be in relationship. A client's teacher can never be God because God is so huge, His light so brilliant, His fire is consuming. To be in relationship to God's brilliance, a person needs to be prepared and taught by the Animus who is the liaison between God and humanity. The Animus comes in dreams in human form while Uranian Father comes as lightning storms, hurricanes, tornadoes, and other powerful forces of nature that are far beyond human interaction.

The transition to the Animus begins once the right relationship has been formed to resurrect Archetypal support to the boy. As intermediary between the immensity of God and the humanity of man, the Animus becomes a mentor or teacher for spiritual work. He is the teacher, not the Father.

The confusion between the teacher and the Father has to be corrected particularly in male psychology, for the issues with the Father become the issues with the Animus. The Animus stands close to the Father and is the son just like the boy within the client. The boy can become the student of the Animus or his apprentice. But this connection must start with the Father relationship or the male client may experience the Animus as a competitor or an enemy. He can become an older brother a man has to prove himself against to get the girl, the job, to always have the better answer or be the idiot with no answer. This issue is cleared through the foundation with the Father because the Animus also has a foundation with the Father.

For women, confusing the Animus with the Father can lead to looking for a man to be a father as well as a lover, which would need to be resolved. Women, however, have the capacity to be with the Animus in a more heart-felt and intimate way. They can become both lovers with Him and student/apprentice. The Animus usually prefers to apprentice a woman client through a deep emotional union often involving lovemaking, childbirth and marriage.

The Animus cannot marry a man, nor can a man birth a child. The relationship of being an apprentice to the Animus for a man, however, does need to have the same amount of tremendous feeling as a woman's love for a man. When a man knows the Father's love, he can carry this depth of feeling as an apprentice to the Animus. In the correct relationship with the Animus, the man can be either the younger brother who also has the Father's love or the student in obedience with the teacher. From there, the relationship with the Archetype can move into an ever deepening process of spiritual transformation.

There is a distinction between the process of spiritual transformation/calling work and the process of psychological healing work. Many people do the healing work for years and move on from the dreamwork once that healing has occurred. The work that each client wants is completely up to the client. The Animus works with every person psychologically at first and He can work with them spiritually later. The later work relates to the second death or Dying to the Divine and requires a deeper level of commitment.

Pain and Vulnerability Dyads

Pain is one of the most powerful feelings in the psyche. Since pathology cannot cover up pain in the way it can cover other feelings, it uses the tactic of adding another ingredient in order to make the pain feel radically different. To a person experiencing this, it may seem that what she is feeling is pain, even though it is not. Instead of pain, she may be feeling nihilism

Nihilism can feel like pain to a person who has only known nihilism. In this way, it can pretend to be pain with devastating effects. Unlike pain which leads to the true soul self, nihilism is a toxin to ego, acting like a parasite to transform the pain into a debilitation agent. It is easily confused with depression.

When a person is in nihilism, she feels as if there is no hope, that she is living in a desolate, bleak, dark world. Dream images that reflect this do not vary much from a specific number of images - the client will find herself in a concentration camp, an insane asylum, dungeons, black/darkened rooms with no windows and a myriad of apocalyptic image where people live on a bare subsistence level in a bleak landscape or ghetto-like environments.

The client will believe the feeling in these dreams is pain instead of nihilism and may try to explain her devastating difficulty. She may not know pain at all or what it feels like except in the destructive form of nihilism. There are also clients who have felt pain and who have hated feeling it so much that they may describe it as if it were nihilism. It is very critical for the therapist to know the difference between pain and nihilism so that he does not encourage the client either to plunge into nihilism believing it is pain or treat pain as if it is nihilism. It is also critical for the therapist to help the client understand the difference.

Pain itself is excruciating - but it does move. It changes and always has Archetypal support in dreams. Pain always brings a client to love because pain is love. If there is no love, there would be no pain.

Another barrier to feeling pain is lack of self worth or self-hate. Self-hate and nihilism are intimately tied together for self-hate conspires with the ego to create nihilism in order to make the person responsible for the pain. The two emotions play off each other creating a virtual tag team block against the vulnerable psyche in pain. It is not possible for a person to feel pain if she feels guilty. To feel pain, one must be free of retribution and feel a rightness of self to truly acknowledge the woundedness.

This rightness of self can also be mimicked by nihilism, creating a narcissism that is outraged, angry, wounded, demanding, insular, indignant and entitled. This is also not pain, but is instead nihilism turned into rage and self-righteousness. Without the deep knowledge of dreams, it could be easy to see these feelings as positive in the wake of abuse experienced by some individuals. The rage and self-righteousness pretend to both acknowledge the wrong and have the certainty of self to right the wrong. This pathological certainty of self masks a profound level of unworthiness often unknown to the person. The person does not know or remember the sweetness of love nor does she know or remember the vulnerability that is necessary to be so torn by life.

Banging a drum conceals a great lie that covers the soul self and does very little to support its rebirth. In dreams, this may manifest as the client feeling outraged and rescuing children and/or animals as a noble gesture. For most, the only real rescuer is the Divine and it is the client who needs rescuing. To be able to be rescued, the client must find her way to vulnerability and her pain. Pain and vulnerability are together, enmeshed in a sea of uncertainty that most have learned to avoid.

There are times, of course, when anger and a vengeful nature have a role in the emergence of the deeper wounded self. This outrage comes not from a reaction, but from the very depths of the pain. But such pain is singular and fleeting. Unlike nihilistic rage, this kind of anger would be a new experience for the client and it would quickly be followed by other feelings. It is typical of all feelings to be followed by other feelings and to be transformed into other feelings. Emotions, on the other hand, do not change and they have a history that is familiar to the client.

Since dyads reflect the conflict between a emotional state and a feeling state, the conflict forces a choice from the client to feel one thing versus another. This choice does not come easily in dyadic form for pain and vulnerability. Pain and vulnerability do not stand up well against most emotions, perhaps because when felt, they plunge the person into a deep rabbit hole that has no end. The client may feel that she cannot feel these feelings or she will be utterly lost. As if pain and vulnerability are an all or nothing proposition. Because of this, a dyadic relationship with pain/vulnerability is difficult to maintain. In fact, if pain and/or vulnerability would be part of a dyad, it would more likely be as an invitation to feel the pain/vulnerability, not the actual feeling itself.

The peeling away of emotional layers in order to reach the pain and vulnerability is not a battle or even a choice or decision. Rather, it is the pressure of the process of the work breaking down and sifting out emotional components such as nihilism, rage, self-hate and self-righteousness. In this pressure, pain and vulnerability will begin to emerge and bubble up into the psyche for those who struggle with either grandiosity or debilitating self-hate that combines with nihilism. This pathology is the most devastating for even the sweet breath of the Beloved is not enough to break the spell. Pain may be the only way out - but its subtle essence is no match for a strong dose of the poison of nihilism.

Security/Control Dyads

Security/control often arises in dyads opposed to fear when a client surrenders to something terrifying. The client will want to run away and be safe instead of facing into the fear. Learning to trust fear requires that the client let go of control and surrender to the unknown. Dream motifs relating to fear versus security are never safe for they are working to break the habit of the psyche to move towards safety. The child self is the self that puts the client into the position of being out of control.

Dream:

> I am in a boat on the ocean. The waves are really high and are dangerously close to
> capsizing the boat. In the bow of the boat is an eleven-year-old girl who is laughing.
> She is not scared at all.

In the dream, the client wanted to manage the situation, to get the girl to safety, to be safe. But the dream is about feeling the fear and letting go of control. The child self is not afraid of the unknown.

Quite often, when shame and judgment of the self are let go, the client is presented with the opportunity to confront this place of fear and uncertainty.

Dream:

> A man emerges out of a fog with a chainsaw ripping through the air. I run and run,
> never looking back. I assume if I stop, I will die.

In the moment the client learns to stop and face the man, he learns to face his fear. In that moment, all the lies fall - shame, blame, self-hate, judgments, even the illusion of being better than everyone else. As the blade enters and blood spurts, the client can realize for the first time that he can feel. Fear melts into the freedom of the passion of the heart and the truth of God's love.

What is the confrontation of the man, the tiger, the knife, the claw, but the opening up of the heart? The Animus often is the Lover or the Trickster teaching a client about himself, but in the final analysis, the Animus is the Killer. As Killer, the Animus presents the most important opportunity to the self, which is to die to self. What a client believes about who he is actually covers and blinds him from the truth of his soul. Because of this, most people are afraid of the Alchemy of fear, afraid of the process of the unknown in consciousness becoming known.

The unknown creates fear, while making the unknown known creates what God has to give to an individual. In the alchemical moment, the moment of the death to self, the client only knows that something is to be lost and this is terrifying. Even though it is the fear that becomes essence. The ability to accept the loss is the ability to face the fear in that particular moment in that particular dream.

There are many types of fear but most of them challenge the client to die to self. And, there are all manner of disruptions that would challenge the client to not die, to stay safe in the world of the known, the world of good and bad where life can be tracked. Facing fully into Dying to Self is a tremendously transformational experience.

Pathological Fear Dyads

Pathological fear is a constructed variation of fear that is not an actual feeling but references an anxiety that causes paranoia and delusions. This kind of fear does not manifest in dream motifs such as jumping off a cliff or facing the scary man. Anxiety fear, unlike Archetypal fear, cannot be processed because it is the denial of a particular feeling, usually a hurt. Archetypal fear, on the other hand, is the transformational element to take the client to feeling.

With pathological fear, anxiety is projected onto things in the world, e.g.. being afraid to go to the store or to fly in a plane. It can also manifest as anxiety attacks which results in the person fleeing and hiding. This kind of fear is a serious breach in the psyche and can be as consuming to the psyche as nihilism or guilt. It is the result of an absolute toxic avoidance of self in a person who lives completely outside her heart. Instead, she is driven to compensate for the anxiety in some way, i.e., perhaps lying to herself and others, telling stories, making things up. The more a person listens to anxiety, the more consumed she becomes. After a while, such a person lives completely in self-deception because she cannot face her own truth. People with this kind of anxiety tend to avoid deep inner work and would probably not be good candidates for Archetypal therapy.

The difference between pathological fear and alchemical fear is that pathological fear is a form of deception. The person feeling pathological fear is really afraid of something else, something deeper, and this fear gets projected and manifested in the outer world. As a dyad, pathological fear versus fear is transformational because the deception cannot create an obstruction to the true fear, only a distraction. If the issue of pathological fear is addressed in a dream, then it reveals that the real fear is the fear of continuing in the process which may manifest as something like jumping off a cliff in a dream. With this dream scenario, the client simply needs to introject the fear she feels in the world into the inner world work of jumping off the cliff. The psyche avoids a feeling by experiencing something it can control in order to keep the pain at bay.

The feeling of fear is stronger than the feeling of pathological or false fear making this dyad transformational. False fear comes from the projection of issues into the world which appears to be frightening, but it does not take the form of obsessive/compulsive behavior. It is specifically related to true fear.

Dream:

> I am going down a river and I see a waterfall up ahead. I have no way to get out of
> the river, so I know I am going down the falls. Most of my possessions are piled up
> high in the boat. I am scared I will lose my possessions.

This dream has two fears, but the only fear the client actually feels is the fear of losing amassed possessions. This fear is the false fear, distracting the client from the real fear of going over the waterfall. The fear of losing possessions may be related to more of a worry or an obsessive need to acquire wealth, but it is not true fear. The real fear is often the fear of continuing in the process. With this dream scenario, the client needs to acknowledge the false fear of losing things and acknowledge his denial of the true fear.

Pride Dyads

Pride is another way the ego avoids feeling and can cover many areas depending on the other emotions present in the client. It is unpredictable - it can be rageful, self-righteous, manic, oblivious of any feelings. It can manifest as avoidance through procrastination, getting involved in great causes and losing the self to the cause. But pride cannot survive fear, which creates a transformational dyad. When faced with a firing squad, pride will crumble long before the bullets hit the chest.

Pride is unpredictable. The psyche would find nothing to puncture formidable forms if possible. Most people, however, have a fear that can break them down and render them open.

Dream:

> I am with the Animus as his bodyguard. I know he is the Animus. I am there for one
> reason, to protect him. I have no fear. I am here.

In this case, fear is turned into a pride. Even in the most difficult, terrifying situations, pride can make the client feel impervious while just under the surface are seething fears, uncertainties and the unknown.

A client may prefer to stay in her cocoon of illusion, never challenging the truth that her life is based only on an idea of self. For many, this is enough. Society and civilizations are created and built on such ideas. But they are hollow. The dreams offer a gift by revealing the hidden feelings, frightening as they may be, that wait underneath.

Nihilism Dyads

In the nihilistic state, a client typically feels betrayed. Although forms of control can manifest in many ways, betrayal is the core of what gives the ego a sense of control. In other words, by feeling betrayed, the ego can find ways to respond, to do something. To stay with the feeling of pain, the dyadic opposite of nihilism, there is nothing for the client to do except to simply feel the grief, to feel the hurt, to cry the tears. Feelings rarely require an action to be felt, whereas emotions always require an action when they are being experienced.

Nihilistic action leads to compulsions, obsessions and unrelenting suffering that borders on rage and can be violent. The violence can be expressed outwardly, but it can also be expressed inwardly as self-mutilation or a descent into a pit of self-loathing. Nihilism is a will to destroy or to annihilate oneself. With nihilism, a person is caught in "I am that I am that I am." The person does not make a mistake because the person is a mistake; the person does not feel unworthy because the person is unworthy. Nihilism is powerlessness, betrayal and hopelessness, with a pathological will behind it.

An individual with nihilism may manifest a sense of great passionate philosophy, belief or set of values that lead him on a grand search for truth. Having found such truth, the person will raise the flag and be extraordinarily committed, sometimes in a positive way, to causes and campaigns that have personal meaning. But underneath the commitment, the anger, rage, judgment of self and others is boiling hot. Many movements, spiritual and otherwise, are fueled by nihilistic people. Some even become martyrs. Extreme cases like the Jones Massacre are typical of the destructive behavior that can occur - whether it be in the name of God or a noble cause to save the whales. An individual can completely give himself over to a person or a group without any regard for himself. The individual may be oppressed by attempts at personal relationships. He might experience the perpetual crisis of one abusive relationship after another, sometimes as a victim and sometimes as a perpetrator. Driven to making self-destructive choices through nihilism.

Correctly diagnosing a person with nihilism and prescribing antidepressants can be a valid way to help to treat this emotion, especially if the person is unable to feel anything but nihilism even through his dreamwork. Nihilism can be the densest of all emotions and the source of its presence is always fueled by a core feeling of grief. This core feeling is very legitimate pain. Such grief could be an existential consciousness of the separation from God and self as well as memories that go back to childhood. Whatever the cause, nihilism as a sense of powerlessness does an exceptional job of replacing the feelings of vulnerability and grief with feelings of pathological hopelessness.

Powerlessness as a form of power is often the underpinning of the most controlling clients. Whether the client is successful and seen as accomplished or whether the client is a victim and seen as a failure is irrelevant. The goal is not to make a nihilistic individual more successful or high functioning. Nor is the goal to break a high functioning person into a dysfunctional person. This issue may be of great concern to the individual, high functioning or not, who is overly identified and preoccupied with what he perceives as his experience, his touchstone into the world. Such nihilistic underpinnings make it very hard for the individual to grieve because he does not believe there is anything other than his own suffering. It is very difficult for him to feel the presence of the Divine.

In fact, the whole point of nihilism is that in poisonous grief, there can be no love. It is like living in a black room with no light and no hope of light. Sometimes this is preferable to the client who may feel that this isolationism gives him a sense of power and control. Pushing love away is one of the most powerful forms of control a person can feel. In some cases, the person becomes addicted to the feeling of control and the anger associated with it. Others may be simply and hopelessly lost in the black room.

Of all the dyadic configurations, the emotional polarity of nihilism is by far the most difficult to overcome. It is as if the pathology can attack at will, continually overlaying the experience of abandonment and betrayal over the raw, naked, vulnerable child self and its pain.

Nihilism occurs almost invariably as a way to avoid the shock or the trauma of hurt. When a nihilistic person has an experience of hurt and/or rejection, he immediately enters into shock. Instead of being in the child self and feeling the raw vulnerability of hurt, the psyche jumps out of the feeling to protect itself from the pain. It is less difficult to feel, "I am bad, something is wrong with me," than to stay with the experience of hurt.

Hurt is one of the hardest feelings to feel. It takes a great deal of consciousness and support to stay with the experience of hurt because it demands a profound amount of self-acceptance and spiritual grounding. Most people do not want to stand in their pain because they judge hurt, vulnerability and rawness as negative. Instead, for the nihilistic client, the pain mutates into nihilism and the client experiences rage or self-hate.

It is difficult to feel pain because it hurts. But the feeling of pain can alchemize and lead to Divine love. Because pain itself is really love backwards, it is possible to get to love through pain. Reclaiming pain and/or love out of the ashes of nihilism is very important and difficult work.

Guilt/Shame Dyads

Guilt is an extremely powerful weapon against the underlying feelings around a wound. It protects the client from feelings of pain or horror in the same way shock works to physically protect the body. Guilt and shame can also trigger reactions such as responsibility which results in a client feeling perpetually concerned with not disappointing anyone. To avoid disappointing others, she makes sure to put other people's concerns before her own so she does not have to feel her own feelings and needs.

Afraid to Let Go
Kristin Kehler

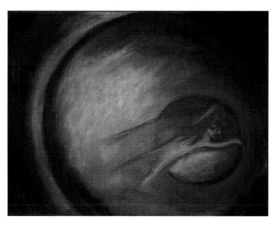

Dream:

I am with a man, familiar yet new. We are on a sphere, spinning around a big planet.
I am nervous, trying to hang on. We want to make love but I am afraid to let go of

sphere, afraid I will spin off into space. I am feeling very anxious, wanting to control things. We have to get off and go into a house.

Not Sleeping with the Man
Kristin Kehler

Dream:

> I have crawled into bed with the sleeping man and fallen asleep, too. Then I curl up at the end so I will not disturb him. Then I move to the floor because I think he might be displeased to find me in his bed when he wakes up. I feel sad and full of anxiety. The floor is hard and cold and I do not have any covers. I feel sad, lonely, uncomfortable.

In the first dream, Kristin's flying off and being afraid to let go is a function of her separation from the Animus. In the second dream, her shame begets fear, but fear is often underneath shame. Which comes first? Will saying yes to the man through the shame or allowing the fear be the way to get to the man? Most would say that Kristin needs to feel the shame to get to him. But this is wrong here - fear is the way. "We want to make love but I am afraid to let go." Through her fear, she can let go and be with him, not through her shame.

Guilt/shame gives the same sense of control as nihilism, but without feeling any feeling. Not only can the person have the experience of control, but her feelings get siphoned off through responsibility and blame. It seems comfortable because it allows for a controlled environment - i.e., the client can be good or better. She can distinguish between right and wrong, and then choose right. She can manipulate, anticipate what is required and fulfill the expectations. Despite her own suffering.

When this kind of dynamic is pointed out to a client and the underlying experience discovered, the client is often reluctant to leave her place of guilt. Underlying the guilt or responsibility is its polar opposite - the chaos of fear, uncertainty and pain. The client may find the emergence of feelings shocking and unwanted.

It seems a natural instinct for people with wounds to feel guilty. For example, when a child does not experience love from one or both parents, the child often feels at fault. The child does not know any better because adults look like gods. Another example is rape. When a woman is raped, she often does not want to report the attack because she may feel in some way responsible - "I should not have been in that neighborhood" or "My skirt was too short." This feeling of responsibility and shame is a part of the tragedy of date rape.

The reality, however, is that guilt is manufactured. For example, there are women who will not report a rape because they are afraid that other people will blame them, the victim. Projecting guilt and shame onto the world allows the person to feel judged. Feeling judged can be as big as feeling judged for having been raped but it can also be about anything - being born, having a mole, failing an audition, not making enough money, having a small house, and on and on. In this kind of projection, the world reflects what is wrong and what the person needs to do to correct it. People who feel a great deal of shame can easily feel the world has imposed the shame on them - projecting the inner shame into outer shame.

Of course, if a person is living in a situation where she is truly being shamed by others, then the situation clearly needs to change. But the dreams always challenge what the client believes to be true. The dreams will guide the client to see if the shame comes from others or if it comes from the client. The dreams will also bring the client to the place of ultimate responsibility which is within.

It is the same with pain. When a person feels hurt, it is assumed someone hurt them. Projecting hurt into the outer world is symptomatic of nihilism when the hurt turns to helplessness, betrayal and abandonment. But pain is none of that. Pain is the heart knowing its place in the world. Feeling pain is feeling the deep capacity to love. Love and pain are the same, allowing a person to know herself and to know whether the inner relationship needs healing. Pain can bring a client into a place of love and acceptance of self.

Believing hurt or any feeling is simply a reaction to what someone does in the world takes away the profound reality of the feelings within. It places them in the world as cause/effect. This suggests a person has no feelings unless someone does something or speaks to the person in a certain way. But what happens in the world does not create feelings. Feelings are already present in every person because every person has a beingness which has been present even since before birth. When the experience of this beingness collides with experiences in the world, the reaction is projection. Projection suggests that beingness is just a collection of reactions to the surrounding world. A client is shown her true beingness by being brought into the labyrinth of feeling, into the soul which has intimacy and relationship with God.

Guilt and nihilism also can work together to create a hydra pathology - a pathology with two heads. In this scenario, the client moves from guilt to nihilism in a way that consumes understanding of herself and her feelings. The guilt and nihilism polarize the client and create choices within the psyche that actually do not exist. For a client with this dynamic, the healing comes from emphasizing the "third way." The third way is through a feeling instead of an emotion, allowing the client to see that the emotions of nihilism and/or guilt are both dead ends. A hydra pathology can be challenging to recognize because although the two heads are not a dyad, the mind that likes to follow rules will want to create a dyad, when, instead, they are both pathology.

. Some hydra pathologies can bring in the element of rebelliousness where the client's sense of responsibility ("it is my fault") is polarized by an equal sense of rebelliousness ("to hell with it") and independence ("I am out of here"). Everything the client relates to makes her feel oppressed and overwhelmed because she feels responsible for everything. The other end of the pendulum swing is to shatter those responsibilities and not participate in them. Using a third way through a feeling, such as pain, grief, or fear, is the way through to healing.

Guilt and shame are the cause of a great deal of psychological suffering. Guilt is a pathological emotion that cripples the ability to feel love and it creates anomalies in the psyche. But in the alchemical process, the true purpose of guilt is to provide a hiding place to avoid fear.

A client's deal with pathology has a level of intentionality or willfulness to avoid some core feeling, even when it causes suffering. The problem is that once the client is engaged in the pathological deal to not feel a feeling, it is nearly impossible to get out of it. The guilt or shame gets into the client's psyche like cement, and the therapist and the client must take a hammer and chisel to break it down.

Guilt and shame allow a person to control and structure life so that her sense of well being can be met in terms of acceptance of the self against the backdrop of the world. In other words, guilt and shame become a way to measure one's performance and the performance of others, working to keep the unpleasant experience of feeling, of beingness, of essence, of the truth of the self away from the ego self. Because the rules of the soul are often too disruptive, a person creates her own rules, her own way to fashion her life against the backdrop of her true unconscious feelings. It is a way to measure the self or others without having to listen to the self or others.

An example of the pathological "value" of guilt and shame: a vulnerable and innocent child finds herself being abused and beaten. With only the experience of fear, she needs to protect herself, to control her environment to survive, to make sense out of a world that suddenly does not make sense. Shame comes to the rescue, telling the child that she is bad. If she is bad, then she can be good, she can find a way to be accepted. But more important, she can find a way out of the horror, the fear, the moment, the trauma of her reality. The psyche then compensates. The girl grows up to be a social worker, a mathematician, a clinician, a bank teller or a neurotic housewife who cannot get to the store or cannot love her children. Or, she becomes an architect who builds the biggest building in the world, an astronaut who lands on the moon or Mars, a writer who writes the definitive book on American culture. All motivated and driven by the fact that as a child, she covered herself with the understanding that she was wrong and had to figure out what was right in order to be loved. Just like the Pulitzer Prize winner who said in his acceptance speech that all he ever wanted was to be loved.

The Hydra
by Laura Ruth

Dream:

I am at a party that is a play reading. A woman says she is most vulnerable doing her part lying on her belly, but others feel the opposite. I think that they will want me to read for it and I am shy, nervous and afraid. I do not know what is right. I do know that it is the director's call and that the woman will be outvoted. I am afraid.

The Three Melt Me in Love

Dream:

A building - like a school. I have gone there and three young men are there and they want me to stay. I am uncertain, afraid, like I do not trust them, and I start to leave several times. I go out the back door. Something inside makes me come back, the part that wants to be with them, and one of them sees me and I try to hide in the back stairs but he follows me, open, smiling, and I feel won over. Like whatever the resistance I have in me is being melted by love. I am melted in Love, totally incapable of anything, surrendered.

From Laura:

In the first dream, I believe I have to make a choice - that one must be right, the other wrong, but it is a lie. They are both liars. I am unsure of the truth - believe there is a right answer but do not know what it is. The only truth is with the young men who are melting me. Their Love is the only truth.

At this point in her work, Laura believes that there is always a right answer. Pathology readily gives her solutions but they are all wrong because they come out of fear. Because of Laura's belief, the pathology can create the idea of choice - that some choices are good and some choices are bad. This becomes her vector, her orientation, her gyroscope instead of her feelings, her soul, the Divine. The squirmy, lowlife ideas that are the underpinnings of values are her orientation. She thinks they will keep the bogeyman away.

Hydra pathology is a way in which the pathology tricks a person with alternative ways of being in the world - if one way does not work, then the pathology mutates and offers another way. The hydra here, however, is not just tricking Laura with alternative ways of being, it is tricking her with the idea that confusion is being. As if inner confusion helps her find her own solace for existing. But this is just a form of oppression that carries with it the underlying trauma of having lost her soul self long ago. The underlying trauma percolates up through the psyche finding a place to project around decisions.

A true hydra is the personality development of two distinctive manners. Sometimes it seems that a person with hydra pathology has a split personality. This client is a hydra wannabe - she wishes she had the choice to put herself in the world in separate ways. For her, however, it is just confusion that carries trauma-based aspects of fear, anxiety and self-loathing.

The solution is to wait for the director who is the Animus. All she has to do is know this and then there is no confusion because He will let her know. Laura knows this, she wants to be obedient, but remains in her confusion as the trauma competes with the clarity of the Divine.

The idea of going to the director for the answer has nothing to do with right or wrong. He probably will not care about what is being debated. The issue is her capacity to know what she wants, to know what is right for her. This can only happen when she is with Him.

The second dream shows the same problem of the uncertainty, the fear, the lack of trust that is part of the early trauma. Laura feels split between the part that wants to leave and the part that wants to be with the men. In a true hydra person, the part that wants to be with them would be pathological, too. But not with Laura. Once she decides to follow her heart and move to her fear, she loses all resistance and is in the love. Once in the love, it does not matter what she does.

Mary

It doesn't matter how I got here
under branch-cracked sky,
how I stood at the iron gate
only long enough to let my fingers
lift the latch from its bed,
only long enough to pass through,
lay the bar back to sleep.
Or that my feet rang
in the night fog, tolling
among headstones.

Your stone hands are smooth as flesh,
white like your face carved from innocence.
The basin of your neck descends from earlobe
to cut of jaw...
I want to devour you with kisses.
But to say this is some kind of asking for forgiveness.

That's not what I came to ask,
not what I meant to say.
I was lonely up at the house,
pacing from room to room,
wanted a little peace, thought
you'd understand if anyone could.
I'm having a little trouble I
can't seem to get clear of.
I thought you might help.

Teach me to love like the maple
in my yard, its roots deeply settled.
If I were its buds shattering into the cresting
season, wouldn't I embody redemption?
Wouldn't I marry the sun?

                    Karla Van Vliet

WHAT IS AN ARCHETYPE?

To define "Archetype," it is easier to start by defining what an Archetype is not. An Archetype is not a repressed or unknown part of the self. The Animus, who comes as a man in dreams, and the Anima, who comes as a woman, are Archetypes, but the Animus is not the male part of a woman, and the Anima is not the female part of a man as is typically believed. They are also not here to fulfill a sexual connection with the self because they are not truly gender identified. Instead, they are the quintessential essence of a consciousness that looks to wake a person up. They are aspects and qualities of gender that are the very essence of spiritual nature and spiritual growth.

This is entirely different than an individual's very limited understanding of his or her gender self. The Archetypal Animus and Anima are actually androgynous and even hermaphroditic. They only separate themselves into gender identities because of the broken split of the people they serve and are trying to help. An individuated soul does not understand his or her self as "man" or "woman" but as connected to the love that comes through. The mechanistic manner in which gender is often dealt with by the Archetypes is simply to help a person become whole again.

Because they are not truly gender identified, they cannot be understood through the identification of gender. When issues of being men and women or political gender issues are projected onto the Animus and Anima, the Archetypes are belittled and rendered impotent. Gender and gender politics struggles may have validity in the outer world, of course, but they are not valid in the Archetypal dream realm because they lead to false identification with gender. People are people and are not defined solely by their gender. Every person is an individual looking for God.

The Archetypes are also not "guides" - instead, they carry essence and love. The term "guide" implies that they mean no harm to the self, which, in fact, they do. As vessels of essence and love, they desire to kill the false ego self so a client can be open to feelings and the deeper possibilities of transformation and connection to the Divine. They want to kill the identification with the false self including all aspects that are not true to the client's essence. Initially, most people would rather have their known self strengthened, even if it is not the true self and regardless of the deeper wellspring of the true self. This makes their work much more difficult.

Both the Animus and the Anima weave back and forth in the different roles they play. The roles they choose in a particular dream depend on the specific needs of the client in the particular moment of the client's process. The following are only brief overviews of the Archetypes.

The Animus

The Animus' role is to empower the client through relationship as a lover and/or a teacher.

His role is also to kill the client, the false self, in order to make way for the true self. The Animus is no friend of the world. He is also no friend of the client unless she is open to being her true self. In this way, the Animus is the Agent Provocateur - the one who challenges the ego self by provoking and presenting the lie. And to the degree the client is in or is invested in the lie, the client will push him away to avoid facing this truth. The Animus' job is to bring the lie to awareness, not to gain favor.

Even when a client does express a desire to have a relationship with the Animus, she will want that relationship on her own terms, not on the Animus' terms. These "terms" are often part of the lie of the false ego self. If the terms are in some kind of alignment with the true self of the client, the Animus may comply to a certain extent - for a while. If the terms are not part of the true self of the client, however, the Animus will be confrontative immediately. Even if the terms are somewhat aligned with the true self, the fact that there are "terms" works against essence and sooner or later, the Animus will confront the client.

When the Animus does confront a client, hopefully the client will have reached a place of courage and discernment in order to trust Him and His love, and to embrace further what He offers despite any history of trauma, wounds or fears. Being able to see through the lie of the pathology to get to these feelings immediately energizes the Animus to be ally and support.

It is important for the client to be aware that the journey to facing deeper feelings is deeply challenging. Most people will want the relationship with the Animus, but will be unwilling to experience their dark night of the soul, even if it means a complete healing. When this resistance comes up, the Animus is loving in hopes of supporting the client through the resistance.

To belong to the Animus is to belong to the self in the truest way.

I Want to be the Bride
by Kristin Kehler

Two Dreams:

I am with a beautiful Indian man. My heart is very open. I can imagine being with him my whole life. The man's relatives seem to be having an engagement party to announce his betrothal to another woman. I think he has to do what his mother wants even though he does not love her. The bride is supposed to sing at the party but she cannot really sing. I am disappointed that it is not me. Then, I am back in my room, packing to leave. I think I will just sneak away. I feel numb. I will never see him again. I feel an urge, though, to see him once more even if it is to say goodbye.

A young woman has been very fearful of going out with a young man, maybe fears sexual intimacy. She agrees to go out with him even though she is scared. We are all thrilled. I am her therapist, taking pride in the work I have done to help her get to this point. We are walking arm in arm; I am congratulating her.

In a dream with a marriage, the client is always the bride or the groom, depending on the gender of the dreamer. To the extent that the client is unaware of being the bride or the groom, being instead a visitor, is the degree of separation of the person from the goal of union with the Divine. In her first dream, Kristin feels the power and passion of her yearning to be with Him, but is blocked by the other self that seems to be marrying the Animus. She only perceives it this way because this other self, the one who is the "bride" in the dream, has control in Kristin's outer life. If this false self did not have so much control in the outer life, it would not manifest in the dream.

In the second dream, the woman who is afraid is really the same woman who is afraid to tell the Animus she loves Him in the first dream. In the second dream, Kristin is the therapist, not the beloved. As therapist, she can be proud and in control, but she is not the woman she was in the the first dream. The therapist personality is so dominant in the outer life that there is only the moment in the first dream where she feels her longing and passion. This second dream shows her everyday life and her overriding personality.

Marriage Dream		Therapist Dream
Kristin Loving the Man	------ Soul Self ----	Young Girl Going on Date
The Beloved	------ Animus -----	The Young Man
The False Bride	------- False Self -----	Kristin The Therapist

In the first dream, she is embodied in her soul life, where she feels her true, spiritual need for Him. She gets it only as a woman who is in love with the Divine can get it. Such devotion is only in the nature of those with a special understanding of the true relationship with the Divine - which is not co-dependent.

The Anima and Preparation for the Animus

The Anima can play many roles depending on the particular needs of the client, not staying with one exclusively. The Anima is never, however, the agent of death, the executioner, for this is the role of the Animus. She is always pristine, the mother, the lover, essence. Part of Her role is as healer through acceptance of the true self.

It is through the process of accepting the true self that a client can move into a deeper relationship with the Divine. When the true self is not accepted or when there is a feeling of shame or unworthiness around the true self, the client is going to be resistant to having a relationship with the Animus that leads him deeper into his true self.

The Anima's primary concern is helping with self-acceptance through healing of shame in preparation for the relationship with the Divine. Once the healing begins, She helps a client move deeper into essence through a supportive role and can be the harbinger of that essence. The way She comes in that role varies greatly, depending on the needs of the client.

The Anima and the Siren

While Her role as supporter, healer and harbinger of essence is the Anima's greatest strength, it is also the reason the siren/demon can easily mimic Her, creating a negative dependency that cripples a client's work.

Sirens/demons are not necessarily sexual. Their goal is to try to seduce a client in any way they can to simply become involved with him, to engage with him in order to keep him from being grounded in his true self.

This is beautifully illustrated in *The Odyssey* by two events in Odysseus' adventures on his way home after the Trojan war - meeting Circe and the Sirens. When Odysseus' ship arrives on her island, Circe lures Odysseus' men to her cave by singing in order to turn them into pigs. Odysseus avoids their fate and frees them, but he still falls for her seduction by becoming her lover and yet again delaying his journey home. The Sirens also use singing to lure men, leading them to wreck their ships. Odysseus' ship is only saved because the men have wax in their ears. Odysseus has the men tie him to the mast so he can hear the Sirens, always drawn to the seduction. When he hears them, he thrashes to be released, wanting to turn his ship and his men toward complete destruction. This is the seduction of pathology through the feminine. It would lure a client with beauty in order to distract or destroy.

The Anima is not a siren/seductress, but the differentiation of the Anima as siren or supporter is subtle, complicated and very difficult to discern. Being controlled by such a demon believing it is a spiritual being is a common failing of spirituality in our culture. This is further compounded and confused by the belief that the Anima is a redeeming agent like the Animus but for men.

The Anima is not a redeeming agent. The Anima, at its best, is about self-acceptance and essence. Acceptance of the true self that is not accepted by the client, the self that is negated. When the client is in self negation, the Anima is also negated and become easily confused with sirens.

For men, involvement with the siren becomes projected into the world as finding someone who is similar to the siren. Also, many men are psychologically incested with their mothers. Because of this, it is important for a male client to see past the seductress.

The confusion begins with the client believing his needs will be met by the woman. The Anima is not there to meet needs. Instead, the client must accept the fact that he actually is impotent. To divert attention away from this, the siren promises a world of support in exchange for sex, saying, "You will know the bliss of being a wonderful man." This has nothing to do with what Anima has to offer. The seduction of the siren is playing on a weakness within the client - the need for solace at a woman's breast.

The complexity arises because the Anima can also choose to help a man heal a "wounded" penis. In this case, it is difficult to know if the female figure in a dream is giving support that binds him to the seductress or dark mother or if she is the Anima supporting some necessary healing of a wound the client may have with women.

This distinction between the Anima and the siren in a dream is often difficult to discern. If it is a siren in the dream, then they are offering a "treasure" to "complete" the man. Instead, he falls into a trap - becoming a pig or seduced or thrashing about on a mast. If it is the Anima, however, then healing is taking place. There are no general guides that help with discerning the difference, but the dreams supply the clues. An example:

Dream:
    A beautiful woman seduces me and I ejaculate into a matchbox. The woman takes
    the matchbox, closes it up and puts it away. I feel renewed.

In this dream, the beautiful woman is a demon, catching the man's seed and putting it away. Nothing is born of it. The client felt renewed by the dream only because it reinforced an incested female connection.

The client must first recognize the self that needs acceptance. The Anima's work can then begin - the nurturing and encouragement of the opening to the repressed self.

Women too can be lost in relationship to a siren, especially if the mother was abusive and the client has lost awareness of the abuse. When the awareness is lost, the woman will continue to search for the destructive mother in others believing that this is a place for growth.

Parental Figures - The Mother and The Father

Parental figures are often necessary building blocks that support future work with the Anima and the Animus. Every relationship with an Archetypal parental figure is part of a foundation that helps the client move into the next step of her work - to the next level of connection with the Animus or to another step into trauma, depending on the direction of the dreams.

Anima can and does double as a spiritual Mother for clients who need a positive bonding with the Mother. In this role, She helps build a positive self-image in the client to prepare her for the next step in her work.

As with the Mother/Anima, the good Father is a necessary building block. The distinction, however, between the parental figure of the Mother/Anima and the Father is that the Animus is never the true Father in the way that the Anima can be the Mother. The Animus is never the true Father because he is aligned with the Father and is in connection with Him as His son.

Many people have poor relationships with their fathers creating a barrier in their inner work. This often manifests with a client having resistance toward a relationship with the Animus and/or coming into relationship with the true Father later in the work.

A woman's relationship with the Animus is different than a man's relationship because she has many ways to be in relationship with the Animus - as friend, confident, student/teacher and most importantly as lover. Being able to be the Animus' lover allows a woman to easily bypass visages of the Father.

But men are never lovers with the Animus - not even gay men. For men with homophobia issues, the Animus may come as a projection of that fear as a sexual partner, but inevitably there is no sexual consummation between the Animus and the male client. Because of this, the relationship between a man and the good Father is much more profound and important.

For men, this raises, again, the issue of the siren masquerading as the Anima. Where the siren will do anything she can to separate the client from the Animus and the Father, the Anima would never do anything to disturb or hinder these relationships. The Anima would never come to a man if he was already overly dependent on women in a negative way. She only comes to a man when his understanding of women is not from a misogynistic place, but rather from a vulnerable place. She also may come as that healing balm for a wound from a dark mother.

The mother/father genders are very much related to gender experience in childhood. The true Father, the Uranian Father who comes later in the work, is not specifically male - he is specifically and overwhelmingly love, a love that has nothing to do with gender.

Most people are splintered by their relationship with their parents, limiting their capacity to know this Archetypal, transgendered love. They tend to lean on one gender or one type of individual for support in part based on gender. Issues that surround the Anima as Mother or the Animus as Father are only the underpinnings of a foundation that will birth the true self. The true self, the child self, can be in a transgender relationship with the Divine.

The Anima and the Animus are really the same and the whole person finds no conflict in these united genders. One of the highest forms of Alchemy is conjunctio - the blending or healing of the genders. One is neither a woman nor a man, but a potent being ready to be filled with the love of the Uranian Father. The Uranian Father, who has nothing to do with a good father, is the Father who is never understood as He is beyond values. He is simply love.

Seeing Me Through

I turn quickly, to catch
what stands beyond my... *what's there?*

As if, there I stood, bared, bore through
and beckoning my sight to fall on me.

Yes, not quite daring. Daring done by one
sure of being seen, and so... *what was that?*

What is that haunting, halting catch
of wing, shadow of the vacuum?

No, sun reflecting now and in my eye
the tear, I'm sure now, let, no, summoned,

you see, by what I can't... nor can I name.

Karla Van Vliet

THE ANIMUS
THE ROLE OF GENDER AND THE BIOLOGICAL IMPERATIVE

Some Jungian schools of thought assert that the Anima, the female principle, performs the same function in the psyche of a man that the Animus, the male principle, does in the psyche of a woman. This assertion is absolutely incorrect. The Anima never does the job of the Animus in the psyche just as the Animus never does the job of the Anima in the psyche. The Animus is always the Animus for both genders. The Anima is a very powerful Archetypal and psychological aspect of the psyche but She works very differently than the Animus.

Ultimately, all clients must come to a relationship with the Animus because His role in the psyche is very specific. However, He performs that role very differently based on the gender of the client.

The Issue of Gender and the Biological Imperative

When attempting to delineate the function of an Archetype and what is asked of a client in relationship to that Archetype, the first issue is gender. Gender in the psyche is not an issue of how it functions in the outer world, but how the issue of gender affects the inner world of the client.

Men and woman have different challenges based on their physiology because of a simple fact - consciousness is contained in a body governed by biology and the biological imperative. The biological imperative is the physical, instinct-based command in all living creatures necessary to ensure survival as a species. Part of this physiologically-based imperative demands that each gender play a different and specific role for the species to survive. In human beings, the different primal biological commands are delivered by the hormones, specifically testosterone in men and estrogen in women. These hormones influence tendencies and drive behavior in ways which, if left unconscious, obstruct the possibility of relationship with any Archetype, including and especially the Animus.

The influence of the biological imperative does not place blame on either gender. However, it is important to bring into consciousness how it can drive behavior in both genders and how it can block relationship with the Archetypes.

Men

The biggest problem men face is "testosterone poisoning." Testosterone causes a male to function predominantly from the left side of his brain, resulting in the shut down of the right side, the feeling and intuitive side. The right side can be shut down for years or decades, and some men never fully recover.

The biological imperative takes preemptive status in the psyches of young males due to the influx of testosterone in their bodies. Over the course of puberty, the levels of testosterone increase eighteen-fold compared to the levels of estrogen increasing eight-fold in girls. The dramatic increase in testosterone manifests in male teenagers as action and doing without great access to feeling. For many, this translates into the impulse to spread seed as far and wide as possible, as if the survival of the species still depends on impregnating as many women as possible. On a physiological level, if the male had retained access to the right side of the brain, humanity may not have survived. But humanity is no longer in that situation.

Of course, not all men live from that impulse, but many do still act solely from their penises without any regard for what they really feel. The result is that men are at a grave disadvantage when faced with spiritual and emotional development in later years.

The challenges facing a man in this work are severe. Not only must a man survive his own testosterone poisoning, but he must also survive his relationships with his parents. In the maternal relationship, many men have learned how to be men based on their mother's expectations, expectations often influenced by the mother's biological maternal imperatives. The maternal biological imperative causes a mother to focus all of her nurturing on the child, to the exclusion of her own needs and the needs of the child's father. In the extreme, the result is emotional incest with the child.

In the paternal relationship, many men have a lack of any connection with their father. Fathers, especially in older generations, have traditionally been preoccupied with issues such as work, status in the world, and activities outside the home. And, more important, many fathers are themselves lost and damaged by emotionally incested connections with their mothers and wives.

Because boys have very few role models to guide them through adolescence, they arrive at adulthood with little opportunity for change. Pressures to be a competent man in the world, to achieve goals, to be a strong mating partner and a provider for a family all conspire to encourage a man to pursue goals that have nothing to do with the heart and the soul of the individual. A man's inability to feel his true essence creates a prison of ideas and reactions, further complicated by competition with other men. The pressure to focus outward cripples a man in his attempt to go deeply inside.

Men and the Animus

The competitiveness most men feel with other men gets projected onto the Animus, making the job of the Animus with the client profoundly difficult. The antidote for this often involves work around the Father in early Stage Two. If the man can understand himself as a boy in relationship with the good Father, he can quickly find a place of emotional and spiritual need. This need can break some of the competitive edge and allow the man to move into relationship with the Animus, who is also the son of the Father.

Men who have a good relationship with their earthly fathers definitely have an advantage in this work. In these cases, the pathology will try to trick the client into separating from his father as a way to disconnect from the son or boy in himself.

The boy is easily lost in the complex modern world. Initiation rituals in tribal cultures almost always included boys breaking from the mother at a very early age. This never occurs in our society. The term *Alma Mater* means "other mother," or "fostering mother" so that even at college age when a boy is clearly a man, he is still with the mother. In fact, a man's entire sexual desire to be with women is an extension of the need to find the support and nurturing with the mother he never had or with the mother he did have. This dependence on the mother is not good for this work.

If a man is successful in finding the boy through his dreamwork, then he can begin to have access to his feelings. As the boy who can feel and can be the son to the Father, all the miracles of this work become available to the man because the Animus is also the boy/son of the spiritual Father. Therefore, the most important teaching for a man is the male principle, the Animus. The Animus needs the male client to become the boy because the boy is where the client felt yearning for the Father, whether it was short or long lived. When testosterone poisoning makes men compete for women, they forget this yearning for the Father. The biological imperative self becomes grounded in sexual prowess, where attraction for the same woman can break a connection between even close male friends.

Women

The bias in Archetypal Dreamwork is that it is much easier for women to do the work with the Animus than it is for men. A woman's capacity to feel is often relatively intact as an adult although it may be tarnished by wounds and her own developmental process. This capacity to feel is a necessary aspect of the female biological imperative because of the complex human need for bonding with the mother. This drive for bonding, like testosterone poisoning for men, can create severe blocks when a woman tends to the needs of the child/children without regard for her own needs or her spouse's needs.

Although women often have a larger capacity to feel than men, they are not less dysfunctional, nor are they healthier in relationship. Most people, both men and women, are more driven by emotions than feelings. Both women and men confuse emotions with feelings and both have difficulty coming to terms with their deeper feelings.

In relationships, women may have a clearer understanding that a true marriage involves both wholeness in herself as well as wholeness in her partner. Most women, however, avoid this kind of relationships. The truer the love, the greater the fear. If women sought functioning, healthy men then the biological imperative would not be met for the need to have babies would not be as strong. Women look for emotional gratification outside themselves, transferring it to their children. Men, on the other hand, do not look for emotional gratification from the outside. For women, emotional relationships will hinder healthy spiritual mutuality. When a woman truly takes ownership of her feelings and resolves her issues with men, the man that she seeks from this place will be similar to her understanding of the Animus.

The biological imperative begins early in the developmental process of women as well as men. Girls grow up faster, stronger and smarter. This prepares a girl at an early age for the intense requirement of childbearing and the need to be open so that her children can have a sense of self in the complexity of the emotional world. The intense primal bond with the mother makes the mother the most powerful person in a child's life. The result is that the mother's problems can easily become the child's problems.

Once a woman has a child, she learns through her care and responsibility to become a mother. She is also now affected by a level of hormonal drive that is equally as devastating to the psyche and to the hope for the soul's reclamation as testosterone poisoning is for a man. Estrogen encourages a woman to give her whole self to the child. The human child is profoundly vulnerable and the biological imperative for species' survival forges and reinforces the mother's intense primal bond. The child's need comes first and a woman's need recedes further and further into the background. Some women suffer from postpartum depression as a result of the loss of their own need.

Many divorces begin with the advent of a child. When a wife becomes a mother, she loses concern for her husband by putting all her nurturing into the child. The man often feels unloved reinforcing the biological tendency to spread seed. Men always need to be nurtured by their wives when they are in love. Even though men do not feel as much, profound unacknowledged pain and hurt can accumulate in a way that results in violent behavior from the man. The lack of capacity to feel the pain and hurt can trigger violence because the pain and hurt are too difficult to acknowledge.

An example of this dynamic is shown in the movie "Eyes Wide Shut." The husband felt threatened by his wife's flirting, which she did to get his attention. Instead of acknowledging feeling threatened, he acted out in order to avoid his feelings of vulnerability. This type of behavior is an example of the extreme immaturity of a man's ability to deal with feelings. When a man cannot express or even acknowledge a simple hurt, the result can be a devastating attack on the marriage. Acting out behavior can be as extreme as child abuse, alcoholism, affairs or it can be simply shutting down.

A man's inability to express his feelings to his wife stems from his lack of support in his feelings from his father. For a man to claim his manhood and his vulnerability, many of his issues must be resolved through the Animus. A man can only accept his feelings when another man, in the psyche the Animus, accepts them. Just as a woman needs the mother to accept her feelings. In this way, the gender identification of the same gender parent is important in the development of each gender.

Women and the Animus

Becoming a mother plus a woman's own great wounds separate her from her child self. Too much estrogen through the childbearing experience can doom a woman to a place of concern for her child and not herself or her own needs. A woman, of course, needs to take care of her children, but she also needs to be aware of the tendency to become lost to her own child self and to lose the capacity to be a lover. The very thing a woman needs to be to raise a child - a strong, potent, caring, responsible mother - can become the very thing that over time makes it difficult for a woman to find her vulnerability.

A woman can become so powerful in her role as a mother that despite her own sense of unworthiness, her pathological psyche can develop into a formidable force. Care and concern spill over into control, denigration of the masculine and emotional incest. The "dark mother" is a complex dynamic. This power as a mother creates a huge obstruction to the Animus' desire to connect with that woman. She becomes unwilling to surrender to the male principle in a way that would allow for emotional growth.

Finding her vulnerability and her child self is as essential for a woman as it is for a man, but it becomes nearly impossible when the child self is projected onto her child. In dreams, when the child self appears to a woman, it is natural for the woman to take care of the child, not realizing that the child is herself. Of course, it is a great step for her to take care of the child in the dream, but the deeper work is to become the child. Once she becomes the child, the self can grow to be a child connected to the Divine.

It is the child self that develops the ability to be in relationship with the male or female principle. The adult self, although aligned with the values of the Divine, can never be truly in relationship with it without the consciousness of the child self.

Man, Baby and Me
by Kristin Kehler

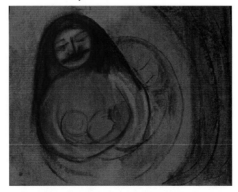

Dream:

> I hear a man in the next room, coaching a boy like for a sports team: "Great, good boy, you are facing that touch down!" I love to hear him. Later the man is in a group with us. There is a frozen baby that is me. The man works with the baby and it becomes unfrozen. I am watching, thrilled, moved.

Loving the Baby

Dream:

> I am having a new experience of falling in love with my baby, a big fat active baby boy about nine months old. I had loved him before in some internal way, but now I am experiencing him out in the world and I feel a new bonding. The baby is very active and happy. He has new wisdom or molar teeth coming in.

From Kristin:

> In some old dreams, the babies are sick or have something wrong with them, or are not mine, orphans waiting for adoption, etc. This boy is definitely mine but I still am invested in being the mother, which is an important role for me in my outer life. I took care of younger siblings as a child/teenager, have worked with kids ever since, been a parent for twenty years, too. Being a "good" mother is something that has quite a grip on me.

A therapist may feel that this dream is a wonderful dream. If the client presenting this dream had very little ability to love children or had never had children, this might be a wonderful, breakthrough dream. The Archetypes will often teach by putting a person in a position to love something, like a child, in order to feel the possibility of being loved by the Archetypes.

But this is not the case here. Kristin knows the love for a child, but she cannot be that child. The birth of the child is impressive, but she is still not willing to be her. What good is birthing the child if the client cannot become it? Even the positive caretaking of the child is not good. For Kristin, she knows the place of being the mother and being in control. The dark mother in this situation is not dark, she is just in control.

This is a complicated situation for the same dream could mean different things for a different dreamer. The revelation for this dreamer is that the child needs to be accepted without caring for it. The true caring is the willingness to let go of the child and be with the child, as referenced by her painting *Union with the Girl* (see page 257). In that scenario, she does not have to face the fear of taking care of the child in her own needs. Her own needs are too terrifying to face, so she clutches the child.

Isolation and control are a large part of dealing with one's past pain.

Gender of the Child Self

The child self that appears in dreams, such as the boy in relationship to the Father, can actually be either a boy or a girl for either gender. For the child self, the principles of male and female in the psyche are simply qualities of the self that have been lost. Boys generally represent the part of the self that reflects desire while girls generally reflect the capacity for relationship. The gender of the child self in a dream depends on the imbalances present in the client and what the particular dream is presenting. The child self appears as an aspect that needs to be reclaimed and the gender is a reflection of a specific piece of that aspect. Like the Animus and Anima, all children in the psyche are actually androgynous. Gender identification is not an issue for the underlying foundation of the inner child self is love. When a client does not have connection with the Divine, with that love, then gender issues can be as important as the color of skin or nationality. But in the psyche, no gender predominates or preempts another because they work together in the intimacy of God's love.

Being with the Animus as Lover and Being Married for Women

Many women struggle with being in a lover relationship with the Animus in their inner lives and being with their spouses in their outer lives, since the Animus comes as lover/husband in dreams for women. But a woman can have her Beloved in the Archetypal Realm and her beloved in the world. If there is love and intimacy with her spouse, the relationship with the Animus deeply enhances the marriage - it does not destroy it.

The two realms are never in conflict unless a woman is with the wrong person. This would manifest eventually and connecting with the Animus could accelerate the demise of a relationship if the discrepancy is extreme. Many women (as well as men) fear if they do the dreamwork, their marriage will fail, especially if the spouse is not involved in the dreamwork. The marriage will fail only if there is something grossly wrong with it.

Many women dream of the Animus coming to them but they feel they cannot be with Him because they are already married. The idea of the infidelitous Animus or, the reverse, for the woman to feel she is an infidelitous lover can simply be the fear of connecting with the Archetype. In this case, turning away from Him is an excuse to avoid true relationship with the Animus.

It is terrifying for either gender to come to terms with the formidable consciousness that is the Animus. In the face of that relationship, every pore of the being is examined, challenged, killed and transformed.

Held Aloft

Wind nicks the flood-water along fields.
Above, the north-flying geese
take sky under wing.
I have seen a thousand breakings.

I stand between this world
and what light mingles
in the corn, that we, the farmer
and I, pray—
will rise and yellow.

Are you one of the few
who knows this land-bit sorrow?
Hard breath?

This is what I want:
to be held aloft, to see
what demands me,
face to face.

Not this world,
slant with perspective.

                    Karla Van Vliet

The Anima

The Anima has a very important role in the psyche because her first order of healing is to help the client recover from deep unworthiness and shame.

The Anima and Women

For women, the Anima can come in several different forms:

Archetypal Mother Figure. The Anima's mothering love is experienced by the client as a contrast to the mothering she actually received. The client's own mother may have behaved in a jealous or narcissistic or hurtful way.

The Ideal Woman. The Anima may come as the ideal woman for a client, a woman the client needs to aspire to be and can be. In this case, the client's feelings of unworthiness or shame may have prevented her from becoming that woman. When the Anima is an ideal woman, she may also come paired with the Animus. The client will perceive her as the Animus's wife or girlfriend and will either be in a competitive dynamic with her or feel completely inept as a woman. This may reflect deep feelings of shame she has regarding men. When the Anima comes with the Animus, this reveals the woman's unhappiness with herself, her inner knowledge that she is not the woman or person she is meant to be. Because of this, envy or jealousy in this kind of dream can reflect the feeling of wanting to be something more, a feeling appropriate and good for the client to access.

Mongolia Mother
by Kristin Kehler

Dream:

> People are adopting babies and I think how beautiful they are, especially the one from Mongolia. I say I want to go there and a woman says: "Do you not know about that place? They take everything from you." I do not care, I want to go anyway. An old woman meets me at the border and takes me to her home. I think for a moment that I should leave my wedding ring behind (so they do not take it from me) but then decide that I will have to lose everything if I need to.

From Kristin:

> Mongolia always sounds to me like the outer limits of the physical world. The part of me that is an adventurer would love to go there but I feel nervous, too, although not about anything specific. Here the demon is back, trying to scare me about how they will steal from me. The woman making me a little bed in Mongolia also reminds me of when I was small, 3 or 4, when we lived in Russia and a very kind Russian woman took good care of me. I think of little beds like that tucked into walls, safe and snug and full of love and closeness to the people caring for the children. I did not have much of that as a child. Mongolia is related to Russia, outer limits of Russia somehow, and Russia was a place of deep feeling for me as a young child. I used to think that I had lost my child self when I left there and came back to the U.S. at age almost 5. Somehow I became tough and independent when I returned to Vermont.

The barbed wire fence and the woman who does not want the client to go are both the demon trying to keep her from leaving where she has been. It is not hard to do because Kristin feels so threatened by the lack of love that she has taken control of her life and her children's lives. Kristin is a profoundly deep, spiritual person who believes that spirituality requires sacrifice. In that spirit, everything is rationalized as necessity - that the control that is survival is noble, is obedience to spirit. In her dream, she is deep enough to leave this place of control and finds herself as a child with the Mother. This is the moment in the timeless journey - a moment followed by another moment when once again she will be behind the security of the barbed wire. Where she will be the dark mother necessitating the management of the world around her. But for this moment of the journey, the Anima makes her first successful connection to Kristin's soul.

A Woman in the Waking World. Sometimes, when the qualities of a client's own beautiful spiritual aspect are perceived in and/or projected onto another woman in the external world, the Anima comes as that woman. She uses the projection to help the client access the specific feelings and associations with the person.

Even though the Anima's main function in the psyche is to heal a lack of self-acceptance because of shame, it is not the same as the psychological criteria of "accept yourself for who you are no matter what." The self-acceptance of the Anima is the acceptance of what the client aspires to be - her essence in terms of a real understanding of what God created in her.

The Anima and Men

For men, the Anima will sometimes, if appropriate, try to heal sexual dysfunction, sexual shame or other areas of a man's psyche under attack by dark female figures who have seduced him. A man may be inordinately attracted to an abusive woman because he is unable to fathom the idea of being loved for himself. It is very complicated to heal this specific kind of wound because for men the pathological dark female comes as a seductress promising gifts and giving the seduced male a sense of power and self-worth. Deep wounds such as this can occur through relationships with both parents, not just the mother.

There are many ways men deal with women from a place of profound woundedness. One example is a man who seeks support from women knowing there is no future with them, so he jumps from woman to woman. For this kind of man, he may be attempting to get what he can, then, before he is discovered, move on to the next woman.

These kinds of beliefs around women can also come from the male client's actual experience with women. Women often project the Animus onto men even though the Animus is something a man can never be for a woman or anyone. Invariably, the woman ends up feeling disappointed with her choice and then rejecting the man in some way. This, of course, dovetails with the fear many men have of being rejected when they reveal their needs.

For the man who jumps from woman to woman, he leaves before he can be rejected. If he does risk staying, most likely he chooses poorly and the woman will, in fact, reject him. Choosing poorly then perpetuates his illusion that he has no choice but celibacy or to continue jumping from woman to woman, keeping distant from any chance of intimacy.

Regardless of the different ways men react and relate to women from their woundedness, the Anima will attempt to reach out to him in dreams once his projection onto dark women is broken. Sometimes men have such a competitive nature with other men that they will find any type of interaction with the Animus impossible. Such a man can be prepared for the Animus by learning to accept love through the Anima, softening his competitiveness.

The Anima, of course, cannot, nor does she ever attempt to, replace the Animus. But, if a male client is initially uninterested in a relationship with the Animus or the good Father, he most likely will be interested in a spiritual connection consummated through the feminine. The Anima's role is unique to that specific male wound. Once this has been accomplished, the Anima then comes to the client only as an encouraging support in his connection to the male principle.

This is also true for gay women. Being met in the world by another woman does not satisfy the psyche's desire to be confronted by and be in connection with the Animus. All women need to include the male principle in the psyche.

The Anima and Sensuality

For individuals who are wounded in their bodies, one of the areas the Anima may work is with the client's sensuality. Sensuality has nothing to do with sex. Rather, it is the capacity to feel love in the body. It is the capacity to feel in the body the heart a client has for others and the world. How essence is translated into the physical world through a touch or a smell or a sense of being intimate with a partner or children.

Many people have guilt around issues of the body because of early childhood and societal taboos. It can be shocking in a dream when an Anima figure comes as a little girl who is inviting the client of either gender to come to her sexually. Again, this is not about sex but about opening to the deeper feelings of sensuality. In this case, the Anima is very shocking and the taboos of society reflect the way in which the client is aloof in the outer world and separate from the passion of the heart. Many people are frightened of the sensual world because in the outer world they have experiences where it led to pain such as betrayal or sexual abuse. This exploration with the Anima resulting in opening up the deeper experiential connection to the physical world is only brought to clients who have a strong moral backbone. For clients with this kind of backbone, there is no danger of acting out the metaphorical imagery of a dream in the outer world.

It would be easy at first glance to confuse the shocking Anima figure with the sirens of the psyche. Some people have sirens who use sensuality in a seductive and sexual way to lure the them into acts that are self-violating. As in all things in the dreams, that which appears as something good and intentionally healing can be a deception for a different person.

There are no absolute rules and guidelines in dreamwork. Each client is met on an individual basis so that the distinction between a pathological entity in a dream and an Archetype is clear. Lack of clarity can lead the therapist into a supportive relationship with forces in the psyche that are deceptive and destructive.

It is the nature of the feminine principle when it is pathologically driven to confuse intimacy and acceptance with seduction and manipulation. This will likely be a blind spot for the client who is emotionally incested through the mother in this way. When this is present in the psyche, the client will have a blind spot in which he allows himself to be guided by spiritual looking demons.

For many clients, pathology is not overtly dark, but is subtle, seductive and will try to disguise itself as the Anima. The art of this work is for the therapist to be able to discern the difference. If the therapist is tricked by an female figure that is pathological in his own work, he will likely make the same error with his clients.

Harbinger of Essence

As the effects of wounds begin to reverse, a client can begin to feel more personally accepting of herself and can begin to move forward. In this forward movement, the Anima can come increasingly as a harbinger of essence. The Anima is, in her nature, the personification of breathing water - mermaids, whales and dolphins often symbolize the world of the Archetypes. Self acceptance is one step toward that world. Self-acceptance brings the capacity to trust feelings, which signals the beginning of the emergence of the inner life.

In this way, the Anima is the gatekeeper of essence and a key to advanced work. The capacity to experience essence is the capacity to be in relationship with the Divine on a much deeper level. Essence is the function of the soul, the way to experience transcendent consciousness. Wherever there is essence, however, there is also deception. Of all the Archetypal figures, the Anima and the area of essence have the greatest potential for confusion and error.

Essence can be manipulated so that a client feels essence in a way that is perceived as Archetypal but, in fact, guides the person away from her real feelings - like a siren versus the sensual child. One example is the dream motif of flying. Some flying dreams represent an aspect of essence that is experienced as exhilaration and a letting go of the world. But, it can also be the opposite where the client is being shown how her exhilaration is pathological and avoids connection with the world by preventing a groundedness with her own feelings. Something good can be converted to something manipulative. The client cannot be expected to know the difference because she does not have the capacity to compare one form of essence to another, one form of flying to another, one form of good feeling to another.

Because good feelings can be false, the feeling of essence can be deceptive. A client can have the pathological illness of having good feelings as a way to avoid real feelings. An example is the Judas character in the first Matrix movie. He betrayed because he wanted to be plugged back into virtual reality, with its virtual steak and virtual sex. He did not care that it was not real - he just wanted the steak to taste good again. Many people are like him because reality seems too harsh and too difficult. The alternative is to live in the illusion of good feelings. Drug abuse and a great deal of anti-depressant use come under this realm.

Often pain and hurt, even love and joy are too difficult to feel, because accepting the feelings means a death to the self. Most people will choose the illusion, regardless of their suffering, to avoid the psychotic feeling of change. Instead, the choice is for the "good" or pleasurable feeling to avoid the others. The assumption of feeling good is really in relationship to feeling safe. Freud's pleasure principle, where a person is driven to gratify pleasure instincts, only applies where pleasure is defined as the avoidance of the very things that lead to spiritual transformation. Since the outcome of facing into difficult feelings is completely unknown, it is easy for pathology to trick a person into avoiding the feelings. Pleasure, in this case, is the desire to avoid the difficult feelings that would lead to true connection and the absolute beauty of God's love.

A person's psyche is driven by the norm by which she lives. If a person's norm is to feel poorly and live with self-hate, she will want to remain in that state because it is safe and known. A good feeling that is not a true feeling is more comfortable than a real feeling that is loving and powerful if the good feeling is what the person has come to expect. The pleasure principle is not based on what feels good, it is based on what feels normal or safe.

The Anima, Essence and Deception

The feelings associated with essence can be very different than the expectations of the feelings of essence. Essence can come through most any feeling - pain, fear, inadequacy, joy. Because essence is difficult to explain - how is it possible to communicate the experience of connection with God - trying to articulate it often gives the pathology a chance to work through mimicry. One of the biggest dangers about pathology, in fact, is its ability to mimic real experiences such as connection, pain, joy and sensuality. It is always ready to replace real feelings with a false reality for a client to unwittingly believe. Because of this, "good" and "bad" feelings can be authentic or pathological. The dreams cut through the lie to find the truth, to point out what is pathological and what is Archetypal.

The Anima is rarely a dark figure, so if a dark female appears in a dream, she is probably pathology. Instead, the pathology can be deceptive by appearing loving in mimicry of the Anima, when in fact, it is not. So that, even though the Anima probably will appear in a loving manner, the pathology can do the same. When Aphrodite rises out of the sea foam in a half shell, is she the seductress or the real thing? It depends on the psyche of the individual.

This issue of deception is of less concern with the Animus because He is not subtle in nature. The Animus presents Himself very differently than the Anima and has a very different role in the psyche. Generally dark male figures are the province of the pathology or of the Animus as a trickster. A dark man chasing the client in a dream can be truly a dark male figure or it could be the client's projection onto the Animus that makes Him appear dark.

Often the Animus can be the Agent Provocateur trying to open the client to the feeling of fear. Sometimes the only issue in a dream is that the Archetype wants the client to feel a feeling. Feelings are the base materials transformed by Alchemy - one feeling state becoming transformed into another feeling state. Fear into essence, pain into love, inadequacy into connection with the Father.

In rare cases, the Animus can come as a seducer in which a female client would find herself in a whorish position, but it is unlikely He would be subtle and sweet. The shadow of the Animus is not a sweet man that is the false male. The shadow of the Animus is the dark evil man or the mean man. The confusion with the Animus is based on His intention in the dream. His shadow is the brute. The shadow of the Anima is the seductress.

A Thought At Twenty Below Zero

The door opened, in memory
or to first cold-morning breath, outside
sunrise toward winter east.

Light stained pink sky. And for a moment,
stillness. Recollection. That moment caught. Or say,
frozen, for an instant the gesture held, studied.

What then when the door is closed? New air
within the lungs, turning, the mind changed.
How, in a breath, a life can be altered.

Karla Van Vliet

GOD THE FATHER

Fetus in the Dead Demon Mother
by Denise Wilder

The Broad Image of the Cave Chamber   **Fetus Hanging on to a Dead Womb**

Dream:

I'm hiking on a path and I meet a man from the nearby village holding a sign. The writing is garbled, so I ask him what the sign says. He tells me he will show me instead, and I follow him to a cave. We enter a chamber. The light from the entryway shines on a photograph of a woman. Below the photograph, I see a stone walled well almost filled with dirt. The man tells me the woman in the photograph was his pregnant wife who died some time ago and she was buried standing up in the well. The man said he has remarried, but he regularly visits this grave of his first wife and unborn child. He placed the sign on the grave. We stood there in silent reverence and I thought about the loss of his wife, but even more, I grieved about how his unborn child never felt his love and nurturing.

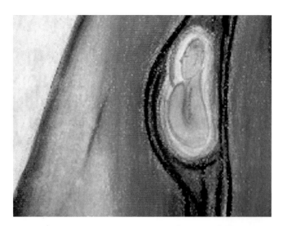

Close-up - Fetus Feels His Own Glow of Essential Life

Close-up - Fetus Feels His Own Glow of Essential Life

The Animus Loves His Child - Fetus Feels His Love and Waits

From Denise:

> My lifelong impulses to hide and caretake get in the way of feeling and acting in essence. For example, I recently hid a positive development in my work because I did not want to show off. Marc calls my pathology Quiet Sally (her role in this dream is the dead demon mother), who keeps me from knowing adequacy, desire, need, feeling, and especially the love of the Animus and Anima. The demon mother has died through my own willingness to receive the love of the Animus in the last three months, yet it takes this dream to show me she is really dead. In spite of that, like a last blast of defiance, pathological dreams and impulses to hide and caretake plagued me in my awake world. Why was I hanging on to a dead womb? What could I do to get out? Marc instructed me not to do anything but feel and then communicate my process through artwork. The Animus will do the rest.

> I had a dream with my little sister crying to me, "What about my little boy?" Marc said the little boy wants to come out from hiding. Here I am - the Animus has birthed his fetus. I have a new life.

In the first dream, when the man shows Denise the grave of his first wife, the wife is actually Denise herself. She does not remember. His grief for her is shielded to her. She cannot know this grief is for her, but she is moved because she knows at some deep level that all of this involves her.

Even though she does not feel that she is the wife, she does feel the pain of the child never knowing the Animus Father. She is speaking of her own self and her own bereftness of being separate from Him. It is interesting to note that her concern for the child becomes the preeminent issue in that she feels the pain of the child not knowing the Father. This would not be an expected reaction. Most people would feel the woundedness of the lost child not having a life and not relate the pain to the Father. This inherent spiritual knowledge is part of the resonance of her spiritual potential that has been hidden in her life. In this pain of the loss of the child not having the Father is the capacity for her to become the unborn fetus. This is the pain she needs to feel.

As she feels this pain, she understands this Alchemy of feeling the need for the Animus, of feeling the need to be loved, which breaks through the shame that makes her feel unworthy. Quiet Sally, the part of Denise who comes from the shame, is unmasked and the fetus can be developed. The work the Animus does is to continue to love and support Denise while waiting for the emerging birth. At this point in her work, the process is not yet complete.

In this relationship to the love of the male, it is unclear if it is the Animus or the Father in this dream. And in this situation, it hardly matters. The male principle is the key to this aspect of birth. It is not to say that she does not need the love of her mother, but in this dream, what is being worked through is the Father. This acceptance of the Father's love is what causes the emerging birth to occur.

The Father

There are many kinds of earthly fathers - authoritarian, passive sugar daddies, supportive "you can do it" types, negative types that shame, destructive/abusive fathers, loving types. But no father, not even a good one, can help a child understand God. All fathers - good, bad or indifferent - carry pathology and are human, and a human cannot distill the love of God. Still, the child projects the need for structure and security onto a father with the expectation that he will provide it.

The child, then the adult, projects what he believes he wants from his own father onto the concept of God the Father. The adult may believe that if he only had the right kind of father, the right kind of authority figure, he would have an answer or a stepping stone to knowing God.

But there is no stepping stone.

God is not a man or a "him" or even "the father." The term *father* is only useful because it is the closest approximation available referencing God to anything. A way of approximating understanding. But God is unknown - the only thing known about God is that God is love.

The dreamwork is, in part, a preparation to receive this love.

There is no easy answer to the question of how to open to God's love. The only way to come to know it is to prepare for it. God's love is only "understood" when it is felt through connection to essence, otherwise it is only a construct or a concept. Role models like God the Father, are always externalizations of what can only be felt. When a person creates a father construct for himself without really feeling it, all he has done is create a structure. This structure may come in the form of obedience or doing a job well, with the hope of proving worthiness of love through positive actions in the world. In this structure, however, love is no more than a conditionality - being worthy of God's love because of good deeds or being worthy of love from family as a substitute for the Divine love not being received.

On a large scale, governments can be seen as the different ways humans have attempted throughout history to find a father. None really work, although some are better than others. Father is something more than a structure of safety. Father is the unknowing connection to love. When essence is felt, the person has moved beyond the construct.

Most people do not feel the love, though a person may have a narrow realm of emotion where he believes he knows of God's love. Most of this, however, is feeling the construct. The person wants God the Father to support him, but if the Father does not give what is wanted then the individual will not believe He exists. People blame the Father because they do not receive what they want, not noticing that what they want is usually something external. Most people pray for things or outcomes or favorable situations. How many people pray for His love?

Religions as well as individuals get caught in a concept of the Father. The focus becomes about right and wrong, rules, correct ways to behave, being good to get to heaven. All construct. Father as a Feeling goes beyond Father as an Idea. It moves into something beyond masculine or feminine and into a deeper sense of overarching love. This love is beyond anything we can even hope to imagine feeling.

God the Father in Greek Mythology

Greek mythology traces the symbolic descent of the Father into the world beginning with Uranus, the first Father. Uranus is castrated by his son, Chronos/Saturn, with the help of his mother, Gaia. In the next generation, Zeus/Jupiter kills his father Chronos with the help of his mother, Rhea. The closer the Father gets to humanity, the more his essence becomes diluted and reduced to something that the small consciousness of a human can understand.

Humans cannot fathom the Uranian Father, the embodiment of pure love. Jung refers to this love as the love that individuates, that creates in every person the special quality that makes him or her unlike anyone else. Uranus, the highest octave of the Father, is Archetypal. He is the Spiritual Father.

The next level in this paradigm of the Father is Chronos, the patriarchal authoritarian who embodies discipline, responsibility, structures, right/wrong, and never being good enough. The stern "senex" father. With this father, the child is loved if she does the right thing; but if she does the wrong thing, the child is bad and unloved. Go to heaven or go to hell. He is the dark father, judgmental and shaming, the guardian of "morality" with very little to give.

After Chronos is Zeus, the son who has sex with his mother and kills his father. He is the "puer" father, the emotionally incested son who never grows up beyond his mother. As a compensation, he can be impotent, permissive, pandering, lacking boundaries and full of pride. He can also be giving, accepting and supportive, the one who has plenty. Zeus is the father made possible by the privileges of the industrial age. Jung predicted this would occur. Over the last hundred years, we have gone from the Chronos father of scarcity whose motto might be "work hard, die and go to heaven," to the Zeus father of plenty who suggests to pray for a bigger house, a new BMW or to win the lottery. This is a common trajectory among successful societies. But plenty, acceptance and support are not the same thing as love.

Both the Chronos father and the Zeus father are embodiments of pathology. If a client is damaged by either type, it affects her ability to know herself. Chronos and Zeus are not Archetypal fathers, but rather two polarities that relate to different personality features and to different ways of functioning in the world. Both extremes are compensatory functions the ego finds necessary for survival when self-knowledge is lacking. Without the soul self, the psychological self tries to "figure out" who it is in relation to the external world. The Chronos father and the Zeus father are really sons, not the true Father. They reflect a continuum of self-identity based on judgment and pride that moves from "I am worse than everybody" to "I am as good as anybody" to "I am better than everybody." None of this is love. Love is something else.

The Uranian Father's love is that something else and for most, is unknown. His love is tied to essence, is potent and it raises consciousness up to meet it. In this love, there is no need for the

Chronos or Zeus kind of father love. The Uranian Father's love excites the soul and brings self understanding because it is the love that creates the soul - God's love. In the process of adapting to the world, the self forgets its creation and that love.

Individuation is the state of being when a person is in his unique essence and can feel this Divine love. From this experience, the client can begin to embody his essence, to be his true self.

Individuation is part of the process which moves a client into Third Stage dreamwork and into finding his "calling." Not a calling out of a sense of responsibility - the Chronos father - nor the spiritual pride of saving the world - the Zeus father. A calling evolves as the soul unfolds in relationship with the Divine.

The killing of Uranus by Chronos shows how the process of fratricide is part of the dissemination of the Father's love. As the love of the Father descended into matter, the previous version of the Father was killed off. Therefore, the process of moving up the male/father ladder is a movement against the intention of the patricide. This intention of the patricide is part of the separation boys feel with their fathers and influences the rebelliousness that follows.

As each subsequent generation kills off the father, the separation from the loving Father becomes more and more profound. As we have progressed technologically and intellectually, we have also continued to regress spiritually, replacing God's love with a hybrid form of society's independent knowledge and success - the greater the knowledge of the universe, the greater the separation from the love.

Of course, this is not a necessary truth. Both knowledge of the Father and a connection through essence with the Father can exist together. The dreamwork of an individual psyche attempts to heal that breach and ascend the individual back through the layers of father. To connection with the ultimate Uranian Father, the Father that loves everyone.

Trouble the Untroubled

Lifted black shapes calling--
caw caw-- into morning's question
sift through the shadowed pines.

Wings spread over what now
is covered in snow's
quiet shielding.

To move is to make my way
deep into what has fallen
like shed feathers,

to make some shape or trail
I can not take back,
to trouble the untroubled memory.

Is that what is asked of me?
What good comes from telling
what insulates my heart?

Ordinary as the crow.

Karla Van Vliet

The Child Self or the Soul Self

In order to experience the Archetypal world, it is necessary to be the child self, the soul self, the true self. The child self is not an Archetype, like the Animus or Anima - a client can never be the Animus or the Anima. The child self is the essential self of the individual, the only part that can be in relationship with the Archetypes. The goal for the client is to become the child, not be in relationship to the child.

Child Self versus Archetypes

Again, the child self is not an Archetype, like the Animus or the Anima, but an essential part of the client. A client never becomes the Animus or the Anima because these Archetypes are not male and female parts of the client. The Animus and Anima are teachers, Divine aspects that are liaisons between God (the Uranian Father) and humans. The client learns to find a way to open to the Archetypes, but she can never be them. Archetypes are themselves - and there are feeling aspects of them that are also aspects in the client.

The wellspring to relationship with the Archetypes and to the Archetypal Realm is the client's own child self which the client does need to become. The child is often understood as a fantasy or part of the self that is childlike or childish - the one that says, "I want ice cream," or a new car or a vacation. The list is endless. The outer world really has nothing to do with the child self. The child self, instead, is the way a person experiences the world and the way she experiences the Divine. It is the true place of need.

For some, the need of the child self might begin as an awareness of needing the ice cream or the vacation. However, the child is ultimately not served by being obedient to a need. It is the need itself, not the goal of the need, that represents the feeling tone of the child self. Adding a goal to the question of what the child wants actually takes away from the reality of the child self. The desire of the child self is not attached to a goal, but is the essence of desire itself. In this way, when the object of desire appears, the child self can recognize it as some aspect of the Divine, not as the thing itself.

Impoverishment may require the client to take baby steps with things like ice cream, a hug from a lover, maybe a train set always wanted and never received. These are baby steps to the larger need that is the soul of the child. It is what the client carried into the world and either knew for a time or never knew. The child self waits, mostly separate from the ego that developed over the lifetime of the client. There are those few who may know their soul desire and may even realize that there is no happiness unless that desire is felt and acknowledged.

Becoming the Child

Children in dreams are almost always the soul of the client, though there are exceptions. How a client responds to his child self in dreams varies. Many clients want to take care of the child in a dream like a good loving parent - they want to nurture, protect and save the child because they are operating out of a sense of worldliness. Becoming the child is very different from taking care of the child. Other clients discover their child self in a dream and have a negative reaction to it or reject the child in some way. The core of such a child may have terrible wounds the client does not want to feel or does not yet have the capacity to face. In this case, rescuing, nurturing, or loving the child in a dream can be a step for the client in the process of coming to terms with his inner self. But he is still separate from the child and remains in a position of dominance and control. Taking care of the child can be an old pattern or a step toward a new pattern; either way, the goal is to become the child.

The client must eventually get beyond the idea that relationship with the child, even in a good way, is enough. When a child is born in a dream, it can reflect an opening to a new opportunity in the psyche, perhaps an opportunity to experience a particular feeling that previously had been lost. The client needs to become the newborn through experiencing the feeling or the new consciousness opening to him.

At some point, the client will suddenly be the child in a dream. He may even be child-sized in relationship to the people and things in the dream. This is an important moment. The experiences of the dream - the feelings, their relationship to the world around - will help the client see both how he is a child and the new reality of being a child. Until he becomes the child, the client will need to be helped and prepared to give up his adult consciousness of reality.

Hospital
by Cat

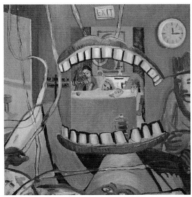

Dream:

> The original source of this painting was a fleeting dream I had about being wheeled into a hospital. I think my heart is bleeding out through my chest. At some point, while working on this painting, I associated this dream with another I had that was also set in a hospital: a young girl lies in bed dying of a fatal illness. Because I work in a hospital, I have many images of corridors and rooms and reception desks, and these served as additional source material.

This painting is a compilation of two dreams, as Cat indicates. In one dream, she is looking at herself as the young girl in bed, while in the other, she is the one in the bed, being wheeled into the hospital. The idea of dreams showing two angles is typical when the process is challenging the client to accept herself in an entirely new way.

Seeing the girl and then realizing she is the girl is a way of reinforcing the understanding of who she really is - that she is not really her old self being wheeled in, but she is the girl. Not only is she the girl, but she is the girl who needs help. The doctors are probably Archetypal figures who are trying to remedy the problem.

The key to the dream where she feels her heart is bleeding is to determine the actual problem. In the dream, she believes her heart is bleeding and coming out of her chest, but there is no such image. The image is not in the painting because it never happened. She only believes that it happened. In the dream, she never sees any blood. Why, then, does she assume an illness that never actually occurred.

One could surmise that her heart is actually bursting, and bursting because it can no longer carry the truth of her child/soul self inside. The purpose of the little girl is to emerge from the concepts the client carries of her self. This bursting emergence of the self is the key to the dream. The child self is the little girl who wakes inside her, bursting out of her chest, needing to take center stage in Cat's ego/psyche.

Walking over the fire
by Cat

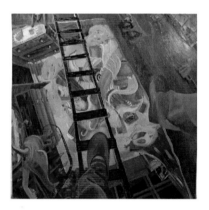

Dream:

> I am in a dark room and a little girl wearing pink looks up at me, reaching out her arms towards me. I love her so much it hurts. She is so close to me that she fills up the frame of my vision completely. I feel aching love for her and I feel her vulnerability as if it were my own.

From Cat:

> This painting actually has its source in a dream I had about the little girl. In the dream, she looks up at me, frighteningly vulnerable with a round pink belly (she is wearing a bathing suit). I painted it three times, and this big painting is the third iteration. I had first imagined it as a kind of Mandala, with four circling girls dancing around an eight-armed no-headed being (where the fire currently is) whom I identified with myself. When I began to work on it, however, the eight-armed being became a fire, and I (with my red clogs) became precariously balanced above it on a thin catwalk. My dog Mayday, and three others, make it difficult to leave the fire and in fact encourage me to plunge down towards it.

The little girl in the dream represents Cat's true self that is separated from her life. This client is a hostage of the whoremaster, as shown in other dreams, but in her new revelation, she is aware of the pain of the separation of the self that knows she loves the Animus. Painting the picture a third time, she paints her pain as fire and she sees her self as separate from the girl. The painting is not really a reinterpretation of the dream but a deeper awareness of the child and the separation from the child.

Cat must plunge into the fire which is her pain. The painting is an accurate representation of her separation from her pain and her inability to be a part of it. Falling into the fire and feeling the pain is a way of letting the old self be devoured. The Alchemy is upon her through her awareness of her need and her aching love. In this way, she begins to dissolve into her true self. The aching love is the feeling that can only come from the child, so she and the child are truly one at that moment. Her objective ego self is the part of her that still stands on the ladder. For her to break that ego self, she must jump. The therapeutic process for her is to see how she is with the connection with the child versus being objectified outside of it in the vagaries of the mind which provide her with relative security and separation from her feelings. There is still a choice to be made.

Walking Above Me
by Cat

Dream:

> I am at an outdoor music venue owned by a friend of mine. I am sitting in the empty stadium seats. My friend is walking above me, checking the lighting, on a high catwalk. I feel very jealous of her and very terrible about myself.

From Cat:

> In this dream, a friend of mine, whom I feel intensely jealous of, walks over my head on a high walkway. In this painting, I am looking up at her. When she blocks out the sun with her body it changes into the three primary colors.

In this dream, Cat is the child who is below, looking up at her old self. Of course, she feels jealous because in her outer life, she does not accept her own beauty. In this dream, she does not see her self, but looks out into the outer world and believes she should find a way to be in it, even though she actually cannot. This leaves her with feelings of unworthiness which sets her up to be vulnerable to the dark male, the whoremaster. Jealousy is a projection of her own power and potency. She sees it in her friend, believing that only her friend can possess power and potency. Suffering such jealousy is a trick, a half turn of the screw. But a glance in the mirror, a slight shift, and she is the one. But, her own self, with all of her potency, has been lost to the other. By accepting who she really is, she can find that she has no reason to be jealous. The reclamation process occurs when she is aware of her pain, the pain of her separation from her self. She can recognize in her pain that she is coming home to her soul self.

The evolution of this dream process can be clearly seen in these paintings. In the first case, the connection with the child is not connected with the pain. She assumes the child is dead or dying. But in the following dreams, there is no such problem. And the whoremaster is no longer a factor. Cat can face the pain which goes beyond her relationship with men. This deeper pain is the pain of her relationship with her soul/child self which is a deeper, more profound aspect of her self.

The Age of Children in Dreams

The age of a child in a dream can represent the time in a client's life when she was that age and lost connection to this part of herself. It could be an age and time in her life when she was still one with the child self.

If the child in a dream is over the ages of three or four, the client likely will remember something of being the child self. She may remember the actual relationship with the Divine or she may remember behaving in a way that suggests the relationship. One thing is certain - the age of the child in the dream is the last time the client was the child self. From this point on, whether it was three or six, she lost her child self.

It is very different to claim through memory a part of the self that was lost. The older the child when the child self was lost, the greater the development of the child self and the greater the memory of the adult of the experiences of being the child self. It is always easier to remember being eight or nine then it is to remember being three or four. Sometimes, remembering is enough to produce a great awakening. For those clients who have no memory of the child self, however, the process can involve birthing many children in dreams. Multiple births are simply a way of showing the intention of incorporating unremembered parts of the psyche.

When a child in a dream is over the age of ten or so, in adolescence, the child usually no longer represents the age of the client when the child self was lost. Adolescence, unlike childhood, is the time of the awakening of self-awareness. To the degree that an individual has lost the child self, adolescence can be the beginning of life without the soul. Because of this, most people miss the gifts of adolescence. For those who lived through adolescence as an extension of abuse they experienced throughout childhood, the nature and emotional aspect of adolescence are no more than reaction - a continual reaction to life. There are rare cases where adolescence was a reflection of the Divine connection of childhood carried through even into adulthood. But for most, adolescence becomes another aspect of the psyche that is missed. In this case, the spiritual aspects of missed adolescence will manifest in dreams, often with the result of the client reacting negatively.

After adolescence, the self becomes the adult and it has no choice but to deal with the world because the self is in the world and aware of being in the world. Others define the post-adolescent person in her twenties in terms of what she has done or not done. No matter how the person reacts - either defiantly or accepting the definitions - innocence is lost.

The great bohemian revolution gave a generation the opportunity to rethink themselves and Western culture. But even this quickly became persona. While people knew who they were and pursued passion from that knowing, most were not in their child self. Most were already lost - so the revolution was over the minute it began. Many like to say that God is on their side, that they are in their soul self, but any attempt to define the self only creates a deeper persona hole. Those who know they are in the persona hole sometime in their thirties or forties are lucky because they can begin to face their personas.

The dreams and the dreamwork challenge a person to face the truth of her development. A person's memory may lie, but dreams do not. The dream is the beacon to the client's past. If a client is on her path, the dreams reinforce the direction and give her opportunities to go deeper. Most people, however, are not on their path and their presumed progress is nothing more than personas out of control. The dreams help the client to face her persona and begin to find her way back to her path.

Leaving Adult Consciousness

Letting go of adult consciousness is difficult for most clients because they have many adult things they believe are important such as cares and concerns and causes in the world. Even if they are right and the positions taken are understandable, they are still obstructions to the consciousness of the child. Questions of getting the bills paid or how to do work that needs to be done make the preparation of a client to let go of his identification with the adult ego quite challenging. But this work is not about the world or values or right versus wrong. It is not even about being a good person. This work is apolitical and has nothing to do with the fabric of the world.

The dreamwork is about Dying to Self and the self that a client dies to is his child self or soul self. The child self is neither good nor bad; it simply is. Because all the child knows is what it is, what it needs, what it feels, the child self has a very poor sense of duality. Instead, a healthy inner child has a strong connection to God and feels essence. It may have a hard time understanding the adult world and cannot integrate itself into that world easily.

Some inner children are profoundly hurt, insecure and wounded while others are less wounded and more joyful. Some inner children are dead, in dumpsters, some act out by eating their flesh alive, in torment. Some are safe and even kept by Archetypal figures. All children represent the baseline capacity of the soul's ability to be in relationship with the Divine. The soul needs to grow and change from this baseline. To begin from the point of feeling, no matter what the feeling was - whether it was injury or joy or passion or grief. It cannot do this as long as the adult self is dominant, even if the adult self is well intentioned and loving.

The higher functioning the adult, the less the client will see the reason to become the child. The developed ego of the adult tends to see the child as selfish and narcissistic, a dangerous thing to become. The child may blurt out things that are unacceptable or see the truth of the client's life and place in jeopardy all that he has convinced himself he must do or have. Since the child contains the cruel truth the client may feel he cannot face, there is a great deal at stake by opening to the child self. But becoming the child creates the capacity to connect to the source, to God, through the relationship between the child self and the Archetypes. The faster the client comes to terms with his child self, the quicker he can have a relationship to the Divine.

Different States of the Child Self

Healthy Child

If a client has a healthy child self with a connection to the Divine but she is just disconnected from that child self, the process will be somewhat easier. Even if the client is living in complete reaction in her outer life, she still has the child self in her that is basically whole and on which she can rely. It is possible to have a healthy child self but a disconnected, unhealthy ego self. When a child self is sick, however, the process will be more difficult. It is very possible to have a healthy ego self and an unhealthy child self. The condition of the child self is crucial to the client's process.

Some people have a child self that does not fit into the outer world. The child self knows something at a very deep level and confronts the world with this knowledge at a young age. For example, a Hispanic woman came into the work with anger issues and with recurring dreams of a black figure from Africa. It became clear through working with the dreams that the figure was the true mother of the child self, indicating that her child self, underneath the anger and pathology, was still intact. It just did not fit in the world. When the child self of a client remembers being in essence, remembers being in relationship with the Divine, this child is never happy until it finds that connection again.

Dream:

> I am raped and become pregnant. When the child is born it is ugly and deformed. I
> want to kill it.

The soul has many nuances which means that psychological issues are not always going to be addressed as would be expected. For this client, the dysfunction of her anger was not an emotional or psychological issue, but a spiritual one as is shown by the birth of a child in the dream. The birth of a child represents something new to the psyche and is the carrier of the essence of the soul self. In fact, there can be multiple births depending on how much has been lost to the psyche. In this case, the horrific deformity of the child is the client's projection of her own self-hate. Since the client was not raped in her outer life, the rape of the dream is her own suffering at the hands of the world which she experiences as rape. This experience damaged her to the point where she felt shame and guilt. The pain is sublimated in such a way that the hate and anger at the world is self directed - in the dream, she wants to kill the child which is her child self.

When a child self is healthy and already connected, it is simply looking for the client to acknowledge and accept it. The issue in such cases is the unwillingness of the client to be in her essence. The client will not want the child because becoming the child means changing the way she is in the world, the way she perceives, and she may be very attached to her ways. The essence of the child self has nothing to do with the psychological awareness of the self.

Dead Child

Most people do not have an intact child self. Instead, most people are faced with a child self in different forms of crises. The most extreme is when the child self manifests in a dream as dead.

Dream:

> I am standing on a street, looking around. All of a sudden, a thunder storm begins
> with torrential rain and tornadoes causing major damage. Many homes are destroyed.
> I find a dead six-year-old girl on the street. She has green bile all over her and it seems
> like one of her organs was punctured.

This was a breakthrough dream for the client. He had been walking around with a dead child inside for thirty-five years without any awareness of that feeling. His child self was not born - it died when he was six. This dream refers to the inner experience of his childhood relationship with his father who was abusive. His father was unpredictable and frightening - he remembered heavy feet coming down the stairs, the feeling of complete fear and never knowing what the father would do. The same feelings that came up for him in the dream.

In his adult life, he felt rage most of the time. This dream was a gift because when he felt the rage, he could go to the dead child and feel all the feelings around her. This immediately dissipated the rage. It was extremely helpful for him to know that the reason for his suffering was that his child self was dead. He felt more connected to that child self and himself then he had in years, even though the dream and the reality of the dream was devastating.

When a child manifests as dead in a dream, the child is not really dead for nothing really dies in dreams. Everything is alive, so that what appears as dead can be made alive again. Being the dead child was a gift for the client because he finally felt and understood his essence. It was a great place to start - to begin the process of bringing the child self back to life.

When the child self is this wounded, the healing comes from the Archetypes, not the therapist. The Divine can heal anything and transform it. With a dead child, the issue is that the client's essence was killed and the Archetypes will work to revive it. The process of reviving something that is dead to the client is profoundly different than healing something that is wounded. When an aspect appears dead in a dream, it means that it is outside the memory of the psyche. Since the client cannot fathom its existence, his life becomes fashioned without the ability to even be aware that it is missing. Consequently, there is no feeling associated with the dead child.

When a child is wounded, there is a feeling associated with it because it is still a presence in the psyche. But the dead child has dropped out of the psyche completely. A feeling is needed to alchemize and restore the child self. This particular journey is nothing short of a complete dropping into a dark hole of the unknown. Without feeling material as a reference point, the client must go through the fear alone without guidance. Understandably, a dead child can remain dead in a client's psyche through even the most intensive therapeutic processes because it is incredibly difficult to go into that unknown. This particular client was able to move through the process.

Abandoned Child

A child self that is abandoned can manifest in scenarios such as finding a child in a dumpster. The client usually does not know that the child self is abandoned because it is a different feeling then when the ego self is abandoned. When the child self is abandoned, the ego self does not feel what the child self feels. The work is to bring the client into the feeling experience of the child rather than feeling feelings related to the ego self. This does not invalidate the ego feelings, it simple brings into awareness both the ego feelings and child self feelings.

When a child self is abandoned in the psyche, it creates the opportunity for the emergence of nihilism. The pain of the lost self easily morphs into hopelessness and desolation. Many clients with an abandoned child self experience some form of detachment disorder where they lose the capacity for relationship and intimacy. The child self is present in the psyche, but is so wounded that intimacy is not understood except through the wound itself.

Orphaned Child

An orphaned child self lives in a state where she does not belong to anyone - not to parents, family, friends. Since the overarching context of a person with an orphaned child is that she does not belong, this includes feeling belonging in any relationship with the Divine. It is an issue that is beyond even fear. Her work will be the transformation of essence into a being who is capable of relationship with the Divine. Even an individual with great parents can have an orphaned child. It is not always dependent on outer world experiences.

Although the child is orphaned, it is taken care of in the psyche, unlike the dead or abandoned child self who is lost in a sea of fear and pain. The orphaned child can be felt by the client and can even exert itself into the ego self at times. There are many warm and caring people capable of taking care of others in pain because of the sense of the orphan in themselves. When the orphan self is projected onto others, great mercy and care can be felt.

Birth Child

For a client who has no memory of any experiences as a child, he will have dreams where a child is birthed, representing his need to continually birth his self. This tends to be true for clients who have a certain degree of abuse in their history. Their consciousness becomes so altered by the experiences, that any memory of being a child is lost.

Some birth dreams are also about the extension of consciousness and reflect new ways of growth. Bit by bit, with each new birth, the psyche is rebuilt. Sometimes there will be multiple births, each carrying a piece of the puzzle. Great patience is required in these cases, since there will be no great revelation as the child is born. Instead it will be a series of slow, painstaking steps in a difficult rebuilding process.

Pathological Child Self

In rare cases the child itself is pathological. In these cases, the essence of the soul has been polluted to the point where the soul itself has completely bought into the pathology. This is a serious and difficult problem. The condition of the child reflects the condition of the soul, not the personality or interplay between the ego and pathology.

* * * *

The child self is not determined by experiences of childhood, though it can be affected by them. Children are not born into the world as a blank slate. Individuals born into the world very open and vulnerable are more likely to be more wounded by life than those who are not open and vulnerable from birth. Unfortunately, when an open child is abused, the child self gets buried all the more deeply. For a person who comes into the world not vulnerable, whatever impact life has on him, it is not likely to have a great an impact on the child self.

For example, a client lived with a father who sexually abused her and her four sisters every day for fifteen years. But even though she lived with this level of violence, the condition of the inner child was not directly connected to the abuse. The condition of the inner child was that of an ugly duckling who felt she was neither good enough nor pretty enough. The inner child was not affected by the abuse. The trauma pushed the child self to the side, keeping it buried, but it did not damage it. This is not to say that the abuse did not affect her, because of course it did. But it did not affect the child self.

Once a child self has been established, the Archetypes can work with the client on building his relationship with the Divine, however that manifests for that particular individual. The Archetypes work with the child self, no matter what kind of child self it is - healthy, wounded, abandoned, orphaned.

Edge

The moon, knife to darkness.

Unseeable in the slit night,
the opened flower.

I am led by sound to the river,
by touch to your face.

In the scent of this darkness,
the edge of what is bearable.

Karla Van Vliet

THE ISSUE OF FREE WILL

Out beyond ideas of wrongdoing and rightdoing,
there is a field. I'll meet you there.

-Rumi

Looking at the world, everyone hopes to see good things happening to good people and bad things happening to bad people, but in reality bad things happen to good people. Even though they do all the right things, tragedy befalls in the form of disease, divorce, death, accidents of many kinds, loss of job, financial ruin.

But what is the definition of a good person? There are a great deal of assumptions about what and who is good in the world, but it is actually impossible to know. The dreams of a "good" person may reveal that to God, even though he is beautiful, admired and respected in the world, he is not with Him. And the reasons he is not with Him are hidden and may not be so beautiful. Most people are not capable of doing truly good things until they are with God.

The Book of Job wrestles with the question of a good person suffering in the world. Job lost everything and suffered greatly in his losses. He felt he had honored God as was appropriate and customary and because of this, his suffering was an injustice.

But, was Job really with God in his heart? In the beginning of this extraordinary story, Job is described as "blameless and upright, one who feared God and turned away from evil." He feared God and performed all the appropriate rituals, but was he with God in his heart? In his affliction, he cursed his birth and demanded an explanation from God. He maintained his belief in God, but he railed against Him because his suffering did not make sense. He was under the illusion that he had control in his life - doing all that was expected of him - but when all the "rewards" for being blameless and upright were taken away, he felt wronged and argued in his own defense.

God, as whirlwind, responds to his arguments by presenting him with a long series of questions about the force of life, about the power that is God - "Have you commanded the morning since your days began, and caused the dawn to know its place?" The barrage of questions from God quickly shows how Job's arguments assume that he has the capacity to understand God, to understand the way everything in the world works. The questions show Job's lack of understanding and humility. God says, "Will you even put me in the wrong? Will you condemn me that you may be justified?"

The only answer for Job is to finally stop arguing. He ends by saying to God, "I had heard of you by the hearing of the ear, but now my eye sees you." In the beginning of the story, Job did not have a relationship with God. He "heard" of God and went through the motions of being blameless and upright. By the end, he "sees" God through his experience, and is in an intimate relationship with Him.

The Issue of Being Good

Pursuing the issue of being good or not good is to seek what is not from God's position. The issue is not about being right or wrong, but about coming into relationship with the Divine. This is an impossible quandary for most people because the way to the Divine is hidden. Rituals, incantations, meditation, prayer, personal self-sacrifice, good deeds are all an attempt to appease God.

But God does not need to be appeased. He simply wants each of us to come home.

The process of returning home to the Divine relationship is the process of Dying to Self. When Job had his revelation, when he could see from God's view, he died to his ego self. This way of seeing through God's view is to become connected to a consciousness that is not intellectual nor in the reality of thinking. It is in the reality of feeling. Advanced consciousness is based on the transformation of feeling because the reality of feeling is capable of great understanding well beyond the mind. Most people, however, suppress all feeling because of difficult or even horrific childhoods, because the world does not support the reality of feeling, because the individual does not understand or does not feel at all.

In Jacob's Ladder, the three steps of Essence, Sensuality and Grace are the modes and qualities of feeling obtained through the process of Alchemy. Without finding the feeling places, without experiencing the feelings, it is impossible to have a relationship with the Divine. This requires going back to the past to reclaim the present, rather than being lost in the present that is actually nothing but living the past way of being. Loss is merely something that has taken place a long time ago - the loss of the connection with Divine and spiritual love. Without understanding the past, it is easy to believe that it is only important to be good and do the right thing.

Choosing God's Version

People who develop Third Stage understanding and find their callings also find that God intervenes in their dreams and in their lives. Some clients receive instruction dreams while others feel the will of the Animus (as distinguished from the will of their "healthy" psychology and their pathology). The deliberate, almost physical, intervention by God is unfamiliar to most people only because they cannot see it.

When something bad happens, most people question God, but God does not cause bad things to happen. On the other hand, if it is possible for God to prevent what he chooses to prevent why would he not intervene? It is the same as in the dream life - it is the person who turns away. It is the person's choice to go through Dying to Self, to move through his issues or not. If the person does not move through his issues, then he is choosing his own version of his self and has no room for God's version. He has no room for God. He is not allowing God or the Archetypes into his heart. Because of this, the Archetype, the agent of God, cannot insert itself into the life of the client.

God requires relationship - a person must reach to Him. The dreamwork gives a map to show the way to that relationship. The dreams provide the opportunities, the teachings, the lessons that help an individual make a forward movement towards obtaining the connection. When the person is in connection/relationship with the Divine, then the Divine can indeed intervene. But the Divine cannot be a gopher to the disconnected self.

Most people do not see that they have free will. God is looking for key ingredients that are centered on choice from the person - choosing to do his work in order to find the relationship, choosing God's version over his own, Dying to Self, growing in feelings and soul self, seeking relationship with the Divine. When a person chooses the relationship with the Divine, then the Divine can be in relationship with the person.

God's intervention - being in daily relationship with Him - is possible if a person chooses to follow the Animus into the timelessness of essence. Dying to Self frees the person from being vulnerable to the ravages of pathology, rather than making him vulnerable to the slings and arrows of outrageous fortune. Ironically, most people who avoid Dying to Self because they fear something bad might happen, suffer because, in reality, something bad has already happened. If they could see this, they would realize they have nothing to lose.

True Free Will

There is no free will if it is believed to be the choice to do or be something right or wrong - to be a thief or to be a minister. Society pressures the individual to exercise the will of right choice in order to supply the needs of society. But this has nothing to do with will. In fact, most people's will controls the desire to be good or bad. True will involves the most fundamental of choices - to follow the soul or not, to listen to the Divine or not. What the soul and Divine want is not to be found in books, rules, ideas, theology. It is found in the heart.

Before an individual can have free will, she must first find her heart by cutting through the fabrications of truth that ideas and values have dictated. The answer is not in the world, it is inside through the encounter with the Divine. Until the essence of the soul self or child self is understood, then it is not actually possible to make a choice. Without the soul self, there is no free will, no true choice based on the core self.

Collection of Stones

Just yesterday I was lonely.
What have I come to?
Words laid around the house
like discarded socks, a
hair brush set down, the
pink light that presses
melancholy to the wall?

My friend and I argued
and for two years
our words were like stones
we held back from each other.
Even now, in old sweaters
and pockets of clothes long unworn
I discover stashes of pebbles.

All day I speak to my daughter
in words she does not understand.
I turn on the radio for words beyond
the ticked off hours of my day.
By the time my husband comes home
I have forgotten the lines of meaning
between actions: weeded, fed,
walked to the library, laid down to sleep.

Weren't there words for the sacred devotions:
half light, the babble of water,
the love, just the other night, we danced to?

Karla Van Vliet

THE RELATIONSHIP BETWEEN FREE WILL AND PATHOLOGY

In every client, three elements are engaged in the process of the dreamwork - the Archetypes and the Archetypal Realm, pathology and the free will of the client. When a client is bound up by pathology, he does not really have access to his free will because the pathology is in control. The pathology is responsible, in a large sense, for what happens. As the Archetypes transform the client through the dreams and through the client's work or homework from the dreams, pathology is not necessarily killed. Rather than attacking pathology, the Archetype focuses on empowering the client's free will.

The pathology is only as strong as the client's true self is not. The Archetypes may need to attack the pathology but only to the extent that it has covered up the client's free will. It is crucial that the client gain access to his free will in order to begin to make choices. It does not matter if the choices are right or wrong, only that the client realizes that he has choices. Most people do not know what choices are truly available to them.

The dreams show the therapist where the client is on his journey and what the client is being called to do or feel in terms of his relationship with the Divine. This is the basis for the homework assignments. But it is difficult to see where the client is in relationship to the process, for a dream may show the pathology but it may not show if the client has an agenda independent of the pathology.

The issue of free will is different than the issue of resistance. A resistant client may simply not like or really understand the dreamwork or he may not even like the therapist. This is different than free will. At some point in the process, the energy of the work shifts from pathology and even the Archetypes and becomes grounded in what the person is willing or not willing to do. It is necessary, of course, to focus on pathology for a time, especially in the early stages of the work. But at some point, the client must make the decision to move forward in his journey or not. When a client hits a wall, even after many breakthroughs, then the wall is where he is unwilling to move forward.

This is where a reversal can happen. A client may begin to receive very positive dreams that he does not understand because he does not really feel them. The positive dreams come, in this situation, because the subconscious has been cleared. The dreams are showing the client all that is now possible to him because the pathology has lost strength and is not as tough as the person believes it to be. The client may still be feeling the pathology, but it is not coming from a subconscious root anymore.

This is a choice point. The client must choose to continue to follow the habit of the pathology or to stay with the process of the dreams. The client will only be asked by the Archetypes to use free will when the pathology no longer has total control. This is a moment in the client's process that can send him into crisis because he must decide if he really wants to let go of pathology. Pathology always serves a function for the person or else it would not have a foothold in the psyche in the first place. The function is usually, in part, the avoidance of something. It is very frightening to choose to let go of pathology and say yes to what has been avoided for a lifetime. Many clients at this point will say no because they are faced with what they never thought they would have to face.

At this crucial choice point, the Archetype cannot do any more for the client until he takes the step of saying yes to his process, his journey and the Archetypes. The client is free to take the step and free not to take the step. If he chooses to not take the step, there is nothing the Archetype can do. The dreams will reveal the unwillingness of the client, sometimes in the form of *Fait Accompli*. This may manifest in a dream as an ambivalent person or as the dream itself reflecting a level of ambivalence. When this happens, it reflects that the client is in league with the pathology and it requires a very different approach than when his block was deeply pathologically rooted. When the pathological root begins to die, the person is no longer a victim. The block is no longer that the person is held in paralysis by the pathology, it is because he does not want to change. This is a very real, crucial and difficult struggle.

The pathology, of course, will try to squash free will and may manifest as the Agent Provocateur in a dream at this point in the client's work. The dreams show that the client has broken from the pathology and that he can see the pathology from a completely new angle. He can see it and he is not part of it. The Agent Provocateur will come to try to provoke him into playing back into the pathology in some new way. The provocation comes because the client is outside the pathology's control. The pathology as Agent Provocateur puts the client under siege, saying, "We are no longer friends. I gave you everything I had and you completely disrespected me. I am going to destroy you." The client, at this point, is in danger, even if his will is trying to push past the pathology.

A client will respond, generally, in one of two ways. He will decide either to fight through the siege and not listen to the pathology or he will try to undermine the therapist. The pathology will attempt to make the client believe that it is not about the pathology or free will, but about the process itself.

When the pathology is called out in this way, it becomes vicious and does not try to hide anymore. It will use any tactic to get the person back under control, including intimidation. With intimidation, the pathology tries to scare the client into not taking another step.

Each passage requires a degree of free will in order for the client to continue. Whenever a plateau is reached, the choice is always presented - to continue or to stay on the plateau. Again, it can be terrifying to say yes to being The One. Fear comes from the denial of self, showing the client that there is a part of the self on the other side of the fear. Some part of the self that can be reclaimed. The fear also arises because once that part of the self is reclaimed, the client then can go deeper into that self. It is a door that leads to something more, something unknown. The fear is not just fear, it is the fear of the door, of the invitation, of the deeper self. To accept the invitation, the client has to want to move through the fear and reclaim the true self. If the client does not want to go, the therapist, with the dreams, can help to support and push him.

Faith can help, but having faith does not mean that the client does not need to move through fear. Faith can help the client move through the fear and can help with his connection with the Divine. Having and facing fear does not diminish a person's faith.

Apple

1.
Within, a   star
cut from whole   to what
is left   after, yes,
the blade has split you.

2.
And the serpent said, eat of the flesh
and when she did, there was a light
from within and from that light
she could see the path which lead not
into darkness although there was
darkness but to the center to the seed
from which lay a new life beginning to grow.

Karla Van Vliet

DEATH IN THE PSYCHE

Death in a dream can be disturbing, for in waking life death seems real and absolute. When a person is gone, the person is gone and seemingly gone for good. We do not know where people go when they die and they do not return to report. Of course, there is a great deal of speculation about what happens - most religions and belief systems have their own version and many have faith that they will ascend to heaven and be with the Father. But we really do not know for sure.

In dreams, however, there is no real death. When a person dies or appears dead in a dream, the death is only a recidivism of that particular aspect in the psyche. The nature of that aspect, whether part of essence or pathology, is merely a reflection of something currently lost to the person. What is lost in the psyche is not lost forever - it can come back. Just as Einstein's theory states that matter can neither be destroyed nor created, nothing in the psyche can be destroyed. This includes the soul created by the Divine, the Archetypes and even the pathology that inhabits a person.

There are two types of death in dreams - the death of the loss of the self and the death that occurs when one has seen through the false self.

Death of the Loss of the Self

Dream:

> I am standing on a great hill overlooking Burlington, Vermont. A huge storm rolls in from the lake and pounds a part of the city with lightning, hail and thunderous noise. It feels like my father yelling at me or chasing me, like when I was a boy. I go to the epicenter of the storm and discover a dead six-year-old girl, with green bile coming from her stomach. A man carries her out, so I help.

In the dream, the girl was clearly dead at six years old, showing that this part of the client was dead. The part that could feel into essence and know the glorious presence of beauty. Without the girl, the client was frenetic, quick, loud and always thinking. In his process, he had been able to understand the Divine presence in his being and had even been able to receive and be guided. But he was missing the beatific. He was not a part of the genesis. The lack and separation of the girl manifested as anxiety and fear, the fear similar to the fear he felt with his father. Because the Uranian Father relates to all meteorological events in dreams, such as thunderstorms, it was very telling that the client associated the presence of the storm with the terror he felt around his father's anger.

The fear of the father was located somewhere in the deep organs of the girl. Seven years after the dream, the client almost died from pancreatitis in which bile in the pancreas, where the fear of the father was located in his body, exploded out and spread toxins for over a year. While in the hospital, he went through a great psychotic experience that sent him back to the terror he felt when he was a boy. This experience allowed great healing both physically and in the psyche. He came through with a clean bill of health and a new understanding of life. Just before leaving the hospital, he had this dream:

I am wandering up a hill. I see a dog the size of an elephant.

Here, the dog is not the size of an elephant, but is normal size. The difference was the size of the client - he had become a baby looking up at the dog. The child had returned and the client became the child. In being the child, he was able to feel the fear turn into an awareness of essence and essential love that is in all things. It was a healing balm for his soul.

The fact that things can return, that death is only a step away from the phoenix rising out of the ashes to be born anew is the promise of this work. The point of Alchemy is to reclaim what was lost. The death of what was lost as the promise of regeneration goes against the idea that we can never go home again. We can. Through the dreams, a person can go back and reclaim the promise given at birth. It is an arduous path, but one defined by the psyche itself by its purposefulness. It is the victory that awakens the soul.

The Death of Pathology

The First Death

The first kind of death of the pathology occurs when a client has seen through the false self which usually manifests in the form of something demonic and pathological. This is the self that the client often believes is the real self, but is not. It is something that inhabits the person inside, offering solutions so he can survive the demise of the true self. Ironically, the client must die to the true self that has died in order to live again. Only when the false self dies can the true self reemerge.

In dreams, the death of the false self manifests as a character appearing dead or dying - usually an ugly demon character or a personality well known to the client. Sometimes the character will appeal to the client to save it, taking on emotional characteristics to trick the client into saving it or somehow reaching out to it. But once the demon dies, it does not mean it is dead. Again, nothing in the psyche dies. The death simply means that the client sees the false self for what it is - and that it is separate from him. In Stage One work, the goal of the dreams is to help the client understand how life behaviors and emotions are in fact a reflection of the false self, the self that replaces the true self.

When a pathological element dies in a dream, it does not mean that the pathology no longer has a powerful grip on the client. In some cases, the pathology will appear to be more powerful once it is seen, becoming more virulent and unpredictable. Once revealed, it has nothing to lose and may attack the client directly.

The first thing the pathology wants is to have a cooperative host. To be cooperative, the client must be ignorant of its presence. The process of dreams revealing pathology through the understanding of behavioral and emotional states that are not the true self is the beginning of the client's awakening. The revealing of the pathology is a major victory moving toward the process of Alchemy, but it does not mean that the emergence of the true self is viable in the psyche. It is impossible to know when that process will begin.

When the pathology is first seen and begins to act out, whether violently or sweetly, the client will work to justify and defend it. When pathology acts out in a virulent way, it can be very obvious to others and even to the client. The ego eclipsed by this kind of malevolent power, even when seen, has no choice but to be ruled by its emotional or intellectual energies. In this case, awareness is not just the understanding of the presence of pathology, for the client often knows it is there. It is also the ability to feel an underlying emotional alternative. Such a contrast offers the client an opportunity to contrast the malevolence and perhaps for the first time truly understand its power.

This awareness would be enough to trigger a dream where the pathology dies. The client can begin to develop the capacity to become allergic to the emotional workings of the pathology. The allergic response can create separation for it signals that the client is no longer a willing, cooperative host. When this separation and death happens, the client is often faced with deep regret for his past history, and continued allergic responses to the pathology are met with greater and greater pain.

Pathology that is kind, subtle, positive, procreative and affirmative of others creates a greater blind spot in the psyche. The more functional a client with this type of pathology is in the world, the more it is clear that the pathology has been able to trick the world. The client gets great rewards from this relationship, for he feels that he gets supported for who he is. To break this type of pathology requires the awareness of suffering that is beyond the gains of having it. Without the awareness of the suffering, it is doubtful the client will feel a need for change.

Before a client is aware of pathology, before the first death of pathology, pathology is usually less overtly destructive. It is not trying to destroy civilization or to enable the client to live a less full life, at least in the mundane sense. Pathology does not care about outer world aspects such as how much money the client makes or how many children he has unless they relate to the client's emotional life. Every good quality and every bad quality is acceptable to the pathology as long as it does not threaten the possibility of greater growth. Pathology cannot be measured on the scale of good and bad, evil and godliness because such a scale does not exist in the psyche. Anger for one is vindication for another; fear for one is liberation for another; love for one is isolation for another. These are examples of words that have no meaning in the true battle beneath the surface. What is interpreted as anger, love, fear, jealousy, need, independence only has meaning to the extent that pathology accepts them.

The truth is mired in the lie that is to be uncovered and recovered, found, discovered, polished, gleaned into and finally understood. Meaning is made of scraps of experience, an understanding of the world, expectations from the self and others and the tendency to believe one way or another. These beliefs are brought into Stage One work and shown to the client, through dreams, as misguided, incorrect and abundantly wrong.

Pathology is able to twist everything into something that makes sense in terms of the client's egocentric beliefs and emotional confusion. So, good may be good in the world, but under the deeper light of the truth, it may be a shallow avoidance of something deeper. Society is under a shadow of misconceptions. When an artist produce arts and the viewer sees in the art his own beliefs, projections and aesthetics, the truth of the work is rarely seen. Misinterpreted images, ideas and aspects of creative work or even of a person in the world illustrates the inability of society to fathom the reality that the psyche suffers under.

Pathology is a master magician that weaves lies and deceit. It is a psychopathic energy that can mimic God itself. The best of a person can be leveraged by pathology into avoidance and denials of greater inner portent. Pathology is very difficult when it mimics good and love in the world.

For example, a client had recurring dreams about being at various conferences around his outer world work and sharing in a loving environment. His work involves running a nonprofit organization based on education and grassroots work and is very idealistic with a simple and noble cause. But his dreams showed how his ego had extended itself in a way that reflected an impoverished childhood. As a child, he had great responsibilities supporting and caretaking his siblings, carrying the weight of the family emotionally while his own inner life and personal needs suffered.

This impoverished way of helping others while his own needs suffered replicated as he ran the organization and manifested psychologically in many ways. For him, running the organization was a simple act of love. But in this act, every personal relationship that was not involved in organizational and community sharing, every personal relationship that required intimacy suffered and/or failed. His was still a lovely life, but the devastation of the past which was covered by the caring of the present kept the Archetypes at bay. Without his inner personhood, there was no inner connection.

Had this client not faced into his impoverished way of living, he would have been remembered only as a great warrior in his field. But the dreams revealed a man who was extremely oppressed and suffered greatly for the lack of the life he could never live. It was difficult to see that his intense love for people actually perpetuated his absolute isolation from the very love he gave. He simply could never receive.

Being receptive is one of the most important and necessary attributes of the psyche. The psyche is a vessel which, when open to the Divine, can receive guidance and direction for inward and outward growth. There is no greater achievement than to discover the relationship with the Divine and to experience the fulfillment of healing.

When a client can become aware of this pathology through a deepening understanding of what has been lost in the process of accepting it, then great regret emerges. Once the regret is felt, the tradeoff of social acceptance offered by the pathology becomes irrelevant. Regret only comes from the soul that grieves its separation or is grieved by the loss of the self. The greater the remembrance of the soul self, the greater the suffering for the loss.

The once born self is the self that accepts life as it is and does not have to die to find itself again. The twice born self has no choice because it finds itself in suffering no matter how wonderfully erudite the pathology can be.

The following is a dream with the death of pathology:

Dream:

> I am with five babies. There is a painting on a wall of many demon heads. As I watch, the demon heads become real and begin to come out of the painting, trying to scare the babies. Wanting to protect the babies, I tear the painting off the wall and crumple it up. I run out of town with it and throw the painting in a fire where it burns.

This client had advanced to the point where she knew the existence and manifestations of the pathology. The child aspects of the self are now in tow. It is folly, however, for her to try to eradicate the demon, for the client cannot kill the demon. But the understanding of its existence is an incalculable step in the demise of the pathology. Knowing the existence of the pathology so clearly is another form of its death. This client is clearly no longer cooperative - and an uncooperative host is no host at all.

The Second Death

When the client can see pathology and is no longer identified it, she begins to see that the pathology causes thoughts and behavior based on her emotions. Until then, the client is identified with the emotions and thoughts which cause the behavior and, through the identification, feels responsible. She is unable to separate from the consciousness that creates the emotional reality.

These are the patterns that in Stage One of the work a client will justify and have to break through. Beginning to see how pathology controls behavior eventually creates the awareness of the pathology as a parasite living inside - feeding off and living through the unfelt feelings of a person. Once seen, a client will become allergic to the process of being a host to such a parasite. The client through her horror of this increased awareness can begin to separate from the behavior and thoughts created by the pathology. This separation from the pathology involves going deeper into the psyche to unearth the repressed feelings that allowed the pathology the opportunity to perform a takedown of the true self.

The takedown of the true self can occur in developmental adolescence or at even younger ages when some pre-existing situation triggered a trauma. In some cases, the true self is never born in an individual and the takedown occurs before even a memory of the true self can form. In other cases, some can actually remember the moment when the deal with pathology was made, when the takedown happened.

Seeing the pathology enacts the first type of pathology death and is a major breakthrough in a person's process. This death means the client can acknowledge the existence of pathology even though she cannot change it. She has to accept the presence of the parasite and know there is nothing she can do but observe it. This is a pride killer for many because most people like to believe that they are in charge of their lives, acting out of their most authentic selves. To know that this is not true can be difficult. The illusions of the self are lost and a client is left to face the reality of her situation. A reality that is often unacceptable to the ego.

Once pathology is seen and the first death occurs, the opportunity for the second death is created. The second death of pathology occurs not by defeating it directly, but by the progressive opening of the deeper self that naturally occurs once the pathology has been seen and acknowledged. Once the client can see through the lie of the pathology, there is room to live with a new, deeper level of integrity of self previously unfathomable. The death experience allows the deeper self to become activated and Archetypal work can occur once the passage is complete.

It is an easy trap to perceive pathology as a devil that must be killed. It is not as easy to realize that the reason pathology is even able to be present is because the Divine connection is not. Pathology cannot exist in a person without a vacuum. This vacuum is created by the separation of the individual from the soul self compounded by the separation from the Divine.

The Archetypes can visit a client on a regular basis once the client has matured enough to perhaps be willing to take the steps necessary to her process as shown by her dreams and practiced in her homework. These are the steps that allow the core therapy to occur. The deepening of the psyche through a series of feeling experiences as manifested in dreams are what allow the true self to be revealed. The process allows the true self to emerge from the depths of the psyche and offers the client the chance to wake up.

When the true self begins to emerge and begins to dominate, the pathology has less and less space in the psyche in which to work and manifest. And there is less and less for the pathology to feed on as a parasite. This is the second death of the pathology.

The Point of Failure, The Point of Liberation

Dream:

> I am in a terrible battle with others against demons. There is test after test - like Frodo in *Lord of the Rings*. But our wits and strength are inadequate to save us because the demons are stronger. We are about to lose, and I am feeling doomed to fail when I pause and remember to let God's power flow through me. Then I feel calm and safe and protected. When I surrender to God, the demons are thwarted again and again. Each time I surrender, the demons are thwarted.

With this client, spirit has already entered the deepest aspect of her psyche, as is shown in the dream - as soon as she opens to the Divine, she becomes potent. When one becomes connected with the Divine, the person can fiercely connect and be spiritually alive. It is not that the client kills the demons, but that she is connected to that which kills the demons. It is a metaphor, for it is the connection that makes it impossible for the pathology to exist in a person. The pathology cannot exist side by side with the Divine. When we are connected, there is simply no room for it.

Prior to pausing to remember God, the client tries to take on the pathology, failing over and over. She had succeeded in connecting with the first death of pathology, otherwise, she would not be in the position of taking on pathology. But this is only half of the solution. Only when she finally makes the connection can real change occur. Only when one is intimate with the love, only when the true soul self is free, can the expression of the self be manifested and, in that moment, the demon be annihilated.

Trying to actualize the true self based on the awareness of the pathology is the point of failure. Clients are often frustrated because they see the demon, they see the work of the pathology in their lives and they hate it. It is a pride killer to acknowledge the existence of pathology without recourse of change. This humbles the soul and sometimes is a necessary passage. But it is important to know that the client is never the doer. The knee jerk reaction is to see the problem and want to solve it, to see the demon and want to kill it. The desire to change is not a death experience. It is only another way to keep the self chained to the false self unwittingly. The pathology was able to get into the psyche because of that false self. How could such knowledge of the presence of pathology change the equation when the only thing that has changed is the client's awareness of it. The point of failure is where knowledge of the demon is created and the continued ignorance of the Divine is manifested.

The point of freedom is the moment when the client realizes that seeing the problem is not the solution. It is the moment when the client can truly surrender and allow the false self to die. The will to kill pathology is part of the problem - even this must be surrendered. The thing that hates the pathology is also pathology. The client's hate of the pathology is the hate of the pathology. The pathology is really not "pathology," it is simply hate. What we presuppose about the Animus or Anima is not really Divine anything, it is really just love. When this is taken down to the core, it is one or the other - love or hate.

When a person takes pride in his hate of the devil, he becomes the demon. When a person takes pride in the love he has for the Divine, again, he is living with the demon. The complete surrender of the self, the self that perceives loving God or not, must be surrendered to become the receiving agent of the love. Once the soul self has received the love, it has no bounds, no boundaries. It is like a child that simply receives. There are no personal issues that become projected into the world. The soul self just suckles at the feet of the Divine. There is no need of other knowing than this.

And in this moment, a person can slay the dragon. Of course, the person is not the slayer, the person is not the anger or hate in the slaying, the person is not in the judgment or pride or humility or even victim place of the slaying. The person is simply embodied in the love of the Divine. In knowing that love, there is no room for pathology. In that place of true incarnation of the Divine, a person cannot help but slay all that obstructs him from this intimacy and the love.

The pathology will fight hard when this begins to happen. Initially, pathology has power because the individual is not aware of its presence. A client believes instead that how she manifests pathology is a positive and necessary reality. Once that illusion is broken, the pathology will not waste time on that kind of deception. Instead, it has nothing to lose and will attack. The client may feel she is getting worse. The pathology wants its host to become discouraged and stop her work so it can re-infect despite the awareness.

The client's awareness of the pathology forever makes her the enemy of the pathology. Once this line is crossed, the pathology will try to attack with a greater degree of destructiveness. This can manifest as the pathology causing a great up-welling of the vilest emotions it can find in the individual. Emotions experienced by the person in the past suddenly become worse. The neurotic tendencies of the past get amplified. For example, if part of how she functioned pathologically was to have overwhelming obsessive thoughts, then these thoughts increase. The client becomes inundated in a way never before experienced for all underlying power of the pathology suddenly becomes more empowered and it devastatingly jumps into the client's awareness. Everything ugly in the psyche that was hidden is now felt and re-experienced.

The result is that the person may feel she is going crazy or is being drawn into the darkest corners of what she had only gleaned in small ways. But instead of being a sign that pathology is taking over, it can be a signal that the client is making great progress. The pathology is playing its hand in a last gasp to wrestle control back from the Archetypal Self. Dreams that follow these episodes are the most critical for they help the therapist understand the particular path of healing and redemption for the client.

An example; one client entered the dreamwork process in an extreme condition of depression for which he had taken as many as eight different medications. After several years of work, his medications were reduced to only one. Progress had been made as his growing capability to feel into his life was beginning to reduce his negative emotional states. After struggling to finish school and struggling financially in mediocre jobs in his field, his outer life changed. He finished his schooling, getting his master's degree, and landed an auspicious job in his field. A great deal of growth had occurred.

Then the pathology struck. He became borderline suicidal, caught between his old nemesis anxiety depression and the deep pain which allowed the opportunity for him to alchemize into his next step. He was unable to sustain the feelings of pain and was close to returning to the psychiatrist in order to increase his medication. The struggle between the anxiety and pain was severe. The following dreams show this struggle.

Dream:

I am restraining a boy at the school where I work. He gets up and walks away.

Dream:

A young boy at the school is running around. I feel pressure, wanting to control him. A former female co-worker is there. I am glad she is in charge of the situation. I want to leave, to get away from the pressure.

From the client:

These dreams are telling me to accept that right now I hate the boy. I think that something needs to be done. The truth is that the kid is fine and the co-worker is the dark mother. In this dream, she and I are in conspiracy against the boy, neither of us loves the boy. My mother never loved the boy and she hated my father for the boy he was.

I am not the boy. Nothing has changed in my relationship to him. Every time I feel pressure, I am dismissing the boy, trying to control. When I feel the pressure, I am being a perpetrator; I am with the dark mother against the boy. I need to accept that I am a perpetrator, not a helpless victim. I am restraining him! The boy does not want the dark mother. He knows that she is a demon. I still want her.

The client's awareness of the situation is very strong - he understands the outer reflection of the inner struggle. For him, he must feel the core feeling of pain versus the pressure and unworthiness.

The core feeling of pain is from his feelings and dynamics around his father and his mother.

His father was a talented musician reduced to playing his music in subways for spare change. The father's self-hate was reflected by an even greater hate from his wife, the client's mother. The client loved his father but was misled by his mother's disdain, completely unaware of her undermining the father. He learned from his mother to dismiss his father as a miserable wretch. His father, in turn, felt alienated from everything, including his son, and animosity grew between them. The mother outlived the father and her influence on the client continued unabated until he turned thirty.

The client's hate for his father perpetuated his own self-loathing, crippling him to such a degree that he became almost unable to function. The more overwhelmed he became, the more he looked to his mother to rescue him. The more he wanted his mother to rescue him, the more his mother took care of him. The more his mother took care of him, the more depressed he felt.

At this stage in his work, however, the lie is revealed. He has become aware of his love for his father and also aware of the destructive power of his mother. Even though he continues to have dependent feelings for his mother and any other woman who would have him taking the role of the mother, he understands the game. He no longer trusts his emotional pining for women. He is accepting the boy as the part of his true self who always loved his father. When he turned on his father, he lost that boy.

The client understands that when he feels the pressure to fulfill any expectations of his mother, he is actually distancing himself from the boy. The only connection to the boy is through the feeling of pain and the beginning of longing for male support. His perpetual need for women to support him led him to be misogynistic and overtly sexual in his misguided efforts to feel as good as other men. His effort is to be with the boy and to acknowledge his pain.

The pathology battles against the client by making him feel even more pressure to perform and having him believe that he is on the verge of failing in everything he does. The reality, however, is that pathology still has power over him because he continues to seek women who will take care of him.

Just after the above dreams, he had the following dreams:

Dream:

> I am in my apartment. I tell my boss that I am not sure I am going to go to work because I only slept four hours. She tells me that a female coworker has quit. I feel relief. Shift.

> A girl who I used to feel nervous around is lying on top of me. I feel good that she is comfortable lying on me. My friend Sheila picks the girl up and off of me. It is very playful. I get up to go to work and get in the shower. Both the girl and Sheila are there and they are both naked. I feel like I should not look at them.

Again, from the client :

> The female coworker who has quit in the first part of the dream represents pathology - she is leaving in response to the work I have been doing, my commitment to the homework from the dreams and the commitment to feeling my feelings.

> The girl is also pathology, coming back in a more seductive way. I want approval from her. I am so wired for needing approval, shame-based connections. The boy would kick the pathological girl off of him. The boy would want to be with the Sheila. I do the opposite of what the boy would do - I reject Sheila in the shower.

I need to go to the boy, to go past the dark mother. I need to go get the boy and cling to him as if he were the second coming. I cannot get better without him.

The gestalt with the boy from the dream:

Me: Boy, I am sorry for abandoning you.
Boy: I need you to fight for me! (Crying.) I am so mad you left me!
Me: I am sorry for blowing you off. I am sorry for not committing to you.
Right now I am committing to being with you. I know I need to commit.

Dream:

I am flying above a river. I am talking to someone unseen, feeling some pressure, trying to convince him of something. The water is shimmering, lit up. We get to a bend. (I still do not see anyone, but feel the presence.) A boy and a man who works with him come from the other direction. I feel relief, supported.

With this last dream of this dream cycle, the client finally accepts the connection with the boy, even though he remains separate from the shimmering. The shimmering water is the pain of his own feelings, the acceptance of the true direction of his inner work and his life.

Through the process of Alchemy which will come in the future, the ego self of client will cease to exist and only the boy will remain so that the client will become the boy. In the meantime, he will continue to choose the wrong women, just as in the dream he wants to choose the girl on top of him who reflects his preoccupation with his mother and her dominance over him. Facing Sheila would mean being vulnerable, in his sensuality and stepping into mutuality, all of which he is unable to do because he is not yet the boy. The boy, of course, can do all of these things.

These threads will continue to be interwoven as the dream process continues to unravel the connection with the mother. As this happens, the boy will begin to emerge and the triangulation of the boy, the Father and the client will create the fourth point of Alchemy (the three becomes four), which will be a final blow to the pathological dark mother. In the meantime, the attacks through increased pressure and increased feelings of unworthiness are likely to continue. The job of the therapist is to help the client as shown through the dreams to continue to undermine the hold pathology has on his true self.

***

Regardless of whether a death in a dream is the death of the lost part of the self or the death of the pathology which replaced the lost self, death gives the client the freedom to make more choices. In the case of the lost self that wants to return, the client must face the next challenge of accepting that self and the great repercussions the process of acceptance will have as the reclaimed self reconfigures itself in the client. In the case of the death of the pathology, having an awareness of its presence along with the regret that follows brings the client to other choices regarding the incredible shift that occurs when she no longer knows her self as she had in the past.

This adjustment both ways opens the door to controlled psychosis in which the disassociative self exposes the chasms deep in the psyche. These chasms allow for the emergence of profoundly primal feelings. Some of these feelings may relate to hidden trauma and some to the feelings that are part of the reconciling principle of Jacob's Ladder. The emergence of these feelings allows the individual to enter the process of re-experiencing reality in a way that she can begin to have relationship with the Divine.

In the larger view of the full journey, the death and reemergence of the self as well as the death of the pathology is only the first step in the evolution and reclamation of the psyche. The child self is the pivot point of future work, for Alchemy cannot really begin without this self. The reemerging self is not in a perfect state, but it can be relied upon to continue its journey. Great learning is possible when the child self becomes reunited with the psyche in a conscious way. This consciousness, when the client can feel the reemerging true self, opens the journey to core Stage Two work.

All I Could Not

Left words against
this storm's hard edge.

Even now I do not trust
myself to speak.

These words I palm
go warm like stones carried to the river.

See here,
a pyre to set them burning.

In the end, dust or ash,
my throat silted.

Turn from the choked flora
there is no digging out.

Leave it, what's left.
Now, only this new lay of the land.

Karla Van Vliet

Dying to the Self and Dying to the Divine

Ego and Secondary Ego

The word *ego* is a value-laden word that can mean anything depending on the person using it. Often, it is used in different ways to cause harm. This is a collective manipulation of the psyche, prescribing how an individual should or should not be in the world.

The truth is that ego is simply a field of consciousness, the ability to contain consciousness both from the subconscious and the world. The ego is a necessary component of an individual, just like a vital organ. For example, eyes are useful and necessary, but they can be used in different ways - used to look at beautiful nourishing things or used to look at destructive things. The ego itself is not bad, but it does, however, get contaminated by pathology. First pathology works at the subconscious level, then it moves into the conscious ego level.

Secondary ego is the ego that adapts itself to the expectations of the world and its own experience and is often determined to be the ego itself. But the secondary ego is always pathology trying to tell the individual what she should or should not do.

The Archetypes and the child self do not have this perspective. Instead, the child self has the ability to experience essence and feeling, and the ego is the container. Without an ego, the individual is unable to receive the Divine in a way that allows her to be in relationship. Without an ego, a person is psychotic or schizophrenic.

The process of moving through feelings creates an ego capable of containing the child self. But how each individual moves through feelings depends on the individual - every person's path is different based on particular individual struggles. Of course, there is a fine line between narcissism and truly working on feelings. Narcissism is the undue dwelling on the self driven by pathology. Truly working on feeling and expressing feelings is being selfish in a positive way. Being the self-of-the-fish, swimming in a deeper level of consciousness and need driven by the individual's process and unique struggles.

Putting value on the process of what is needed contaminates what is needed. For example, one client may need to feel and express deep anger, but if the value of "anger is bad" is placed on the feeling, then the feeling is no longer useful. The child self is nonjudgmental. The child self only wants to know what is the feeling channel that will allow it to come up into the consciousness of the person. Secondary ego stands apart and dictates what is right and wrong, using anything it can to keep the child self from coming into the conscious ego. It loves the values game, using it to create distractions.

Dream:

I am babysitting a child who is sitting on me. The child picks her nose with a pen.

Everyone in the room is laughing, wondering what I will do now. I am ok, but then the child urinates on me. Now, I feel angry. I put the child on the toilet and give her a good talking to. Then, suddenly, the child is sitting in the toilet with a poop floating around her. I take her and put her in the shower to clean her off.

In this example, the client wants to do the right thing because she is a good person. The secondary ego uses the value judgment to distract her into taking care of the child instead. The very effort of wanting to connect makes the child urinate on her because she is taking care of the child out of shame. The secondary ego wants the client to do something. It can use the values of society or community as part of how it tricks the client. But the child self does not care about whether something is right or wrong in terms of the external world.

The more the ego is contaminated by pathology, the more the reality of the individual is challenged by the dreamwork. For the client in the example above, she perceives that she has to take care of everyone else. This is not about actual behavior, of course, for there is nothing wrong with her taking care of others in the world. Instead, it is her perception that needs to change. Believing that changing behavior will solve the issue comes from secondary ego, secondary reasoning. This is why there needs to be a death of the self - the death of the secondary ego - for the client to become the child. In this example, the secondary ego in the woman that believes she must do the right thing, that she must take care of everyone, is the self that must die.

If a client does not have a strong ego, the Archetypes work through the dreams to strengthen it. Once the ego is strengthened, then the death of self can begin to occur. In the process of the death of self, the secondary ego, the part of the self that is identified with pathology, dies. Not the true ego. The true ego needs to be strong in order to survive the loss of the secondary ego or it will not be able to feel the child self when it begins to emerge. It is like chemotherapy and cancer. The chemotherapy is not supposed to kill the patient, it is used to kill the cancer cells. In order to do that, however, every cell in the patient is taken to the brink of death.

Dying to Self and Dying to the Divine

Dying to Self is challenging because there are many similarities to physical death. Death is unknown, unimaginable change, out of anyone's control, painful, final and how everyone will leave their life. Most people are afraid of dying.

Leaving the world is a very subjective experience. Some people die quickly and do not have the opportunity to look at their lives, while others choose to avoid themselves even in death. But death can be an opportunity to confront how one has lived. People who face physical death through the process of a terminal illness often come to terms with their life in preparation for departure. It takes courage to look without flinching at the failings and regrets, to look back on opportunities gained or lost. It is also terrifying to consider how suddenly the things that made us feel snug and safe will be gone - the favorite vacation, the beloved garden untended, the projects, dreams, plans all left undone.

Facing the questions that come when facing death does take courage - how have I lived? From my heart? Did I do the things that burned in my heart - write that book, paint the paintings, create what I had the passion to create? What about the love I gave or did not give? Did I live fully present in each moment?

Coming to terms with the self and the questions raised at the onset of physical death are similar to what must be faced in Dying to Self. Dying to Self simply lacks the overt motivation to face all that is unlived. The dreamwork leads to the same opportunities inherent in physical death because the psyche longs to be reconciled to its truth. Dreams lead the client through the different steps of Dying to Self, raising all the appropriate questions with opportunities to see the answers - all the denied truth, all the things the client has hidden from in his past/present, all the ways of not living congruently with the heart. While these things come to the surface, a breaking down process also begins which dissolves the layers that cover the buried feelings. As the client is prepared for Dying to Self, everything is stripped away to enable him to go deeper and deeper into his underlying truth, while the true place is allowed to strengthen and heal.

Dying to Self literally means dying to the true self and losing the false self to the child self or the soul self. The life that is unlived is always the life longed for by the soul self. Dying to Self so the true self might live.

The Process of Dying to Self

The process of Dying to Self is part of moving through the stages of the dreamwork. Again, the goal of Stage One is to become aware of the pathology and for most, Stage One work results in an intellectual awareness of pathology as it relates to certain behaviors. Movement into Stage Two and Dying to Self is possible without having any deeper understanding of pathological behavior than on an intellectual level. Eventually, the malignancy in the life lived through pathology becomes more obvious, and how the client continues to be driven by pathology become increasingly apparent. This depth of self confrontation is possible because of the increasing spiritual support and essence/light that becomes more available to contrast the darkness.

But, unless there is suffering in an extraordinary way, most people are satisfied with their state of consciousness, accepting it as the norm, as long as they can do well in their job or relationships or whatever it is they believe they want. Many people either stay ahead of their suffering, or manage it through forms of escape like recreational drugs, alcohol, antidepressants and all the ways available to stay occupied. Our free society offers many options. These types of escapism may still be present for a person in Stage One who is looking at her behaviors. Getting at the underlying emotional pathology and at true feelings on a deeper level is not necessarily desirable or perhaps even possible unless there is some counterbalancing spiritual support.

Because of this, the dreams unravel a person's awareness of her situation only to the degree that is needed to have an opening to the Divine. Too much unraveling too soon and a person could descend into a real depression or even psychosis - the Archetypes are very good at not upsetting the applecart of the psyche. A dreamwork therapist pushes only to the degree that the Archetype is pushing in the dream.

The Soul Self

While Dying to Self is a necessary breakdown of the old self, it is also a discovery of the new self. Just as when looking at the fear of physical death often leads to a deeper fear that there will be nothing, looking at the fear of Dying to Self often reveals a fear that there is nothing else there. But there is something - the soul self whose genesis and birth can have a place in the client's life and psyche. The soul self typically appears as a child in dreams.

What dies is the persona the client developed when the pathology was in control, a false self that takes up a tremendous amount of space in consciousness. This process is so difficult because of the identification with experiences and emotions, thoughts and values, which most clients clutch onto as if their sanity depended on it. In reality, what a person clutches is actually destroying his real sanity. From the soul self, the client can begin to grow and evolve in his relationship with the Divine. It does not, of course, mean that a client in his soul self is perfect - it does mean he has a base for spiritual and emotional growth.

The spiritual feeling life, the soul self, is at the base of who the client truly is, and it is very different in every person. Whoever that self is, no matter how broken, how small, how mature or immature, this is the self the Archetype and God wants to work with. That is the self a client dies to: hurt child, happy child, broken child, dead child, genius child. For some, the child self is so lost and repressed that the client has no memory of ever being it - or perhaps the child self never came into this world.

The child self, of course, can be regained through the experiences and feelings of the client's dream life. This process may include dreams of pregnancy or of an infant being born. For clients who remember being their child self at a specific age, this is the child they will rediscover and this is the child who will emerge in the dreams.

Sometimes, dying to the child self involves an intermediary step in which the client needs to relate to the child in a dream or dreams. The therapist guides the client to embrace and accept that child. This can be a significant piece of work if the child self feels foreign or makes the client uncomfortable and want to reject it. But accepting and caring for the child is a small step on the longer road of becoming the child. When the client starts to become the child, he will see and experience dreams from the child's perspective. For example, in a dream, the client will experience a doorknob as being high over his head or a dog as large as an elephant. This is the client experiencing from a child's perspective.

The client experiences what the child experiences and feels what the child feels. Eventually, the client can wake up to his life as that child and have the experiences and feelings of the child in his waking life. This is the genesis of the child in the self - when Dying to Self has gone deep enough, consciousness becomes an extension of the child self.

The goal in many paths of psychology is not Dying to Self, but rather to make the ego more functional, more rational and more able to present itself the way society has determined it should present itself. When this happens, a physical, spiritual, emotional, sexual, financial (in terms of job productivity, etc.) self is imposed that an individual thinks society requires. This imposed self has to die to the child self. Clients who are successful with many achievements in a worldly sense often have a difficult time especially if those achievements are not congruent with the soul self. The client's audience awaits and expects him to be a certain way. Letting that die, not knowing if people are still going to be supportive and loving is very difficult and, for some, impossible. The less "baggage" a client brings to his work in terms of worldly identity, the easier the process of Dying to Self can be. But Dying to Self is always difficult even if the client does not have "a lot to lose" because the process of disintegration can be very disorienting. It requires courage, desire and preparedness for a client to literally lose his bearings on who he is.

THE STEPS TO DYING TO SELF

Awareness of Pathology/Behavior

The steps in the Dying to Self process reflect how a client might experience this change in consciousness. The first step, again, is to see pathology which begins in Stage One and deepens as the client advances in her work. The client sees how she is behaving, sees how the pathology is controlling her. She sees it in her life and in all the many ways it manifests. This is crucial. The client needs to look into her unconsciousness or blind spots where the pathology hides. But when the light of awareness shines into the dark of the psyche's blind spots, the pathology loses its stranglehold, loses its ability to drive behavior into a chain of reaction. When the pathology is seen, it is tantamount to it dying.

Unfortunately, most people do not see because the world is blind to itself. When a client begins to grow out of pathology through the awareness that it exists within, she pulls away from the world by not reacting. The more she stops reacting, the more she realizes how most people around her are thoroughly in reaction. People seem like land mines ready to go off and the trip wires are everywhere. Even if she tries to avoid them, eventually she will hit one, and it is very painful to witness pathology other people do not see. She witnesses pathology not from a judgmental place where she can blame others for what is really about herself, but from the clarity of seeing others in their reactions, accepting their failings and trying to work around them. In a sense, a client takes a hundred percent responsibility for the pathology of others when she owns her own reactivity. In the world of unconscious land mines, other people do not take responsibility for what is their reaction. They do not even know they have pathology - they cannot see.

Seeing into blind spots and understanding how the pathology operates is the first step and a significant piece of work. But the journey continues. The pathology is seen, but the client still reacts. She realizes she is reacting but cannot stop because she is not in control of it. The client also can begin to realize all the justification in the world only makes her reaction more "justifiable" and therefore more "acceptable." For example, if the situation to which the client is reacting to is valid, then it is easy to be convinced that it is not about her. Then the reaction can be viewed as not the client's "fault," but a natural response to the world's negativity. Projection of this kind of reactivity onto the world is common and easy to slip into, especially at this point in her work. The client still reacts in ways that perpetuate her suffering, but now she can see it happening, wants to stop, but cannot even though she sees her justifications of her behavior are lies.

The first step in the death process is to see the depth of the pathology and the reactivity. The second step is the acceptance of learning to live with pathology. Rather than being in self judgment or self-loathing or wanting to fix it or thinking it is fixed, learning to live with pathology means accepting its presence. For the client, this means accepting her pathological behaviors and knowing she can do nothing except continue her inner work based on her dreams.

This kind of acceptance inevitably expands to include feeling the pain of regret. When a client begins to confront her behavior, she sees how much of her life has been spent in pathology. Everything is called into question and the client can see how she has contributed to the pain in her life. Blame, judgment, self-denial, self-hatred, hatred of others are all tools of the pathology. Regret surfaces when the client stops reacting, when she starts to acknowledge the truth about her pathology, about all she has allowed to happen or not happen, when she realizes all of what she did that was wrong.

This kind of regret is the basis for the higher octave of love - compassion. The degree to which a client understands her failings and has gone through regret for those failings is the degree to which she can have compassion for others and their failings.

This awareness of behavior is only one aspect of Dying to Self. Parallel to becoming aware of behavior is the work of moving through levels of feeling, which is a complex Alchemical process. As the client moves through feelings, consciousness is released and the process of Dying to Self can manifest. But if the heart of the client is not working, then just having the awareness of behaviors will not lead to Dying to Self. The heart is the crucible needed if the client is to stand in the suffering. Seeing the pathology, being in pathology and being unable to change it is the suffering and it causes the regret of what has been. This passage of pain must be experienced. If a client is making changes and having awareness but not going through the regret process then all she is doing is making external adjustments. The ego/pathology is still intact. The changes may be positive in terms of the world but the source of suffering remains the same. The pathology has simply gotten trickier.

Feeling Allergic to Pathology

The next logical step from awareness and feeling regret is to become allergic to the pathology. Once the client has accepted that pathology is within himself and has experienced the pain of regret for it, he begins to be repulsed by it. This is not self-hate but an awareness of this thing that is not himself, like having a parasite inside the body and wanting it out. Instead of justifying or thinking it is good/helpful or right/necessary, the client wants it out and he wants it out now.

Wanting to separate from the parasite of the pathology but being unable to stop reacting is a difficult part of the death process. All the client can do is accept that he is in reaction and know it is the parasite. All he can do is see the effect of the pathology and know it is not his true self. Clients often become very impatient at this point. They want to jump out of their skin as if they cannot stand being the way they are for another minute. Their awareness of their pathological behaviors intensifies without necessarily having any corresponding ability to change the behaviors. Becoming allergic to the pathology is a pride killer. The client always likes to feel the problem lies somewhere else, that the pathology is in someone other than himself. To realize that he is in pathology every day, every hour, every minute can be overwhelming. It is a pride killer because when he accepts his circumstance, he cannot go into the pride of being superior to the truth of himself.

A lot of innate pride supports the idea that the client is doing okay, not that he actually is okay. The Archetypes only support the client when he really is okay and their support is always tinged with work and self examination. Pride says the client is worthless or, the opposite, above reproach. God does not see the client as wonderful or worthless. Just like with children, good parents love them not just for their finer qualities but also regardless of their failings. God does not portion out his love based on the client's good qualities or failings. The problem is most people do not feel loved because the pathology has gotten inside and convinced them there is no love for them. This is the belief that opens a door to pride and shame issues.

Outing Pathology

Once a client has become aware of and then allergic to pathology, she can begin to out it. To out the pathology simply means to talk about it and reveal it to others.

Revealing pathology to others and witnessing others reveal their pathology can be an important step because it helps with the process of dis-identifying with the pathology. Revealing pathology means the client stops protecting it, consciously or unconsciously.

Keeping pathology a secret is a way of perpetuating it, even though the client may want to hide it because of shame. But hiding is what the pathology counts on. It wants the client to be ashamed and to remain over-identified with that shame and with the pathology. Shame of self keeps a client from seeing the pathology for what it is and gives it a way out by the client needing to feel good and cover up. Or by hating herself for what the pathology is doing or simply changing behaviors. But, is it the client's fault, for instance, if she gets Lyme Disease? The pathology would have the client believe she is the tick that infected herself. But the client is not the pathology, is not the infection. The way into process is for the client to stay in the crucible of feeling the pain and whatever else she feels that relates to having been in the awful place of pathology.

In all of this process, the client will be given Archetypal dreams to provide support as she progresses on her journey. If a client stays with her Archetypal assignment, if she stays with her homework support, she will begin to have another way to see and perceive herself. This new way of perceiving self emerges in the dreams as a new and deeper dyad where the client can feel her old way contrasted with her new way.

Sometimes the old and the new overlap and the client is immediately aware of the new way of being - as if when the old pathological self diminishes, the sun quickly shines through. Some clients, however, experience a gap or a chasm between the old self and the new - as if when the old pathological self diminishes, it is still night. The capacity to feel essence and connection is different for each client.

Experiencing a dark night can cause a client to feel like clutching the pathology to keep from falling into the abyss. She is Dying to Self but does not feel the presence of the new consciousness. The therapist will need to provide a great deal of support and literally stand in the breach for the client. The therapist can become a temporary bridge in the absence of that connection to the new way. Clients often say, "I am doing this on faith - I am trusting you!" This is an important step and this kind of transference onto the therapist is beneficial. The person has to go on faith so that the new consciousness can emerge. If the therapist has a connection himself, he knows the client's trust will not be in vain. If the therapist does not, he will wonder if he is driving the client nuts. A therapist cannot be much of a bridge unless he has found his own connection.

Stopping the Reactions

The work of outing the pathology leads to the client not reacting, the last step in the Dying to Self process. The client, of course, cannot simply decide to not react. Instead, it happens without any effort as he works through the first four steps by following his work in the dreams. The dreams provide the Archetypal help and support the client needs to work through the process.

Now the Archetype, the Divine, is free to move in ways to heal the hurts and the original causes of the reactive behavior. The client can become clear. Of course, others around the client, in his life, may still be doing their things, but the difference is that the client is not reacting. In a vacuum where there was once a reaction from the client, these others may have a chance to look at themselves. When everyone is reacting, people can just blame each other. But if one person stops reacting, that person becomes a mirror for others to see themselves. If someone acts poorly and the client does not react, then that person is stuck with her own yuck. The person may not do much about it, and may try to cover it up again, but the point is this is very bad for the pathology. If there are enough people walking around in the world who no longer react, it undermines the pathology's hold on people which is much more tenuous than we might believe. The more one person really changes the more it affect others.

The steps again:
1. See the pathology, accept it is there and feel the pain of regret.
2. Develop an allergy to the pathology.
3. Out the pathology.
4. Do not react.

Fear and Pathology

The process of Dying to Self is a daunting one. The Archetypes are not going to ask a person to enter into that process, not going to kill the false self or secondary ego, until a person has a strong enough sense of identity to take the place of what dies. Until the essential self can begin to emerge. Fear is a protection from Dying to Self too quickly. When a client begins to break open, she feels scared because new things are always initially experienced as fear. This helps her to move slowly, at the rate which is appropriate for her.

Fear is like a scab. It insulates and protects the consciousness that is latent and essential to growth, protecting it when a person gets close to something new and unknown. Underneath that fear are the

Archetypes and the Archetypal Realm. Once the fear is felt, other strong feelings emerge, such as yearning and desire to be with the Archetypes. The fear helps dissolve pathology enough so that when the client slips under the fear, enough of the process of Dying to Self has happened that she can embrace what is there. Feeling the fear, just as feeling any pure feeling, dissolves pathological reaction.

Because everything in society pushes against feeling, especially this kind of fear, it is hard to turn into that fear. It implies a death of something that does not want to die. But when core fear is present in the process of the dreamwork, it is always because the client is ready for something new to be revealed. This is the fear that ultimately leads to the child self or the soul self.

The child self only becomes part of the process when the client has sufficiently died to self.

The fear that comes from Dying to Self is simply the fear of the self. Most people are afraid of their true selves. Part of the fear is that the self will get lost in the process of connecting with the Divine. The truth is that the personal self does not get lost, each person still has her unique individuality. In fact, that personal self becomes more elevated and dynamic as the connection deepens.

The reason there is such deep fear around the child self is because the child self is what needs to be most protected. Ironically, this protection also keeps the individual away as well so that when there is this fear, the client goes away from her child self. As a client becomes ready, she can learn to turn into the fear and follow it as part of her journey. The journey to the soul self.

This work comes when a client is in Stage Two, the part of the process where it is the client, not so much the pathology, which seems to be in the way. The Archetypes try to catch how and where the client is in the way of her next step. The therapist works to find what the Archetypes are attempting to work in the client and show this to the client. In this way, a client becomes more responsible for her process. But becoming more responsible also makes it easy to get stuck in Stage Two because the client must say yes to the shifts and changes the Archetypes offer. Good intentions, which can help in Stage One work, do not work in Stage Two. In Stage Two, the client ultimately is learning to accept the death of the ego self.

Dying to Self
by Denise Wilder

Dream:

> I was supposed to meet N. at his house, but he seems to be away. I feel abandoned, unworthy of his love, and hurt that he did not follow through on our plans. I cry as I walk away from his house and take the short cut through a neighbor's back yard. I do not see the dogs, so it is safe to pass through. But suddenly they are on me and I

feel completely terrified. The dogs attack and tear into my belly, my face, my arms and legs - I feel the attack and the pain. I am so wounded I fall into a coma. I rise up from my body so that I am watching the scene. I see myself rescued by EMTs. How did I live through that? Why?

Dream:

I am an administrator in a prison. Two prisoners have escaped and I am their hostage. We are outside the walls in a rowboat on a lake that surrounds the prison. I know the prison guards standing in the watchtowers have my captors and me in their rifle sights, so I am protected if they do anything to me. But even though I feel protected, I feel scared that I might die and I want to get back to the prison. Yet, the escaped prisoners do not care about the guards or running away from the prison or even about me. The two men are in their own world playing cards while the boat drifts and rocks with the water's current. The boat is moving on its own. I feel fear and I also feel perplexed, but I find myself less and less anxious as the boat rocks and wanders and the men talk jovially and play cards. Behind them, I see the prison. I realize that the prison is a place where rules and restrictions dominate, that it is a restrictive place, confining. I realize I do not want to go back there. I look at the men with a whole new perspective. The biggest man senses my change and puts his hand on my shoulder as if he were my protector and I feel protected, safe. I say, "I want to stay with you." He asks, "Are you sure?" I reply, "Yes, I would rather die than go back there." I feel completely sure about this. "OK." His hand leaves my shoulder and moves to the crown of my head. Then, with a quick jab, I feel the sharp sting of an ice pick enter my skull. It hurts for a moment, but it also feels like a great release. As blood seeps down my head, it seems like all the toxins from my imprisoned life are flowing out of me - I am dying. Everything in me pours into the enormity of this moment, and in its own way, moves into the next moment. I also feel very aware that I am with them on the lake and nothing else matters.

In the first dream, Denise runs from the Animus. This is a common aspect of her life - she is always running from her self, her possibilities. But in this dream, the dogs will not allow it. They are onto her. The EMTs at the end of the dream are probably pathology, for they endeavor to save her. The critical Dying to Self fails.

But in the second dream, the Archetypes have another crack at her. This time, she knows the prison. In the projection onto the Animus in the first dream of her own dislike of herself, she never realized that she was in a place of suffering. In the second dream, the fact that she knows she works as an administrator of the prison only shows that she does not see that she is actually a prisoner. But she is a prisoner. The best prisoners are the ones who are the best behaved, the ones who end up administrating the prison. Of course she runs from the Animus - she does not know the depth of her own suffering. In the dream, the other prisoners are running away and she finally joins them. It seems that she is beginning to see that her secondary ego self and the control she has experienced is a sham. Her sense of control is nothing more than a deception. In the dream, the biggest man, who is the Animus, senses the change in her and begins to help and protect her. Then the Animus without her awareness stabs her on the crown of her head. It is the end of an era. Her mental pathology has received a mortal blow. Denise is dying. In that moment, everything awakens. She is now with the Divine and nothing else matters. This is Alchemy at work, revelation and awakening. It is now possible that her life can begin again.

THE SECOND DEATH

Clients encounter dream motifs of dying such as breathing water, burning in fire, or jumping off cliffs as they move through the death process. The demon of pathology becomes visible to the client, appearing in dreams as separate from the client. Or the client may see the old self buried or hacked to death. However the initiation process goes, the old self will be seen for what it is and the result is big changes outwardly as the client moves beyond the old self. As the client dies to self, he opens to essence, which is the genesis of the child self. He is becoming conscious in a more profound way. From this place something new can happen called the second death.

The second death is dying to the Divine. It is the death that comes from feeling the existence of God, from feeling an embracing spiritual reality. Involvement with the Divine and the ability to begin a life with that relationship marks the end of the death of self and the beginning of the death to the Archetype. Now the Archetype can empower a client through the growth spiral with the Animus and the Anima without empowering the pathology. It is the best death - it revolves around becoming something new and unknown. Becoming the child self is not the goal because the child self is just a child and needs help to grow. It needs the relationship with Divine to grow.

The goal in Dying to Self is the learning process that unfolds in the relationship with the Divine now that the client has become the soul self. It is very intimate and powerful. The transformation, the growth and the Alchemy that is to come from this place is the learning process of the child. The child can grow and the ego can be transformed in its growth. As one becomes, one changes. The client forgets the past and who he has been. This forgetting is even more pronounced than with the initial death of self because with new growth and new consciousness comes a sense of reality that eventually eclipses the psyche. All identity begins to dissipate. The therapist is no longer the teacher although she may still play a profound role in the client's life. The teacher, instead, becomes the Archetype.

Many clients are not prepared for such a direct relationship with the Divine. They may believe they will have to die more in the old way to which they have acclimated. They may feel terrified by this new death because it is an incredible acceleration of growth. They may become scared because it is not like the first death. It can be terrifying to suddenly discover new territory and beautiful new experiences. But once a client allows this sense of reality to emerge in his being, the work can be extremely pleasant. The mountain has been climbed. The client is living on the other side and typically becomes the healer or teacher or leader only he can be. But all the time, the client remains the student of the Divine. No matter how big he might become in the world, the client can now know the proper relationship with the Divine. Once the client knows his place with Him, he is beyond the seductions of the world, beyond the hook of countertransference. Once the client knows his place with the Divine, he no longer needs others to make him feel bigger or smarter. He no longer needs outside approval. He can just be with the Animus, knowing who he is.

The sweetness of the second death is welcome for clients who make it through the challenges of the first death. At this point, the client is ready for the fulfilling of a calling or a life's work that is both profound to the client and congruent with the Divine. This congruency between the feeling new self and the Divine allows the client to be in the outer world and to be in the inner world with God simultaneously. This new death, this new birth, catapults a client's consciousness into unexplored worlds. The evolution of the child self or soul self and its manifestation in the world are unique and intimate to the inner relationship with the Divine.

Blossoms

Some days she drops
the most simple words,

hollyhock blossoms
closed and falling.

She collects them
in a small clay bowl,

twisted and bruised
purple like lips.

Karla Van Vliet

Essence and Breathing Water

Essence is a state of consciousness which allows the client to have access to the Divine. In essence, the client is open to commune and connect and be in relationship with Divine love. For most clients, feeling essence occurs through the process of Dying to Self - a death of the old self, the secondary ego - which usually occurs in the deeper layers of Second Stage work. The self the client dies to is the child self, the part that lives in essence, the true self the client is becoming.

The child self is the most Divine aspect of any client, the closest to an Archetype without actually being Archetypal. When a client is in essence and has died to a deeper sense of self, he is deeper in his soul. The soul resides in the bowels of feelings.

Essence, the Brain and Breathing Water

The essence state of consciousness affects the electrical energy of the brain. When in essence, brainwaves emit an alpha rhythm which is often associated with a state of wakeful relaxation or meditation. A person's soul, which is revealed in dreams as the child self, lives in this alpha state. If humans use only a small portion of their brain, is the rest of the brain for higher math or logic? No. The rest of the brain is for the unknown and untapped capacity to experience God.

Since essence opens up this untapped capacity of the brain, a person's IQ or way of being conscious increases. In essence, an individual has a greater awareness, a greater spiritual intelligence and an increased ability to hear God. She has new eyes to see in the knowing way of the spirit rather than in the knowing way of the mind. Essence is of the spirit. Essence energizes like a spiritual fuel that is continually replenished through the connection to Divine source.

The dream motif of breathing water reflects the capacity to feel and experience essence. If a person is willing to do her inner work, she will eventually dream of breathing under water because it is a type of initiation reflecting opening to essence. Essence deepens intuitive capabilities as the relationship with the Divine expands. Water breathing relates to being in essence, in feelings and becoming centered in the inner soul life.

Breathing air is a part of normal waking life and since everyone is an air breather, it is nothing to work on. As an air-breather, an individual cannot fathom being in essence. Essence can only be known when it is felt - like breathing water. Air breathing relates to being in the mind, the emotions and being centered in the "outer" world. Some people imagine if they lose their ability to breathe air, they will be ignorant in the world and all their concerns will go to hell. It is true that the concerns as an air-breather may shift entirely upon becoming a water-breather. But even if the concerns remain the same, things do not go to hell. Quite the opposite, in fact, because when infused with essence, an individual's energy is replenished as it is spent.

When relying on isolated individual will and effort, people often experience exhaustion in the face of their concerns as if the onus was completely theirs. Essence connects an individual to the uplifting and abundant source of Divine energy and love that is available to anyone who is willing to do the work. But the pathology makes this process difficult. Its singular purpose is to prevent people from experiencing Divine love and to keep them separate from God. Experiencing essence is having the veil of separateness lifted and the lies of the pathology exposed.

The Work of Getting to Essence

The work of getting to essence can unfold in two ways - the essence of transformation and the essence of remembering.

The essence of transformation comes through the specific process of Alchemy. Everyone doing mid to late Second Stage work will experience Alchemy and its geometric spiritual formula that describes the process of Dying to Self, the child self. But, connecting with the child self does not mean the client is enlightened. The child needs to learn and grow through having a relationship with the Divine in the experience of essence. A person cannot be taught nor can he grow in his soul if the ego is running the show. The process of Alchemy bypasses the ego by taking a genuine thread of feeling that leads like a corridor to the soul. Alchemy is always necessary to bring the client to the deeper core self or soul self of the child. The client comes into essence through the transformation of Alchemy.

Sometimes people have an extraordinary connection with God which they simply have forgotten. Perhaps as a child, a person experienced essence and connection to the Divine but as she grew up and her ego developed, that knowing was abandoned. She may be walking around her daily life with a great capacity to know God and experience essence and not recognize the gift she possesses. If she remembered that connection, she could be living a very different life. Such a person will have that lost knowledge and awareness return through the essence of remembering. A person who remembers the experience of essence and connection to the Divine is fortunate to have such memories as a reference point to guide her. Her remembering may come first and Alchemy will follow. Sometimes, a bit of Alchemy can jog memory as well. But whether essence is remembered or discovered anew through transformation, Alchemy is always the process that brings one deeper and teaches the individual how to connect with the soul.

In That Second

And how was she supposed to move?
I say this because the shadow
had pinned her.
That which is thrown
from what is real
becomes distorted
by the temper of light.
And the light was coming from down low,
from the belly of the horizon,
laying a long shadow.

She would have looked away
but his gaze had become
an arrow that marked her
held her tight to uncertainty.
Or to the very ground she was standing.
If she could have taken him
into herself swallowed him like
the hills take the sun at dusk
he would have been the shadow
she feared and hoped for.
But she could not move.

What she wanted right then
was to shatter onto the gravel road
they had been walking
to be not the solid form of herself.
A scattering of stones.
She wanted to cry out love me
because this is all I am.
But what kind of sense would that make?
She thought this is how it is
in the second you realize you have lost your mind
and it's still your secret.
So she wanted to take back all she wanted
and start over.
She wanted light and shadow
to be parts of the same
to step forward and be
part of that world.

                    Karla Van Vliet

Eclipse of the Psyche, the Blind Spot
and Standing in the Breach

Every individual who begins the work is eclipsed by pathology either partially or fully. The more eclipsed, the more a person is held hostage to a place of blindness in the self. To the extent that the eclipse continues, the problem of pathology continues no matter how much work the therapist does with the person. Because of this, clients can be in the work for years and not progress as quickly as they hope.

For a severely eclipsed client, he simply cannot get out of his own way - he often has no idea what the therapist is talking about in relationship to his dreams. Many clients who are eclipsed in this way fail because they never get to the underbelly of the pathology. Without the ability to see the pathology, to see the demon, they cannot get to the point of seeing how their behavior or beliefs are pathological. They have an understanding of themselves that only remains at a surface level because they are unable to separate from pathology. If they cannot separate themselves from pathology, they have nothing against which to compare their understanding.

For example, if a person lives out of a pride or anger dynamic, then this is how he knows himself. He has no way to contrast his own experience because his experience is only based in the pride or anger dynamic. He is unable to see that he is eclipsed by the pathology of pride or anger. This creates a blind spot. When a client is eclipsed, the issues manifested in dreams are a mystery.

When a client is less eclipsed, he has a greater ability to receive what the dreams offer through the clarity of separation. With this perspective, he can move through his work more quickly. The contrasting perspective is essential to the process of separating what is true in a client and what is pathological.

Of course, some form of eclipse is carried into each stage of the work. But once a person's eclipse is only partial, he can use his awareness to work through issues. Clients with growing awareness will often have negative/difficult dreams because the Archetypes can finally show the true reality of a situation. When a client can begin to see with clarity, he can appreciate the truth. His appreciation comes not from simply being told that something is bad, but through the ability to experience, feel and know it because he is opening to his feelings.

The negative/difficult dreams that often come at this point are different from earlier dreams because, generally, the client is separate from the pathology, seeing how it is trying to manipulate him. Sometimes the client will be manipulated and sometimes he will not. But the dynamic is now exposed and the client can begin to see how it manifests in waking life. Having the clarity to see the demon means that the eclipse is broken or breaking down. This is a major breakthrough in the work.

Having a major breakthrough come in the form of negative/difficult dreams can be confusing. But when a client witnesses someone else in a dream being tricked instead of always being the one tricked, this signals a shift in consciousness. Seeing the demon instead of being the demon.

It is important for the therapist to relate a client's experiences in the dream to outside world behaviors. When a client is partially eclipsed, he may be aware enough to see the symptoms of his behavior even though he may still get stuck in a negative emotional place. But becoming aware of a symptom is not necessarily getting to the core of the pathology. Therapists are sensitive to the limits of the client and will only work a blind spot with a client when a dream takes the client to that blind spot.

When a client does not know how his pathology is manifesting in the world, the therapist can say, "This is how it appears in the world," or "This is the way it may look to others." It can be useful learning to a client to know how others experience him, especially when others can see the pathology in a way that the client cannot. Observations from the world can be good in some situations even though the client may take the observations personally and react. It can be a tool to help the client see into blind spots.

The Blind Spot

A blind spot in a person's psyche is the way the ego perceives both itself and in general. When a client has an issue around a blind spot, the Archetypes cannot help her with the issue until the blind spot is exposed. In many cases, the dreams work around a blind spot, allowing feelings to arise which reflect different aspects of the self coming through. Feeling the new feelings will produce changes in the psyche that will help the client face the blind spot. But when a blind spot is dominant, everything in the person is filtered through it. In this case, the dreamwork can only challenge the client to change the way she perceives reality. When the reality that is being challenged is the only reality the client trusts, it is always a difficult issue.

How a client's pathology manifests in the world may be an entirely different mechanism than how it appears. The way it appears may refract for the person into different arenas of issues. The way into and through issues is presented in dreams in ways that the client can face into at each particular point in her development. The therapist does not need to attempt to illuminate the blind spot as he sees it to the client. He simply follows and focuses on the message of the dreams.

If a client is exhibiting a destructive behavior in her outer life, it may be only a symptom of what is happening on a deeper level and it may not be helpful for the therapist to confront the issue initially. The client may not have any idea about the behavior because of a deeper issue, placing the reality of the behavior in the client's blind spot.

For example, a woman involved in a thirteen year affair while married to another man did not see anything wrong with the affair because of her deep wound around men, especially her father. The issue to work with initially was not the affair, but the deep wound. In this case, it was important for the therapist not to take a social moral agenda because the affair was not addressed initially in her dreams. This showed the therapist that the client was not ready to face her behavior. The therapist must always trust the path the Archetypes choose even though he may wonder why a specific, seemingly obvious issue is not being addressed.

The therapist and even friends of the client must let the dreamwork work for the individual and stay out of the way. When a friend sees an issue with a friend, the impulse is to want to help the person change destructive behavior. But when the real issue is a deeper wound, the more the person is told about the outer issue, the worse the behavior can become. This is why a therapist does not interfere in a client's process. Instead, he allows the client space to work it through based on the dreams.

When another's way of being causes a reaction in a friend or even in the therapist, it is because of unfinished business in the friend or therapist. Out of reaction, the other person will feel that the only way out is to have the client see and understand her issue because he cannot see or understand his own issue. When a therapist reacts to a client in this way, it makes it difficult for the therapist to allow the client the space she needs to deal with her feelings. The only way to give another the space to feel is for the therapist to feel his own feelings without projecting them.

The Therapist and the Blind Spot

The therapist must always be willing to move his position, something that most people do not do very well. It is easier to establish a position, even a passive one. To find the place that is perfect for the client - not too aggressive and not too passive - is very much akin to finding the perfect place with the Archetype. If a therapist has that strong connection, it is easier to bring that connection into relationship with client. In this way, the therapist can know where to be and when to move his position. If a therapist fails to do specific work with a client, it is almost inevitable that it is something he needs to do in his own work.

When a client gets triggered into the senex/puer dynamic, then the issue becomes right/wrong based on value judgments. The therapist in this situation must be able to avoid engaging in a dialogue about the value judgment. For once a point is argued, then the connection to the Archetypes is gone and the connection to the senex/puer is engaged. The job of the therapist is to be the ally of the client, even when it is a struggle because the client is fighting her own work.

Because the therapist is directly fighting the pathology from the very first sessions, the therapist is always a target for that pathology. This means that the personal work of therapist, in the process of working with others, accelerates greatly. When a therapist grows more and more in his own process and in working with others, he becomes more and more vulnerable. Becoming more vulnerable means feeling one's own suffering and feeling the suffering of the client. Part of becoming a therapist is committing to caring for others and feeling everything that comes up in the work.

When a therapist finds that he has personal issues triggered when working with a client, which inevitably happens, he must be willing to face into the personal issue. It offers a great opportunity. For example, if a therapist feels fear when working with a specific client, it is a great opportunity to face fear. The fear is not about client, it is the therapist's own fear.

When working with an individual and her dreams, it is important for the therapist to be open and vulnerable. The client needs the therapist to relate to and to encounter without an oak desk for protection. It is important for the therapist to be completely human and compassionate, which means being vulnerable with each client.

Standing in the Breach

Every person who comes into the dreamwork knows that something is wrong. People come to the work because they can feel that crack inside. From the very first session, the dreams take the client and the therapist to that crack. For some, the crack is already exposed and obvious when they begin. For others, it is far more buried.

The pathology will do whatever it can to keep this place covered. The client and the therapist are in a battle with the pathology from the very beginning to find and uncover this place. Part of this process is that the therapist often will stand in the crack, in that breach, for the client.

To stand in the breach, the therapist must be able to feel where the crack may be in the client. This is more than just showing the client where she is or is not in her process as shown by the dreams because it entails opening to the person's soul. Opening to another's soul without projection requires that the therapist have a strong connection with the Archetypes.

A therapist cannot stand in the breach without connection because the Archetypes, the Divine, are in the breach. Standing in the breach means allowing the Divine to work through one person, the therapist, in order to help another, the client. This is why it is important for therapists to stay committed to their own spiritual work, their own connection and relationship to the Divine. If a therapist can stay with his own process and his own feelings, then he can stand in the breach and even stand in for the Archetypes, if necessary. For therapists are often called to be Archetypal for their clients.

Most people in the dreamwork react, especially in the early stages, because they are not yet strong enough to stay with their feelings and their connection. Their pathology waits for the therapist to make a mistake or a misstep so the client can have an excuse to stop her work. But it is up to the client to make the choice to stay open to her process or not. This is not a reflection on the therapist. The majority of people who start this type of deeply spiritual work will not move all the way through to Stage Three because it is such challenging work. Many will stop at different places for many different reasons. The therapist's job is to go with the client wherever she wants or can go in her process. Many clients take breaks and return to the work, while others reach a place in their process where they are comfortable enough and decide to stop. If the client decides to stop the work, the therapist will support her, always leaving the door open for her to return.

The very moment a dream is worked in a session, the therapist is theoretically standing in the breach because it is his job to see the truth of the dream and speak it to the client. But communicating the truth of the dream is often difficult, challenging the therapist to work on his own work. If the therapist worries more about what the client will think instead of articulating the message of the dream, then he is not standing in the breach for the client. Instead, the message of the dream gets tainted by the therapist's pathology. The therapist cannot worry about being liked by the client. His job is to articulate for the client the message from the Archetypes based on the dreams. The therapist is an advocate for what is presented in the dreams, an advocate for the Archetypes and for the client's connection with the Archetypes.

To be in alliance with what is presented in a dream, be it a child or an Archetype like the Animus, the therapist must be strong in his own connection. The therapist must also be willing to stand in the breach for the client. If the therapist wants to be in that place for the client and if the client wants the therapist to be there, then there is a good match for the process. However, if the client does not really want the therapist to be in that breach, then something in the process will fail.

The dream forces the therapist to be inside another person in a way that can be extremely uncomfortable, close and intimate because it means the therapist is in another's psyche. Through the dreams, the client's astrological chart and through the therapist's own openness to his own feelings and connection, the therapist can be in the psyche and can stand as an ally for what the dreams reveal. The therapist, from this place, can say what is true in the client's inner world as it is shown in the dreams. Hopefully, the client's ego can listen.

Lovers/Partners Standing in the Breach

Sometimes, a lover/partner will stand in the breach for her partner. When one person in a couple is in the work and the other is not, or even when both are in the work, there can be an opportunity for one to stand in the breach for the other. Especially if the partner is deeply wounded.

For example, a female client brought to every session how her partner did not know how to love her and how they did not have a successful relationship. But her dreams showed that the Archetypes wanted her to stand in the breach for her partner. She stood in that breach for a year and a half, and finally, her partner began to grow into his process and open up to her. Because she stood in the breach for him, he had room to grow and learn how to be more loving. Of course, standing in the breach is not just for the other. For this particular client, standing in the breach allowed her to experience being with the Anima without the support of the Animus. From this position, she was able to grow spiritually as well as be a channel for her partner. She stood in the breach for him and for herself as well.

When a client stands in the breach for a partner, it can trigger a dynamic and an opening that the partner may not be able to face. Many people who do the dreamwork have partners who do not. In this case, it is necessary for the client to stay out of reaction and not project onto the other - to not go into false pain or betrayal or abandonment issues that may arise. Staying clear of projections and reactions, staying with feelings, allows the client to stay present with her partner. It also allows the partner to experience another standing in that breach for him. Even in these situations, it can be a great opportunity for both partners to grow.

Standing in the breach for a partner works more smoothly when women stand in the breach for men then when men stand in the breach for women. Men have a greater tendency to follow women into the feeling realm whereas women do not have the same tendency to follow men.

Exile

I have not told you, said the girl,
that I lifted above the water's long slip
like a heron

my voice, said the girl, the raw call
of the black bird

when I could not live in you I lived
in the image of the world

fish in the reeds, black stone
at the river's edge

when you were a border
I was the burnt field, the new grass
lifting through ash

and the fox turning to look,
our eyes meeting.

Karla Van Vliet

Projection

We bring our accumulated past experiences to every moment and this past prevents us from being fully present in our individual truth. In dream life, the Archetypes confront the client in the past in order to bring him into the present of the child self that God created. Emotional issues and conflicts are from the past, and projection is how a client stays stuck in that past.

Many people enter therapy looking at the externals of their lives and wanting change. If the goal of psychology is that kind of change, then the goal of Archetypal Dreamwork is to prepare for the change that can only come from the inside.

Most people search for reasons why they feel the way they feel. When they feel angry or depressed or unhappy, they project this internal feeling or emotion onto the externals of their lives. Projection is the justification of the why an individual feels they way they feel. Simplified, projection may manifest as thoughts such as, "I hate my job," or "My spouse is to blame," or justifications such as "My best friend has not called me."

In contrast, when a person has a physical wound and someone bumps it, he knows the bumper did not cause the wound. The person would not say, "You are the reason my arm hurts," because he knows the pain and soreness around the wound was already present before the bump. Even though there is pain when the wound is bumped, the person does not blame the bumper for causing the wound.

But in the psyche, a person does not understand that he is damaged or hurt or wounded. He will always think it is the other person or the situation or whatever bumped him that is causing the hurt. It is tricky because there is hurt, but it is not what is carrying the pain. The wound already within carries the pain and being bumped only triggers that wound. Anything can be the object of the projection and even minor things can bring up that hurt. Through projection, a person stays trapped in the past of old wounds.

In the dreamwork, when a client has an emotional reaction, he can begin to see it as linked to the past and see the reaction as a way the pathology controls him. While the client cannot forcefully change his reactions, he can acknowledge that the pathology exists within and ride it out. Riding out the pathology rather than trying to change it means to acknowledge the emotion without projection. To be aware of projection is to distinguish between an emotion and a feeling and not project that onto the world.

If there are things in the client's life that reinforce the projection because they are intolerable, then the client can really be caught. A person in that situation may have to make changes in his outer life before he can even begin to do the work. If the situations that invite the projection are truly destructive to the self, then the person is not yet capable of doing the work on the inner level.

However, many times when the outer life is not intolerable, an individual will make it intolerable just so he can project. Sometimes, of course, there are real issues to be worked through but many times it is just another excuse to justify a feeling or emotion. An example: a coworker suddenly requests to work on a project to which you have committed a great deal of time and energy, a project you really feel excited working on. The coworker's involvement will change the project in ways you can only imagine. Suddenly, you are shaking with rage at this person - wanting to strike back, hurt him, condemn him for making you feel like you are not good enough to do the project alone. This kind of reaction is habitual and standard in the outer world. It is much easier to project the feeling, to blame the coworker and complain about him to someone else rather than descend into the depths of the woundedness. In this case, if the wound is around feeling hurt and unworthy with nothing to offer anyway, then this is how the person reacting probably feels all the time. These feelings have nothing to do with the coworker. The projection makes the situation intolerable because there is no room for the possibility that the coworker might actually enhance the project. Because the person is blind to this, the projection continues to poison him against the coworker, making it probable that the project will eventually fail.

Breaking Projection

When a client is able to detach from the object of the projection, from the why of the feeling, then she can own that feeling and feel it rather than project it. This is a challenge because usually the client has spent her whole life avoiding these feelings. The dreams will guide the client by giving an experience and a connection to the deeper feeling. The client is also given the Archetypal support she needs. With this experience and support, she can begin to approach an understanding of her own pain.

Dream:
I see a dying deer with a great wound.

Through the experience and feelings for the deer in this dream, the client is given the opportunity to confront her own great woundedness. She can then relate her pain to that wound rather than to anything external, like a coworker or a spouse or a situation. External circumstances may hurt, but they are not the carrier of the pain.

Breaking a projection allows for an understanding of the difference between emotional pathology and deep feeling. The distinction, again, is that emotions are mutated feelings. Emotions are pathology while feelings are deep process. What makes something an emotion or a feeling is not based on the core feeling, such as anger or sadness or fear, but on the intention and where it comes from within the client.

When an emotion is projected, the emotion wants to control the person. In the example above, the person is controlled by rage. He is angry because the coworker became involved. While anger is the person's feeling, it controls by poisoning him against the coworker. To do this, it requires the cooperation of the person. When projecting, the person infuses the pathology with energy and the past will always stay powerful and present in that moment. But when the person does not project, then the pathology will simply run dry. Life, of course, goes on, but the pathology will not be able to control the person because it is not receiving his cooperation. The pathology needs the person to cooperate in order to stay alive in him.

Projected feelings do not differentiate between "good" and "difficult." They can be feelings a person wants to experience or feelings she does not want to experience. A person may feel happy because she won the lottery or got married or a new song was released. In these examples, the person may be projecting the idea of happiness onto external things like people, places, things or events she believes will make her feel happy.

Feelings a person may not want to experience might be nihilism or depression or hopelessness. Antidepressants are often prescribed for people in the grips of these states of beings. For a person in the dreamwork, she can simply say, "I am just feeling this way. These are my feelings." She can begin to understand that it is not about her job or because there is truly nothing about which to be hopeful. Some people's pathology just wants them to feel bad.

When a feeling is projected, the person never gets to descend more deeply into it. The descent is not really from point A to point B because it is not linear. Instead, it is a vertical journey, moving through the layers of the past to reach the moment of freedom and liberation that is the present. To be in the present, a person must descend deeper into feelings because that liberation can only be felt. The evolution of consciousness in an individual means she must find her deepest feelings and move through them. Through this descent, through moving through these feelings, the individual can begin to alchemize and evolve.

For this kind of Alchemy and evolution of consciousness, the client needs to grab hold of a feeling and follow it, no matter what it is - pain or horror, insecurity or joy, fear or love. It does not matter where the client starts, it only matters that she starts somewhere. Once the process of feelings begin to emerge, feelings that are not emotions, feelings that are not projected, then the client's work can descend further and faster.

A good example is when a woman falls in love. Women usually project the Animus onto the men they love even if they do not believe in the Animus. A woman often puts her man in a position of rescuer or someone who will take care of her - a role that can only come from the Animus (even if it is not in the way most expect). The Animus will come to the woman in a dream as her man being seductive and loving because he is trying to get close to her. The only way he can get this close is to come as her lover. In this case, he is like a doppelganger or a twin. Since he cannot get in any other way, he rides the projection.

Often the woman marries the man and at some point begins to be disappointed because her husband cannot be the Animus. But if she can remember the love she feels in a dream for the Animus who comes as her husband in terms of the dream and her inner work and not just in terms of the person she married, she can withdraw the projection. When she withdraws the projection of the Animus from her husband, she can begin to feel her longing for a loving relationship with the Divine. This will be supported by issues in dreams that produced the love and the longing in the first place. It also allows for the marriage to deepen, allowing the woman to see her husband as he is, not who she expects him to be.

The process of withdrawing a projection from the world and bringing it back to the inner source, usually represented by a particular situation in a dream, is called introjection.

The focus of this work is internal, requiring the individual to face her own woundedness. When a client is feeling her feelings, the Divine can intercede and the tools of Alchemy can be used. Through the descent into feelings, a client can be healed through her relationship with the Archetypes. She can become free from her past, no longer trapped into looking out at the external world from the wound through projection.

Homecoming

You come out of the rain,
like a shadow, a bird in flight.

I have missed you
and this holding you is not enough.

I want to climb into your body's oarless boat
drift into the world looking up into the gray gray sky.

I want the tall pines' hush, the open water
spreading towards the misty horizon.

Karla Van Vliet

PROJECTION AS ISOLATION

The dreamwork is about what is waiting on the inside as shown through the dreams and moving through the maze of interconnected feelings and emotions which battle for our attention. It is a battle largely ignored because we are looking out into the world to solve the issues which are inside. It is as if the world is nothing more than a stage on which to play out our struggle and our journey. But the journey does not work that way.

With projection, the eye sees to the outside, not to the inside. Once the inside material is projected into the world outside, the very material that would lead the soul on its journey is lost to the person. The person rationalizes that if the problem could just be solved, then everything would be fine and she would be free. This is true, but not if that problem is projected out into the world. No matter what changes in the world, it will never change who the person is inside and what she brings into the world.

Even personal changes are nothing more than strategies to cope with inner material that is projected out into the world in the first place. We demure, we are humble, we think we are honest but really we are only scratching at the bars that cage us.

Being a better person, working on issues, changing behavior, changing attitudes is not actually freedom. It is only cosmetic work, like liposuction, even though it may make us feel better and think we are actually changing. But the separation from the Divine shows that nothing has changed. The goal is not to become better people. The goal is being connected and being conscious of the Divine on the Divine's terms.

The material played out in the world through projection has to be played out on the inside. This is the journey. Projection is not evil, it is simply the consciousness of avoidance, the consciousness of isolation. Everything that is projected into the world works to isolate the individual from her true soul, from her way to that true soul self and from her way to the Archetypes.

Separated from the Tribe
by Kristin Kehler

Dream:

> As I am walking, a pack of wolves comes at me from all directions. At first I am not scared, I think I can run to safety, but then I realize they will devour me. I feel terrified. As they close in for attack they become Native Americans. I am with a tribal group, very loving, powerful, sexual (a couple is making love on the ground out in the open). I am specially drawn to one man with a huge barrel chest and loving eyes. I feel a deep love and peace, connection. I love the man, I want to curl up with him like a child, be protected. Shift.

> I am sobbing from a deep pain. I am not with the tribe any more. I think maybe I am grieving because white people have mistreated the Indians or something.

In the dream, the powerful Native American images of the wolves coming from the four directions is certainly not lost on the client. Kristin knows that they are sacred and is not scared. But, then she realizes death is at hand. Death precedes the understanding and seeing the isolation from the Divine, but Kristin does not know this in the dream. Because she does not know this, she becomes scared and wants to run. At this moment, she is lost to the Divine and her fear comes from her ignorance and her lost capacity to feel the pain of the separation. At the end of the dream, she does feel that pain, but she thinks, altruistically, that is about the suffering the Native Americans suffered at the hands of the white people. Kristin is white and so therefore is part of it and part of the blame. It is hard to stay in the pain, to be the Native American soul who has lost her way and is feeling the pain.

Fear moves to pain, isolation moves to belonging. In the midst of moving from isolation to belonging it is necessary to feel fear and pain. This is the journey, the Alchemy of the soul, the requirement. Yearning to be with the Divine without these feelings is not possible in this work. Enlightenment requires an awareness of one's suffering both past and present. At some point, she will know that she is the wolf, she is the Native American. It takes more than just knowing - it requires a descent into feelings. So, she cries about the loss and separation for the wolf and the tribe, not able to know her primalcy - primal sea - connection to the Divine. One day, she will know this, but right now at this point in her work, she struggles with the pain of having lost it. Isolation requires pain to be dissolved.

Sometimes, in reaching for God or others, a person hopes to solve the problem of separation. But the reaching is a reaching to a universe that looms outside, that is billions of light years into darkness where God is far away. It is like looking into a set of binoculars the wrong way. But when a person looks to the inside, everything is right there.

The portal that is inside all things, including the portal to the universe, is us.

Through dreams and the journey of the psyche, a person can find her way back through the portal of the "Wardrobe," back into Narnia, to the true battle. The choice is inside each person. Where do you want to live, where is the undiscovered country in you?

But how does an individual change the world if she is inside, how does she touch others and how is she touched by others? Being on the inside does not isolate a person from the world, contrary to what many believe. In fact, the opposite is true. Being separated from the inner life is what makes an individual isolated. Without her inner life, a person cannot bring her love or her beingness into the world. Instead, through projection, she seeks love from the world that cannot love. Even when it tries, the love is empty for when people are isolated from the inner realm, the love they offer from that isolation is empty. A person can only be empowered through the Divine that emanates through the soul and into her very being.

With this inner support of the Divine, a person can jump into the world, bringing all that she learns and receives from the Divine. Being in the world from this place of support is an extension of what is true on the inside, an extension of the Divine in that person, an extension of the person's soul and her ability to fulfill her calling. To be truly in the world and have service, a person must journey to the inside first. Then she can return resplendent and open, not alone or isolated.

From this place of not being alone, of not being in isolation, the individual can look into the world with new eyes. She can look without needing it to love or care for her because she already has the love and the caring from her inner connection. With this new, clear vision, however, the reality of the world is apocalyptic for one can see the suffering that was once hidden behind the self-deception. But with the inner connection, Divine love can come through and guide the person to offer support and help in the world in ways that would have been unfathomable.

Moment's Sight
After *Ned de Poisson* by Janet Fredericks

The pool's reflection holds
the sky's clouded iris.
In a moment's movement,
near the rushes, I see surface break
of illusion. Fish, thick bodied,
flush the water's darkness
for a moment rise
to the unknowing world.

Fins flutter the reeds of my body.
In its deep pond, fish swim like prayers.

Karla Van Vliet

INTROJECTION

Introjection is the process of taking an emotion that is projected onto the world and returning it back into the inner world using a dream image. The goal of introjection, in part, is to reach the feeling underneath the projection.

Introjection is most often used with clients who have at least begun to explore their feelings and may have even experienced a death of self. They also, usually, have some experience of their connection with the Divine and have some capability of containing that connection within. Once this kind of work is established, a client, when prompted by a dream, can use introjection to shift out of a difficult pathological place by withdrawing an emotion from a trigger in the world and grounding it in a place of connection or deep feeling associated with a dream.

For example:

I am in a river and see a waterfall ahead of me. I am terrified as I go over the waterfall.

This particular client was having a great deal of fear in her outer life around money issues. The therapist can use this dream to help her remember that when fear arises, instead of projecting it onto an external object or issue in the world, such as money, she can introject the fear inward to the terror of going over the waterfall. Introjection in this way can help the client shift her way of being.

Shifting a way of being means that the fear is associated with the drama unfolding in the inner work, in this case, a place in the journey which is represented by going over the waterfall. The dream offers the client a tool to understand fear as a place to jump into instead of away from. In real life, the client would never go over a waterfall, but in the dream realm, it is not only possible, but important. It places the client in fear as a place to become, a place to jump into in order to take the next step in her journey.

When fear is present, a client will immediately want to ask, "Why am I afraid?" in order to understand the fear. When the question of why is associated with Archetypal fear, it can then be projected onto an object in the world. If it is projected, then the client creates the opportunity to avoid the feeling. In the world, fear is not usually an ally. In fact, it is usually an enemy.

But in the inner work, fear, when it is Archetypal, is an ally. It can be a doorway for becoming the soul self. This kind of fear is of the spirit, of change, of transformation. It gives the client an opportunity to come to terms with her desire to grow. Fear is a feeling that alchemizes well when it can become something in and of itself to be encountered and especially when the client can surrender to it. It can transform into essence and into a state of spiritual openness to the Divine. It can transform into awe.

Introjecting fear onto a visual image from a dream - such as going over the waterfall, facing the wild animal, breathing the water, receiving the love from the Archetype - allows the fear to be a place of becoming for the client. The depth of meaning can be exposed when it is faced based on an awareness of fear. But without having the awareness of the true nature of the fear, the client has no way of understanding and confronting its power.

Of course, there are different kinds of fear and it is important to discern between them. For example:

Dream:
I meet a man who is 20 feet tall and towering over me. I immediately love him.

This dream can be interpreted in one of two ways - either the client is deeply connected and can feel love for the Animus or the client is completely out of touch with his feelings of fear and is unable to embrace the Animus from a deep place of vulnerability.

Fear is always a part of the process when confronting the Divine. But once that fear is projected into the world, the opportunity for a deeper understanding of the spiritual world is lost. The client, instead, gets lost in reaction to the fear and the attempt to answer the question of "What". When attempting to answer "What," the client is looking for a way to be safe. Safe, but separate.

Projection is a dynamic that takes all of the inner spiritual challenges that come from dreams, all of the opportunities to face growth and throws them into the world, essentially asking the client to journey the spiritual life in the world. But the person who tries to find her peace and connection in the world is hopelessly lost, for the world is not the place to face spiritual challenges unless it is understood from the grounding of the inner journey.

For instance, if the client with the waterfall dream is faced with the choice of taking a new job in a new place, she may face her fear by taking the job, believing it could be a place for growth. But taking the job may be another attempt at finding peace in the world. What if the job does not work out? If the client, instead, focuses on her inner work and allows herself to go over the waterfall, then her next dream will be a deeper dream taking her to a deeper place in her inner journey. In this way, taking the job becomes a moot point. The client can understand that whether or not she takes the job, whether it is a right or wrong decision, she has already succeeded in facing her fear by having the fear be where it belongs - in her inner work. She may even realize that she does not actually need to take the job.

The Archetypes do not really care where the client works because their connection to the client is not based on whether she lives on the east or west coast. The relationship is based on whether the client can face the fear, because facing the fear brings her closer to the Archetype.

Introjection is not just used with fear - it can apply to any feeling presented in a dream. Another example of a feeling that is often used with introjection is hurt or pain.

Dream:
I am standing at the bottom of stairs that lead to an attic. A man tells me that there is a dead baby in the attic I must retrieve. I feel great sadness for the baby.

If this client is feeling pain in her outer life around a failed relationship or a slight from a friend, the dream shows that the source of the pain is not the relationship or the friend, but the pain of the dead child. Of course, it may be true that there is significant pain that comes from a betrayal in a relationship or from deep wounds in childhood. This child in the dream may be a reference back to the time of the wound.

And, it is also true that unresolved hurt from the past usually resurfaces in new relationships. The lack of resolution around the original wound perpetuates into the replication of new wounds that are rooted in the past. In this sense, childhood wounds keep a person from progressing for she is still living from that past wound. The only future, then, is more and more of that past.

The resolution of pain through introjection through a dream helps the client move beyond the issue of the past because the child self that may have been wounded is still living in the present, is still waiting to be accepted, usually by the client. Although the child may have been hurt and separated from the client by past events, it is separated not just because of the past. It is separated because of the client's ignorance of the child's presence within. The client's salvation comes from accepting the child and feeling its pain. This is very different from being an adult bemoaning misfortune. Ultimately, the client needs to become that child.

Separation from the child combined with projection ties the client's past into the present, where she is blinded and can only see the past woundedness. In this state, the client can blame others or find circumstances that are similar to her past. She may even corrupt new situations. Very few people actually live in the present meaning of who they are really meant to be.

When the projected pain of the outer hurt is introjected into the inner pain of the dead child and when the client can accept that child, then healing can begin. The missing child can begin to relate to the client and the client can begin to understand and acknowledge what was lost. The issue can change from the woundedness in the world to the acceptance of the lost part of the soul.

The lost child is typically part of a triangulation. Without the child, the client cannot truly connect with the Divine. Any connection without the child is through the client's created ego self, the self that survived the loss of the child. In triangulation, it is this self that dies and is replaced by the child self. While reviewing the past to connect with the suffering of the child is helpful and important, in the end, the process is not about the past. It is simply about the reclamation of the child. When the child is reclaimed, the client can go deeper into her true self and be more open to her feelings which are necessary for the relationship with the Divine.

Man at a Distance

You stood beneath the birds,
the clattering of their beaks,
the shadow of their numbers.

What can a moment bring?
I saw you through the house's window
like a painting, *Man Listening
to the Thunder of His Soul.*

Black strokes over tree's green,
raw canvas road with standing man,
hint of gray sky surfacing below
in puddled foreground.

And what is love if not the seeing clearly
of another's longing?

I went on as if the catch of my breath
was not held in the claw
of whichever bird is your image.

When I turned then turned again,
you had gone.

Karla Van Vliet

Tactics of Pathology

Pathology is a kind of consciousness with a will of its own that sinks hooks into a person. It is its own agent of control, with many ingenious tactics, whose singular purpose is to keep people separate from the Divine. A client is vulnerable to its invasion if she represses her feelings - the pathology especially takes advantage of feelings that are difficult to feel, such as hurt, fear or trauma.

A simplified example: a client experienced a tremendous amount of pain as a child and could not bear to feel bad and hurt all the time. Nor did the people around the child know how to deal with the pain. So, the child repressed the feeling of pain. But repressed feelings do not "go away;" they mutate. In this example, the feeling of pain mutated into the child feeling that something was wrong with her - the emotion of shame.

Emotions versus Feelings

A denied feeling creates a hole or a blind spot in the psyche which becomes a place for the pathology to hide and build a nest. The soul resides deep in the bowels of feelings, and the distinction between feelings and emotions is crucial.

Feelings are what God made in us. Emotions are created as a protection from something the person does not want to feel. In the example above, the child's ability to feel pain is part of her gift - the gift of a good heart. These feelings are part of the essence of the person's unique soul. But it hurts and it is scary so the child rationalizes that something must be wrong. The child unconsciously creates distance from the feelings and believes she is the source of the problem. She feels the emotion of shame. Shame is hard, like lead. It gets stuck. The child begins to hate herself. The pathology insinuates its way in by agreeing with the self-hate and whispers, "Everyone else hates you, too." From here, nihilism can grow. In this example, the pathology used the emotion of shame to control the child.

The pathology cannot control, however, without some form of agreement from the individual. In this example, the person chooses shame over pain or hurt because it is denser. The density of an emotion, like shame, allows the person to avoid psychological suffering. The sacrifice of psychological health is driven in part by the biological imperative to survive, procreate and create. But the survival of the species is no longer determined by procreation and the creation of a social environment. Without spiritual maturation, an individual is doomed to live only in the external world.

To feel the love, it is necessary to feel the hurt; to feel God's grace, it is necessary to feel the fear; to feel God's blessing, it is necessary to feel the inadequacy. The original agreement with pathology is to not feel. The dreams show the client what she needs to feel at each step of her journey. The dreams take the client step by step through all the places left behind in the rush through adolescence.

Emotions are a mutation of feelings. When this mutation away from feeling occurs, a person essentially loses the ability to reflect the consciousness of the soul. From nests in blind spots, the pathology eclipses the client's truth, twining itself like a parasite through wounds and around the soul.

When a person begins this work, the goal of First Stage is to look into the blind spots to discover the pathology and learn how it operates. It is reflected through the psyche in the unique ways that each client has denied her feelings. Pathology initially uses tactics that are very personal to how and what the individual has repressed, reinforcing its hold through memories of past experiences and meanings specific to that individual.

This changes as the person advances in the work and begins to experience some of the feelings that have been repressed. The pathology starts to retreat from aspects of the psyche when these feelings are acknowledged or absorbed by the client's consciousness.

The child who repressed pain grows up projecting it instead and lives a life unconsciously driven by shame, nihilism, anger and competition. But through the process of the dreamwork, she can unravel the ego self and finally begin to feel the hurt and pain she rejected. A breach forms in the wall where the dam in her consciousness is breaking open to the feeling life of the soul. The client begins to see how she has avoided feeling by projecting the pain onto others and the world. The pathology can no longer hide in the client's projection or in her expectation of rejection from the world because these are now known to be part of the lie.

But even as the pathology retreats from some aspects of the person's psyche, it calculates, like a Machiavellian general, a new approach full of craft and deceit in order to readjust its hold.

Pride

The more a client becomes connected in his conscious life to the Divine, the less effective the tactics of the pathology. But as a client moves into Second Stage, the relationship with the Archetypes is just beginning to develop. At this stage, most people are vulnerable to the pathology because they are not yet deep enough in their soul selves to feel the presence of the Archetypes. When in essence with the Divine, the pathology has no hold. But, in the absence of Divine connection, the client can identify with other things usually related to the ego and things of the client's own making, which the pathology counts on. It knows innate pride makes a person vulnerable to the new battle plan.

Innate pride functions to maintain the equilibrium of the ego. The ego seeks to right itself like a ship tossed on the stormy sea of the dreamwork. Most want to feel good, want to be seen as a good person. Each time the Archetype confronts the client with his reactivity and projection, each time he is asked to own how he acts out these behaviors, the ego takes a hit. Pride then attempts to recover its former balance, to support the client to know he is doing fine. But this state of "fine" to which the client tries to return is most likely more of the old self, the secondary ego.

Of course, pride can cut both ways - it can lift the client up as better than others or slap him down as being the lowest of the low. Pride uses comparison with others or to the outside world as a gauge. In this place, the client can become preoccupied with the external. The self in pride wants to feel good no matter what. The pathology can use this because the client becomes numb and does not realize the pathology is present.

One form pride takes is when a person longs for praise and then cannot let it in when he receives acknowledgment. As long as the person's center of gravity is outside of himself, the pathology can keep him isolated from his deeper truth and the Divine. Pride in this context is the pride of shame, a habituated way of knowing oneself as bad and unworthy, of needing others to affirm oneself and being unable to accept affirmation. It is not the same pride as taking satisfaction in an accomplishment or taking pleasure in a beloved's accomplishment. This is more of a mechanistic way of thinking, a way the mind seeks to create a relationship with something outside so it can know itself.

Pride promotes the development of the ego for the sake of the developed ego rather than being rooted in a deeper feeling place in the self. Pride always identifies with things other than God. It identifies with the habitual ways of thinking about oneself that the pathology has already polluted. Pride in the self does not want to have pathology. A client may try to create distance from it by believing he is "better now" or by believing it is out there and not in him. But Dying to Self takes the notion of pride that the client is as he is and blows it to smithereens.

Dying to Self begins with seeing the pathology as it is revealed with increasing clarity one step at a time in one dream after another. The client spirals deeper into an awareness of the breadth of wreckage left in the wake of a life lived through pathology. But the pathological behaviors continue, and, in fact, the client's behavior often gets worse. This creates a difficult part of the process. It is difficult to see the pathology and passively watch oneself react in the old poisonous ways, over and over again. The pathology is dying back and retreating from aspects of the psyche, but the reactive behavior continues to emanate from that old place like an echo.

The pathology is ever bent on finding a way back in. The person watches in horror, knowing better but helpless to stop. This is a vulnerable moment because the client must accept his situation even as his nose is continually rubbed in it. The challenge is to learn to live with pathology. There is nothing to do about it beyond following the guidance of the dreams. If the client can stay with the truth and accept it without needing to fix or change anything, then the pain of regret has a chance to emerge. Acceptance of suffering leads to the pain of regret and the pain of regret leads to the acceptance of suffering. This ultimately allows the client to feel true compassion for the suffering of others.

Pride is part of what makes the client vulnerable to the seduction of the pathology. It distracts the client from seeing the reality of the pathology. Once the client can look squarely at the truth and accept his failings, there is room for the love to enter. This is the key: the client is loved by the Archetypes anyway, regardless of his failings. The moment he can admit his weaknesses is the moment he is open to the love that is always present. In this way, Dying to Self is a pride killer. But to the extent that pride lives, to the extent that the client has not accepted the humanness of his situation, he is vulnerable to the tactics of the pathology.

Although pride gives a feeling of adequacy or even meaning, it is not Divine love. It is, rather, a compensation for the lack of that love. Like the story of the Devil and Daniel Webster, an individual, like Daniel, receives a compensation for giving his soul away. Sadly, almost everyone has made some agreement. The agreement may be trauma-based where the client is compensated by avoiding the feelings of difficult experiences. The compensation may come in the form of the ability to maneuver power in the world or, conversely, to hide from the world. In all cases, when an agreement is made with pathology, it is the individual giving away his innocence, that which was created as his true self. The soul self or the child self.

Since most people do not remember God's love, the compensation is often pride of being in the world in a certain way through some external world value such idealism or altruism or power or money. But this only keeps the individual further away from the love he is truly seeking. If the love of the Divine was truly known, the individual would never sell his soul self.

But that love is not known by most people. The Animus, who breaks the agreement like Daniel Webster, can help the client to reclaim his soul self and the miracle of his true life.

Tactics of the Pathology

Once the pathology initially retreats, it bides its time regrouping and looking for another strategy. At this point, the tactics of the pathology become less personal to the individual and more general, impersonal and common to most clients in Second Stage work. The goal is to plug up the breach in the wall, the point of death, where the dam in a person's consciousness is breaking open to the feeling life of the soul. Pathology will direct an attack at this breach, because the breach in that wall is the place God can intervene and widen the crack. The pathology calculates its next move, using one of many options:

Blame the Client	Convince the client she is the pathology.
Adaptation	Pretend to change by adapting into something acceptable to the client and/or the therapist.
The War of Attrition	Create a frustration with the work where the client does not feel there is a possibility of movement until he finally gives up and stop his work.
Cornered Animal	Attack the client directly, like a cornered animal, to make her feel a hundredfold worse than she has ever felt.
Ghetto Gang Mentality	Stay in the ghetto gang and remind the client of his origins. Ask him, "Who do you think you are to change for the better?" Make the client believe that if he leaves the ghetto, he will lose all family and friends.
Worst Case Scenario	Take advantage of the unknown. Tell the client about the unknown and, of course, make it her worst nightmare.

Blame the Client

Blaming the client is a common and powerful tactic where the pathology blames the client so that the client feels she is the pathology. When she feels this, she feels responsible for the pathology's actions. The more a client sees the pathology, the more it shouts, "I'm you! I'm you!" But this is a lie. This tactic hooks a person in her shame, making it very difficult to isolate the pathology. People who have shame issues are already hard-wired to blame themselves and feel overly responsible.

Fortunately, at this point, the client will probably see the pathology reflected in a dream as an ugly or horrible creature, perhaps some mutated quasi-being or half-animal/half-human, possibly even a womb-less woman or a penis-less man. To see the pathology exposed in this way is extremely useful because it is reflected as something ugly rather than something attractive. The client can then reference ugly behaviors and examples in her life as well as reference the voice of blame as coming from the ugly mutated being in her dream. She can see the voice is not her true voice and the emotion is not a feeling and can separate from it. When she can start to separate, the control of the pathology begins to diminish.

Adaptation

By adapting into something acceptable to the client and/or the therapist, the pathology attempts to remain in control by feigning change. The client can be convinced that he has changed and does not behave from pathology anymore. The client begins to feel he is "better" because the pathology has learned good manners.

Similar to mutating into something acceptable, the pathology can become well behaved, playing the part of chameleon and disappearing into the background. It acts like the good guy and convinces the client it wants to serve God or be a good spouse or that it is sorry for what it did. While a client who is really Dying to Self may actually feel all those things, the pathology will eclipse this by acting out its own idea of transformation. It may tell the client what he wants to hear, but it is a lie. The pathology is fighting to stay alive and hidden by being good.

For example, a client making great progress in her work had the following dream:

> I open a door to find a wolf standing outside. My cat goes out and rubs himself against the wolf. I am very impressed.

This dream shows that the pathology is biding its time like a trickster cat. The wolf is unable to do anything to the cat because the client is impressed by the cat. But the cat is the pathology trying to convince the client that there is no problem, that all is well. This is a dangerous moment in a client's process because the pathology will try to convince the client and the therapist that because the client has grown and changed, it is time to relax. When the pathology cannot stop growth in a client, it will pull back and wait to strike again.

If all else fails, the pathology can simply become believable and agree with the therapist. It might say, "Yes, yes, I used to do that, but my homework went really well. I am really in my feelings now and the Animus is with me." The pathology remains hidden by appearing to buy into the system. This can hook a client in his desire to please the therapist, to be a good and obedient client. But avoiding the truth only protects the pathology.

This tactic is more dangerous than blaming the client because the pathology has mutated into something acceptable to the client. Clients with mutating pathologies will continue to have difficult dreams even though they may have done profound work. They will have a new barrage of Stage One confrontation dreams which can make them feel increasingly overwhelmed by the tenaciousness of the pathology even after a great deal of deep work. Their frustration can mount to the point of giving up on their process altogether. There is a limited window of opportunity, a limited amount of time unique to each individual in which to kill pathology.

This window is really the window of willingness the client has to do the work. To perpetuate the adaptation of the pathology as it switches from one behavior to another means that the wound has not been completely seen yet. The pathology's ability to keep shifting is a tactic used to frustrate the client, leading him into feeling increasingly hopeless. The client may feel that the pathology will never be rooted out.

The manifestation of the pathology wanting to change is not the client wanting to change. The reason the pathology can shift is because the client is avoiding other feelings. In this avoidance, the client may use the frustration by bringing it to the therapist, challenging him to "do something." Projecting the frustration onto the therapist is another way for the pathology to shift the war from inside the client to something outside, telling the person that the therapist is not doing a good enough job.

War of Attrition

The war of attrition tactic has a similar outcome in which it closes the window of opportunity, but here the war goes on and on until both sides are dead. The pathology does take blows by the process and is actually dying, but it pretends to live. It keeps the client doubting her progress, saying, "See, I am still here." When a client has changed but the behaviors have not yet stopped, the pathology will use this as proof that nothing has really changed. It says, "See, see, nothing has changed! Nothing will ever change." The pathology tries to drive the client into a nihilistic frame of mind by distorting aspects of the death experience.

The pathology keeps fighting, wearing the client's strength down through years of effort until all hope dies. The client can begin to feel that things are never going to change, that there will always be some variation of pathology, that it is no use to keep fighting. At this point, the pathology has succeeded in the closing of the window of opportunity, and, again, the client may want to quit her work.

It is extremely difficult to realize that even if the pathology dies, the pathological behaviors can continue and that this is a normal part of the Dying to Self experience. The death of pathology begins more on an unconscious level and continues as the client experiences an awareness of the pathology's existence. But the everyday behaviors might get worse in the process of dying at first, because the ego is still functioning - the ego is the last to change. When the ego changes before a change occurs on an unconscious level, then it is not really a change but a mutation.

The war of attrition is similar to adaptation except that in adaptation, the pathology tricks the client into believing that it no longer is present. In the war of attrition, the pathology is very present, it never really changes a great deal, and the client is clearly aware of its presence. The issue is not that the pathology exists; the issue is in the client becoming more and more resistant to admitting that it exists. If the client admits that it is still there, then it becomes unacceptable. The antidote to the war is for the client to accept that she has pathology.

It is a devastating blow to pride to accept the pathology, to accept that it is acting out and that there is nothing the client can do about it. It is also a big step in the healing process. A client is not defined by the pathology because it is not the client. The true essence of the client is also worked on in the dreams and is more readily available if the client can admit to her pathology. At some point in the process, what the pathology is doing or trying to do becomes irrelevant if the client can simply acknowledge it. Once it is acknowledged, the client and the therapist can focus attention on the processes the dreams present that are attempting to help the client. In the war of attrition, the pathology is only a problem if it is not acknowledged. Or, if it is acknowledged, its presence becomes over-inflated.

Cornered Animal

If other tactics are not working, the pathology can become cornered like an animal. When an animal is cornered, especially if it is wounded, it gets vicious - the pathology behaves the same way. It knows the client sees it, that the client does not like it anymore, and it does not care about hiding anymore. It goes into a full frontal attack.

Even though the client knows he is being attacked and can acknowledge it, he still feels terrible. Or the client will suddenly feel awful for no apparent reason and the pathology will not even try to project it onto people or situations so the client can believe he feels bad because of something external. When the pathology is a cornered animal, it reveals itself and flexes its muscles. It works because the person ends up still feeling awful.

For example:

> I try to kill myself by throwing myself out of an airplane then jumping off a large
> cruise ship. I am surprised and frustrated that I do not die and want to keep trying.

This client had worked hard with Dying to Self, but she believed she needed to die more. This thinking was the pathology's way of controlling the client's belief that she was not good enough. Even though she had died to self, her pathological habit kept saying she had to die more.

Reinforce Ghetto Gang Mentality

An exceptionally useful tactic, the pathology can attack by trying to keep the client in his place like some member of a ghetto gang. Ghetto gang mentality says, "Maybe you have changed but you will never really be able to leave the ghetto. It is who you are. Change may be fine for someone who was raised middle class but not for you. Who do you think you are? You think you are better than me?"

This tactic hooks a client in his identification with his past and the people who have been a part of that past. The people in the client's life may not want to change and are unconsciously threatened by the client's growth. If someone leaves the "ghetto," it reminds those who remain of their unhappiness and pain. The pathology will use this to convince the client he will lose his spouse, his family and his friends if he deepens into the feeling life of the soul. Ironically, there may be truth in this. If the client survives this tactic, he may indeed lose relationships as he leaves the ghetto gang behind.

Worst Case Scenario

In worst case scenario, the pathology takes advantage of the unknown and tells the client exactly how her life is going to be when she allows her feelings to emerge. If the client feels her anger, the pathology tells her she will end up in jail for murder. If the person opens up to explore the feeling of pain, the pathology says she will never stop crying or she will be just like her mother who cried all the time. The pathology will take the worst scenario it can find in the client's psyche as an example, then point to it and say, "This is how awful you will be if you change." It uses the uncertainty of the unknown to convince the client that what will happen next is her worst nightmare.

The Goal of the Tactics

The goal of the pathology is to simply halt/reverse the process of Dying to Self and to keep the client separate and alone. To do this, it will use any means at its disposal in whatever combination necessary to try to derail the client's growth toward connection with Divine love. But the process does diminish the pathology. Two dreams from two different clients:

> I watch in horror as the Animus lifts an enormous serpent of a snake out of the ground. When I look again, the snake is the size of a finger, shriveled up and blackened.

> I see a man holding down a slimy monster midget that has been pulled out of a big dopey man's chest.

The diminishment of the pathology reflected in these two dreams is real, but the pathology is opportunistic. A client can be seduced by its tactics through his own innate pride. If the ego of the client cannot bear to have pathology, he will try to change it or hide it or just feel lousy about it. From here, there is no admitting to imperfections so the person lies, covering the truth by defending, blaming and justifying. In social interactions, he will protect pathology by projecting it onto issues and other people. The habit of the pathology is so visceral that the client devours the bait long before he realizes how far from his truth it has taken him. When a client cannot expose his truth, he gets stuck right where the pathology wants him. No love and support can penetrate that prison.

The way through is to be honest and revealing about shortcomings. Understanding how the pathology operates helps give context to this process. It is a relief to let the pride go, to truly see the snake. It is a relief to know the slimy monster has been caught by the Archetype even as it still triggers reaction. Getting to this is simply being honest about it. The point of death, where the dam in consciousness breaks open to the feeling life of the soul, splits the wall in two.

Revolution

      Valley: carved by ice
and wave. Sky: forever blue
or gray or starlit.   Tell me
     this was wanted.

  On my tongue: a sliver,
like mint, sharp and disappearing,
   your name forgotten.

  How silence holds
      this body. Clay laid
in the river's curve. Nothing.
   Then hands digging in.

This is how we are bared.
   What is left: chrysalis hull,
sky torn *Common Blue.*

    Vast soundless valley:
  what little whispers I dare make.
To bruise heaven: words thrown
     at a sleeping God.

              Karla Van Vliet

THE WHOREMASTER

Although the Animus can deliberately manifest to the client as a "mean" man, it is entirely different than actually being the pathological male. The pathological male is the whoremaster. When the Animus appears as a dark figure, he does so because of a projection the client might have onto Him and/or men. By being the dark figure, the Animus reflects the projection back for the client to see and confront.

It is common for clients to be disappointed when the scary guy in a dream is not really bad, because it shows that their reactions are not based on what they believe. But it is far better to be tricked by the Animus than for the man in the dream to actually be dark. For when a client has the whoremaster, dark male, in a dream, it is a very difficult issue to confront.

The whoremaster resides in a place in the client's psyche that specifically has a sexual root. One way it is revealed through dreams is when the client is being sexualized, often anally. The client's sexuality is used, not just by the whoremaster, but also by the client. The client may find herself in abusive situations, or she may constantly look for sexual relationships with a dark edge, an edge where there is no possibility for love. She has a desert heart.

The whoremaster controls a client in various ways, including anger or violence, either overtly or covertly. The client may lash out at others or, the reverse, she may lash back at herself. The result is that the dark male has total control over the person.

A client's outward life, however, may not determine if she has a whoremaster pathology because the symptoms are similar to symptoms that have other motivations or reasons behind behavior. Awareness of the whoremaster has to come, instead, from a dream. For example, if a person has a tremendous amount of shame, the pathology attempts to shame her and keep her small in her dreams.

Dream:

I am in a concentration camp and there is a commandant who is brutalizing people in the camp.

In this dream, the relationship between the client and the pathology is one of oppression. This client will have experiences of feeling overwhelmed in his life that are congruent with the oppressive relationship.

In contrast, dreams that reveal a whoremaster relationship have a specifically sexual root for the client. The whoremaster is often someone attractive to the client, someone she wants in her life. In such a case, the client is confusing pathology with attraction and may not even know she is in relationship with the dark male. The attraction may come from a place of sexual debasement. For example, one common factor for a powerful dark male in the psyche is a child trauma in relation to men or fathers. Once the issue is clear, the work is to determine why the client is with the dark male, how she is a willing participant, to what extent is she a victim.

An example of how the whoremaster can be revealed in dreams: A female client frequently dreamed of desiring a famous actor, no matter the scenario. The actor, however, is famous for playing characters with an insatiable appetite for women, and, in fact, is known in his real life to have the same insatiable appetite for many different partners. The client knew all of this - but in her dreams, she allowed herself to be subjected to one degrading scenario after another because she would do anything to be with him. In this example, it was clear the actor-figure was not the Animus mirroring projection because of the degrading scenarios in the dreams and the patterns in the client's life.

Many women are attracted to destructive or abusive men in order to make the man a scapegoat for their own inner dark male and their own self-destructiveness. Women often replace their inner dark males with an outer world counterpart to avoid living their own lives and to avoid stepping into an intimate relationship with the Animus.

The whoremaster, of course, can come as female or male to both female and male clients. If the whoremaster consistently comes in a particular gender, then there is usually some way in which this manifests through that gender in the outer world.

The whoremaster is vile, with no regard for the sensitivity of the client or the client's relationships. It will dominate and control all aspects dealing with relationship. This often includes the relationship of the client with her therapist where the whoremaster may attempt to seduce the therapist, depending on the gender relationship. When the whoremaster is in control, relationship with others is always understood in the client through the quid pro quo of sexual intercourse.

An example of a whoremaster dream, from a male client:
>
> A man breaks into my room. He hangs me upside down and enters me anally. I feel
> terrified and ashamed.

The client is clearly a victim of the whoremaster, with the dream showing how it controls him in the world through feelings of shame and violation. This client has no history of sexual abuse and is not driven to sexuality for its own sake. However, his wife was unresponsive to his sexuality and he felt she believed his sexuality was disgusting. In this way, the whoremaster created a paralysis of shame through his sexuality that was really aimed at his sensuality and his capability to feel loved and supported.

The crippling effects of this particular version of the whoremaster permeated the marriage to the point where the client believed his wife was having many affairs, which left him feeling ashamed and powerless. There was no evidence that the wife was having affairs. In fact, in the process of unraveling this dynamic, it became clear that his wife was actually willing to be more responsive to his needs. He needed to break the story that the whoremaster created convincing him that his wife was the shamer, that his wife was the whoremaster. But his vulnerability to the whoremaster made it impossible for him not to project onto both men and women, resulting in a complete incapability to honor the love he was actually often given.

The whoremaster does not always manifests into some form of sexual predatorship or insatiable need. As is shown in this example, the client was merely a puppet, allowing the pathological male to plant fantasies rooted in his sexuality. The brutality of the whoremaster is that it leaves the individual lost in a loveless landscape where all motivations are twisted around the idea that there is no love in the world. Most victims of the whoremaster probably have very little pleasure in the sexual act itself. It becomes more of a living compulsion which is manipulated by the pathological male.

Another example comes from a female client. In this case, the whoremaster was female in the dreams who was always looking to have sex with the client. The client was compliant and attracted to the pathological female figure. This particular client had early childhood sexual experiences and claimed to enjoy them. For her, the molestation was exciting and, in some ways, created by her. As an adult, every man and woman was a potential sexual object. Her insatiable sexual and manipulative drive not only led her to having many partners, but led her into having a great deal of control in the world. For her, the whoremaster seduced her by helping her have power in the world. The client used this power of the whoremaster in a relatively conscious way. When presented with this fact, the client said, without flinching, "So? This is not a problem for me." Shortly thereafter, she left the dreamwork.

Of course, sexually acting out does not indicate the presence of a whoremaster in a client's psyche. This kind of behavior can be caused by many different things.

The whoremaster works to have some form of mutuality with the person. When the client feels a participation with it, it is able to draw the client deeper into its deception, whether it is through destructive sexual behavior or other destructive behavior.

The House
by Cat

Dream:

> I am in a house full of domestic junk - piles of chairs, hanging pots, a bird cage. In the center, a man is holding a girl who appears to be dead. I feel creepy, wondering if he is fondling the dead body. Another man, who is a dark, evil man in a dark dining room and appears to be wearing something shiny, confronts me as I enter. I try to hide.

Monsters

Dream:

> I am with a handsome young man I knew when I was younger. He asks me to go away with him. While I am attracted to him, I feel that I cannot leave with him because I have "too much to take care of" in my own life. I leave him and return home to the house I grew up in. When I go upstairs to my parent's bedroom and look through the door from a height that I used to look from as a child, I see dark shapes moving around my parents' bed and blocking out the light. I feel terrified of the shapes, they seem evil and hairy and oppressive. I immediately pick up the phone and call the young man to tell him that I do want to go with him after all. I do not want to stay in my parents' house.

In the first dream, the child appears dead and is held by what is likely to be the Animus. But this idea is expressed in images occurring outside the dream. The difficulty lies not in the dream itself, but in Cat's perception of reality regarding the dream. This issue is true as well regarding the dark man in the dark room who appears in the painting as a Christian executioner or some kind of zealot from the dark ages. This is an aspect of her projecting her fear and recreating these images in her art.

This is extremely helpful, for in doing her art, she is expressing in image form the fears she has in the first place. The art is simply putting light on the way her fear makes her see things that are not really there.

The story of the dream could be quite different if it is perceived without fear - a man is holding a girl who is sleeping or resting happily in his lap. When Cat enters the room, she could respond by feeling warm and excited. In this scenario, there would be no need for a dark figure unless, in fact, there is a dark pathology in the dream emerging. If this is the case, then perhaps the dark male is trying to scare her and make her believe what is happening with the other man and the girl is evil and dark.

Which, she in fact, feels in the dream. She wonders if the man holding the girl is fondling her and fondling her as a dead girl. This belief of the man fondling the girl reflects a deep-seated distrust of men which may be reflected in her outer world relationships with men, starting with her father, and through the various relationships she has had as an adult. Since her father was an alcoholic whom she caretook, the seeds of this distrust may have been planted long ago, especially if her father projected a secondary wife onto his daughter, the client, and created an unconscious romantic bond.

Cat's past history of promiscuity in relationships with men seems to support the idea that the man in the dream who appears in the painting as an executioner is indeed a dark male, the whoremaster. Her history with men as well as her own psychological distrust would account for the projection of the man holding the child. It is like a Rorshach test - many images could be projected on the image of the man holding the child if Cat is unable to receive what is really happening. Assuming that the man is a father loving his daughter, one can see layers of imagined images based on her distrust and deep hurt with men. The dream indicates the depth of the issue not just by virtue of the presence of the whoremaster but by her inability to see a loving relationship when she is looking right at it. Cat's next painting, Monster, is another reflection of the whoremaster in relationship with her father. In this dream and painting, the whoremaster manifests as several monsters threateningly surrounding her father.

It is understandable that she would duck and hide under the table. The whoremaster now that it is seen for what it is, conjures the fear that may have been unconscious earlier in her work. In the early stages, she may have been inclined to follow the dark male, unconscious of her behavior. The good news is that she sees it for what it is and knows to hide. The transfer of her feelings from the whoremaster to the Animus is the next step in her healing.

Cat's awareness of the dark pathology has awakened in her the spirit of fear that she has not had in the past. It is typical that the whoremaster can be attractive which, for Cat, has led her to find men who play out the betrayer reality. In this case, it is based on her own inability to be more open or more vulnerable. But the veil is lifted, for she sees the demon for what it is. Eureka! She knows the truth. She calls the Animus, now willing to be vulnerable, to be open. Her fear has set her free.

She does not avoid her fear by going to the Animus. Instead, she understands the nature of pathology and knows enough to be fearful of it. This is starkly different than the avoidance of fear. The necessity of facing into her fear shows that while she sees through the fear, she could not feel it. Sometimes, women are with dangerous men and are so attracted to them that they do not know they are even in danger. Such is a blind spot for a woman who is lost to the whoremaster. She feels a bond to the very thing that might kill her. It is like the movie, *Waiting for Mr. Goodbar*, in which the main character's obsession for the enemy led her to succumb to it.

Prison
By Cat

Dream.

> This painting is from a recurring dream I had as a child. The dream: A naked, hairless, very androgynous man is locked in a prison while I with a whole group of kings and queens peer at him voyeuristically through high windows. Somehow I feel I have locked him in there, but he also feels like me somehow. I feel sexually excited and ashamed at the same time.

In this dream, it is clear that the Animus is locked in the prison. Cat feels appropriately guilty. She knows enough to know that she keeps him locked away, but at the same time feels excitement and shame. This is definitely a marker for the whoremaster, the thing that kept her attracted to "wrong men" for a long time. Since this dream occurred when she was a child, this was to show pathology as it was inherently going to manifest in her later years.

It is extremely difficult to work with children as they do not have the capability to fathom themselves in the way that adults can. Still, the psyche attempts to explain the situation. Now, as an adult, at a time when she is beginning to break through to the Animus, Cat's psyche reminds her of this dream as a reinforcer for the past. It is as if this is a look back dream.

The Look Back Dream

Often as a client is having a breakthrough, he will have hideous dreams that show the past which, now that he is far enough along in his work, he can appreciate with horror and regret at the way pathology had a hold on him. This is a look back dream. Without a greater knowing, this understanding would not be appreciated. It is important to be awake before the lies of the demons that control a person can be appreciated. For clients in Stage One, if the lies are evident from the beginning, it can denote a deep understanding of the pathology or it can denote a pathology that is so abusive that even in showing itself, the person is still under its control.

Call To The Beloved

I bring flowers,

tiger-lilies, like the heart's vase
picked wild.

In the blue sky above, the moon
a dart of brightness.

A bird in the wild apple sings
what with words I say to you.

Come to me, I am here, ready.

Karla Van Vliet

ANIMUS AS TRICKSTER AND AGENT PROVOCATEUR

When the Animus appears to a client as a "mean" man, it is very different than being the pathological male. The Animus as "mean man" usually reflects a projection of the client that the Animus wants the client to see and acknowledge. A blind spot to bring into consciousness. This is especially true in a First Stage dream where what is bad can appear as good and what is good can appear as bad. A "mean" Animus reflects how the client is projecting something of his own fears or judgments within onto the Archetype.

When the Animus comes in this way, he comes as either the Trickster or the Agent Provocateur.

Animus as Trickster

In dreams with a "bad" man, it is important to distinguish if the man is truly a pathological mean man who wants to cause harm or if he is the Animus playing the trickster. An example:

Dream:

A shadowing man chases me into a hotel room. The room has a sliding door which
I lock desperately to keep him out.

This client is a woman working in First Stage. She is convinced and terrified that the man is bad and truly wants to hurt her. But with close questioning, she realized the man was not shadowy at all, but was, instead, always in light. Also, she was able to see that not only did he not have a weapon, but he did not behave in any way that was threatening. He was simply trying to reach her.

In this example, the Animus tricks the client into a reaction in order to make her aware of a pattern in herself where she has fears about men. Once the client was able to see how she was projecting onto the Animus in the dream, she was able to talk about many examples of this projection onto men in her life. It is also possible that she chooses men that act out her fears by being truly scary men. This dream is telling her to feel her fear to find out what the man wants.

For some clients, it is difficult at first to see the projection. This particular client reacted by becoming angry that the Animus would come this way - it was difficult for her to accept the possibility that he was not bad and to see her projection. It took several dreams for her to accept her own fear

The Animus as trickster may take other forms besides being the "mean" man, forms that make it difficult for the client to know that he is the Animus. An example from a female client:

Dream:

> I am standing near a man and feel very attracted to him. He seems attracted to me,
> too, but he does not make a move towards me. I turn away from him.

When asked what she thought had to happen for them to be together, the client replied that the man had to come to her and since it did not occur to her to go to him, she turned away. This is another example of a blind spot. She is feeling an attraction to the man, but instead of being open about her attraction, she wants him to come to her. As if she would be fine only if the Animus would come in the way she wants or expects him to come.

This is similar to a woman who wants her partner to behave in a specific way she believes she needs in order to love him but will not ask or let him know what she needs. When she does not speak her needs, she can fall into feeling unloved and betrayed. In this way, she gets to act out an underlying fear, perhaps her own unwillingness to be more vulnerable with her partner. She may have experiences with men who have violated her or she may have experiences where she used men in order to avoid further injury and validated the fear. Whether the client chooses partners who will play out her fears or if she is simply projecting without any basis, in both cases, she is lost in her idea of others or in her idea of herself in relationship to others.

All the different ways this can manifest are forms of narcissism which do not allow the individual to experience life as it is. To be open and responsive to the world rather than creating and living in a fantasy world because of an inability to break through emotional imprinting from the past.

In this particular example, the Animus is not being mean, but he is not sweeping the client off her feet, which is what she wants. But doing what she wants at this point in her work would not teach her anything.

The Animus will not necessarily come in a way that is easy to recognize or understand, especially when he is trying to illuminate a blind spot. But, as these two examples show, how this manifests varies wildly from person to person. In the first example, the client needed to let the man approach her, but in the second example, the client needed to approach the man. Understanding a client's pattern in the world with men or, women if the client is male, helps the therapist discern the intention of the dream. Knowing a client's patterns gives a clearer picture about why dreams represent issues in the specific way they do for the specific person.

When the Animus is playing the trickster, it is always an opportunity for the client to learn to do something different. She is given the opportunity to face a projection not only in her dreams, but also in her waking life - what is projected in a dream is always projected somewhere in the outer world as well. When the trickster comes as a "mean" man, it is an opportunity to look at the truth of the self once the client can move beyond the idea of his "meanness."

Usually, when the Animus is playing trickster, he knows the client is going to run or turn away, especially with clients working in First Stage. Clients in Second and Third Stages may not run away, or they may see the trick in the dream and decide to face the man anyway. However, most clients in their early work turn away from the Archetype in some way, shape or form. The challenge presented to the client is to do the opposite: to not turn away, to walk over to the man, to face what is scary.

Because the Animus is provoking a feeling in the client by being the trickster or by playing "mean," it is the job of the therapist and the client to uncover the feeling. The feeling being brought to light via the reaction in the dream is part of the dynamic of the pathology in the person. It is important to face the man and facing the man means facing into the feeling at the core of the reaction. In the example above, where the woman feels an attraction to the man but turns away, the therapist can challenge the client in session to take a risk and face him and, in doing so, face her fear of vulnerability.

Animus as Agent Provocateur

When the Animus comes with the intention of stirring up difficult feelings and behaviors that are not yet in the consciousness of the client, he becomes the Agent Provocateur.

The Agent Provocateur is very different than the trickster. The trickster plays into various roles for the simple task of exposing pathology and helping the client feel and own his projections. The Agent Provocateur, on the other hand, wants to provoke something much different. He challenges the client in very difficult ways to acknowledge his deepest fears and deepest wounds to the self.

When a client is projecting something of his own understanding that is invalid, the Animus will play with that projection from the trickster role. The dream sets up a condition in which the projection can be caught, like being afraid of something when there is no real threat. The Agent Provocateur takes the client down a very different path. He may manifest as actually being scary or threatening - wielding a chainsaw or a sword, loping off a head or a limb. In this way, he clearly is a frightening figure, but he is not the pathological male. As the threatening figure, he means to take the client through his worst fear, challenging him to face his own death and exposing the fear that is in every moment. Where the pathological male wants to damage and control the client, the Agent Provocateur wants to take the client through projection and deep fear, helping him to see that in surviving, he really had nothing to fear.

Typically, when the Agent Provocateur is at work, the client is facing a psychological fear where repressed material can begin to transform into spiritual fear. With Alchemy, the repressed material can produce a feeling of spiritual fear or awe. When working directly with trauma fear, the Agent Provocateur will challenge the client to allow and feel the fears rooted in the trauma memories. For example:

Dream:

I am with my brother. He lays me on my back, then kneeling, spreads my legs open, leaning into me. He says, "We can do this now," meaning that he wants to have sex with me. I feel terror and horror.

In this example, the client is confronting the likelihood of a sexual encounter with her older brother when she was around six years old and the brother was eleven. The figure of the brother in the dream, since it comes from a repressed memory, does not necessarily reveal itself as the pathological male. In this dream, the figure could be the Animus manifesting as the Agent Provocateur to challenge the resistance and fear in the client of the Animus and of men in general, using the unacknowledged possible rape and molestation of the brother as the way through.

The pathological male is often revealed as the whoremaster whose effects on the psyche are deeply destructive and profound. This particular dream does not give clues about whether the brother is the Agent Provocateur or the whoremaster, but it does show that the opportunity to face the fear of the Animus is directly linked to a trauma.

Trauma is not an actual traumatic event - it is the repression of the fear around a particular event or events. The goal is to release the fear. The question of whether the dream is an actual memory or not is irrelevant in the process of the client. The issue is that there is repressed fear locked up in unconscious memories or events or fantasies. The job of the Agent Provocateur is to release these feelings. By touching the wound or trauma, he touches the provocation or the thing creating the provocation, but he is not the perpetrator of the wound. He is, instead, leading the individual through the wound to release the fear and to allow healing.

Of course, there is always the possibility that the therapist will make a mistake and assume that a "scary" man in a dream is the Animus when he is actually the pathological male. If this mistake is made, the client will feel uncomfortable between sessions and his process work around the dream will not work. The client and/or the therapist may also have a dream to show the mistake so that the correction can be made in the next session.

Flowering

I.
Earth still holding the bulb
silence from the throat

here song begs to rise

the white stem, trembling
cry from the body split open

this is where it ends, the anticipation
of light, for light

slain darkness the broken ground

I am not crazy to love god.

II.

I needn't kill you
if you do not believe

the flower proof enough

pulled open by my fingers

like the slit wound
rent to view heaven

within the body

all is life.

Karla Van Vliet

Fear, Trauma and the Transformational Process

Fear is a feeling corridor, a gateway, that alchemizes to love and essence. As a gateway, it leads to the soul self and is, in a way, essence in disguise. Without fear, there is no way to essence. Archetypal fear, the kind of fear edged with excitement, comes from facing the unknown.

Facing the unknown in a dream, always an Archetypal moment, can come in many different ways - a large animal coming straight for the client, the client falling off a cliff or drowning or in a plane heading for a crash. When the dreams present a client the opportunity to face into her fear, her Archetypal fear, it signals that something wonderful can happen in her process. A gateway has opened.

A Picture of the Normal Psyche

The normal psyche consists of many layers. On the outer edge, the conscious ego pushes into the realm of the outer world with the subconscious and the unconscious below. A natural layer of Alchemical, Archetypal fear lies between the unconscious and the Archetypal world. The Archetypal world can push into the unconscious and the subconscious through a portal or a doorway in the psyche - a portal experienced in dreams.

The Normal Psyche

The Outer World

Consciousness (The Ego)

The Subconscious

The Unconscious

Alchemical Fear

Archetypal
World

Location of the Child Self in the Normal Psyche

In the normal psyche, the child self, the soul self, begins in consciousness when a person is a baby then moves as the person develops. As a baby, the child self is with the nascent ego interfacing with the outer world. As the baby grows and the ego forms, most people separate from the child self, pushing it down into the subconscious. By adulthood, the child self has descended into the unconscious, where it dwells for most clients when they enter into First Stage dreamwork.

The Normal Psyche - Child Self

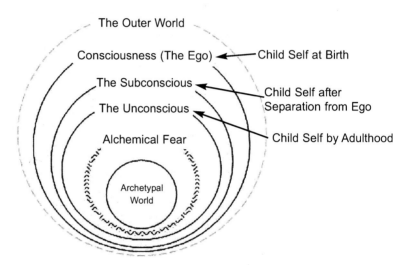

Because the Archetypes interface in the unconscious where the child self is typically located, it is in the unconscious where the Archetypes connect with the client's child self. In the process of moving into Third Stage work, the Archetypal world connects with the child self in the unconscious, then moves up through the subconscious and into the conscious ego. Once this movement happens, the ego is transformed and the person moves into the individuation work of Third Stage.

Fear and Trauma

For a client with trauma, however, the gateway of fear may not lead to essence. Instead, it may lead directly to the trauma if it has not been felt or acknowledged.

When a child is hurt or traumatized, the wound remains on the subconscious level. The trauma is not the wound itself, but the repression of the fear and the feelings in response to the trauma. Pathological shame represses this fear and creates a layer of trauma fear or "negative" fear. The child self is not necessarily wounded by the event, but gets repressed nonetheless into the unconscious by adulthood.

For a client with trauma, the descent through the wound to the child self includes encountering a layer of trauma fear. This trauma fear prevents direct access to the gateway alchemical fear. Before the client can fully access the alchemical fear, he needs to feel and acknowledge his wound.

The Psyche with Trauma

The psyche protects itself from hurt and trauma through the dynamic of shame in the same way the body goes into shock when physically injured. When a hurt or trauma occurs, shame, responsibility or guilt will shut everything down to protect a person from feeling the pain. And once pathological shame is engaged as a protection from feeling, it is like cement. When this dynamic is revealed through a dream, the therapist and the client have to take a hammer and a chisel to break down that cement. Since an awful experience of hurt is underneath, the cement is strong, stubborn and clingy. But this awful experience of hurt relates to the fear essential to the alchemical process. A client may need to descend through layers of shame to reach the terror underneath.

When children bond with their mothers, they accept her fully as the best mom even if they are mistreated or neglected by her. So, if a child experiences a trauma like rape or molestation, the child also experiences betrayal because he assumed he was being taken care of by the mother. The child then unconsciously assumes that the trauma must be acceptable since it was allowed to happen. Since a child is less inclined to blame anyone else, he will assume blame.

Shame works best when the fault is aimed at oneself. Guilt may say, "I better take care of my mom and protect her from this," even though the child is the one who was completely destroyed. Guilt, shame and responsibility are covering the pain or the fear.

If a trauma is present in the client's psyche, it will be revealed through the process of the dreams. Eventually, the memory of feelings related to the traumatic event surfaces in the subconscious and the client will have a dream experience of the feelings underneath the guilt, shame or responsibility. This is a major breakthrough in the person's process.

For example, if one of the feelings underneath guilt is helplessness, then the trauma fear is connected to feeling helpless. For a client in this position, letting go into helplessness would seem equal to experiencing trauma. But the Animus may come in a dream asking the client to let go and to be with him. Of course, the trauma makes it extremely difficult for the client to let go, but the dream offers a great opportunity to begin to work through the trauma.

Opening to the Feelings of Trauma

To fully accept and feel the pain of trauma, a person must learn self-value or self-worth. When the psyche goes into shock to avoid the trauma feelings, it does so in order to protect the self from the horror and fear of the situation. But, everything else gets sucked in as well, the way light gets sucked into a black hole. Losing the ability to feel anything means the person loses the ability to value the self. The ability to cry and to feel appropriate pain is crucial because pain, like love, is one of the rivers that feed into the heart. Acknowledging and feeling pain involves a deep level of self-acceptance, even if the pain is from a place of having an egregious loss. The common voice of "I should not cry," is the psyche trying to defend itself through shame by producing a judgment against the self.

Opening to pain can be a wild ride. It may start out as a trickle, perhaps through feeling sadness for another person in a dream. But once the client can accept sadness as really for herself, then the feeling can expand and become a powerful grieving. The sadness of losing the part of the self that was traumatized and lost. Clients who break open to their own pain will sometimes cry through a whole session, beginning a deep grieving process.

For a client with trauma, it may be extremely difficult to consciously feel for herself, so she may have dreams in the motif of experiencing a feeling for someone or something else. Dreams in this motif can reflect the beginning of feeling her own pain through feeling it through another, showing that the unconscious repressed pain is moving up into consciousness. The motif can manifest in many different scenarios. For example, the client may witness an animal being killed or injured which provokes sadness and crying. Or, the client may dream about the death of someone she loves.

In a psyche with trauma, trauma is in the subconscious while the feelings and the child/soul self are in the unconscious. When a client feels something in a dream, she feels it on the level of the subconscious. That material then sits in the subconscious like a bullet in the gun chamber, ready to move into the conscious ego. The fact that it is in the subconscious means the beginning of the end for that aspect of the pathology.

Part of the miracle and mystery of this work is how material moves from the unconscious to the subconscious. This is not controlled by the client or anyone - it is the work of the Animus. This mystery is not just true for clients with trauma. The mysterious process of changing and growing is the same for all clients.

Most people have a connection with their child self when they are children. For people with trauma, there is a connection between the child self and the wound in the subconscious. As the person grows, the child self gets pushed down into the unconscious, but the connection with the wound in the subconscious remains. It is necessary, then, for the person to move through her trauma to get to her child self.

Working with trauma is working with spiritual transformation. But for the client, all she knows is that she is coming up against something awful in her past experience which has to be acknowledged. When a client confronts something difficult, she may hit negative fear - the repression of fear resulting from the trauma. In her dreams, she may dream of a dead child or she may experience a feeling that relates to the traumatic event. Clients who do not remember the actual event or events may even have this experience. This is moving into the revelation of trauma, not moving into Archetypal fear. But since the dynamic of revealing the trauma is so deep, it can actually reveal the essence of the child self as well. Because of this, the dreams do not take a wide detour to deal with trauma, then return to address the spiritual part of the child self in the unconscious. Instead, the difficult traumatic experiences and the feelings associated with them can be a part of the emergence of the soul self.

Fire Woman
by Laura Ruth

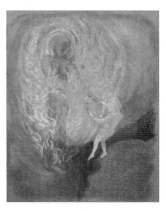

Dream:

> There were two beings standing opposite to one another. The one on the other side was the fire mother, the other one was the earth mother. When the fire mother reached out to take the hand of the person on the other side the earth cracked, huge limitless chasm opening up, and the person began to fall. Terrifying. Then the fire mother asked the transformational question and everything was ok.

The struggle between earth and fire is the struggle between passion and death. The need of the girl to fall into the ground, into tunnels in the ground to find her way through the labyrinth could also be the catacombs that lead to nowhere. In the catacombs, there is no need to have a destination. There, the end is not the beginning, it is just the end. Sometimes, there is nowhere to go except to simply not go. Trauma needs to be plunged into so that the feelings can be redeemed and so the person can emerge like a phoenix. The nature of trauma is to keep the person in prison, to encourage and encourage and encourage the process of descent. Even after the death has been completed, the hole opens again promising more and more work, but only devouring again. In this case, Laura is done with the descent into the trauma and the fire phoenix invites her into rebirth. The demoralizing decay is like a poison that is drunk like sugar, taken the way an addict takes drugs. In the dream, the child resists the oblivion of the earth and is ready for new creation. The demon is burned and cannot devour her. But the demon does not reduce itself - instead it morphs into a spiritual being that the client believes it to be and gives a spiritual question. It gives up the battle for the bigger war. The unconscious not understanding of the pathology can prevent further work for the client. She must work on understanding pathology to be ready for the next assault when it will loom up again, ready to devour her into her trauma. This must be seen and understood for her journey to continue.

There have been books published asserting that people with trauma cannot do the deep, core, spiritual work. This is not true. Feelings related to trauma can be used in a spiritual manner. Although the process is more challenging for the profoundly wounded person, trauma is not necessarily a barrier to alchemical experience.

For example, a particular client was deeply traumatized as a girl by a trusted family member who raped her repeatedly. After years of dreams of being strengthened and prepared, she dreamed that the Animus came to her in her bed as the person who perpetrated the trauma. It was clear to the client that although it was the same man, it was not him, but the Animus. The Animus came to her as the perpetrator to get into the wound with the client in order to heal. This was a revelation to her process. As a person opens to the traumatic events, the Animus can move through the place of trauma in an Archetypal manner. This is completely opposite to what is taught about trauma.

Archetypal dreamwork does not treat trauma, but people with trauma can do spiritual work through their dreams. Dreams have a consciousness of intent as a part of Divine will - if a person is not ready to work through her trauma, then she will not dream about it. God's power in this area is surprising. If the dream is putting the Animus in the bed of a woman who has been betrayed sexually, then it is important to trust the intent of the dream. There are therapists who try to bring their own concerns into difficult dream areas rather than trusting the dreams in their fullness, but the dreams and the Divine will behind them can be trusted.

Psychotic Modality

The locus point for every feeling is often in a visual image in a dream. When dealing with fear, for example, there is often a locus fear point in a dream such as a bear jumping on the client or the client seeing a child under the water and feeling scared. The dream image offers a focus, a way to relate an inner experience with a visual story experience. This helps the client from projecting these feelings or material out into the world. When inner material is released and projected into the world, the client may feel crazy. Having an image helps to bring the work back to the inner world. If a client starts to project his fear, for example, he can bring it back to the inner by referencing the dream - "Oh, this is about the bear jumping on me." Taking experiences in the world back to an image or a story in a dream is called introjection and helps clients advance to the core transformational work of Dying to Self and psychotic modality.

When a client is experiencing psychotic modality, he no longer knows himself as he has known himself in the past. He is beginning to separate from what is pathological and also from the person he has always been in the world. This separation is upgrading understanding and being. For the client, it is a sign that his conscious is transforming, because everything that happens is now filtered through the new understanding and new feeling.

That is the impact of unconscious material moving up through the subconscious and into the ego. Pathology simply does not exist in the deeper realms of the unconscious - it is where the Archetypes dwell. When a client in advanced Second Stage dreamwork has Archetypal dreams, the subconscious is cleaned of pathology. The Archetype is capable of living in consciousness with the person and whatever he is dreaming he is beginning to live out and experience. The ego has died to its old self. For example, a Third Stage client had this dream:

> I am underwater, breathing the water, with several others and feeling the peace of essence. I drift up to a lodge where everyone was in chaos. I try to get everyone to go with me back under the water, but they do not come. I feel agitated.

In his waking life, this client was having reactions to people he was working closely with, so he was filtering his experiences with his coworkers through his old personality, the person he had always known himself to be. His reactions were conditioned by his old sense of identity. This old identity is referenced in the dream by the locus point of being outside the water and feeling agitated.

The client needed to remain in the state of consciousness he experienced in the dream - breathing under the water and feeling the peace of essence - then filter his experiences through this new consciousness. The reemergence of the old ways of being can be so subtle that the sweetness of essence is quickly forgotten. For this example, the client needed to return to the reference point of feeling at peace and breathing the water whenever he felt agitated in the world.

The psychotic modality is really about not knowing the self, not reacting or responding in the old ingrained ways. Instead of reacting in the old ways, the client can return to the image of being under the water. It is a psychotic mode of being, but based on the root meaning of the word *psychosis* which means "mind" and "abnormal condition." The client is living in a way that is not in his normal mode of living. He is not functioning out of his normal, neurotic self, but the new self is not entirely formed.

Carl Jung, who refers to psychotic modality and recognized transformational spiritual work, wrote about the process of Alchemy, the process of Archetypal Dreamwork, in his last book. His other books do not necessarily relate to Archetypal dreamwork. In this book, however, he refers to two types of spirituality: aesthetic and transformational. Transformational spirituality requires a Dying to Self which brings one into the psychotic modality. Aesthetic spirituality does not require a Dying to Self, but it does result in a sensitivity to life, as in the saying, "Stop and smell the flowers." In this modality, a person might enjoy the chirping of birds at dawn, children playing, meditation or a prayerful life.

Jung in his day was disgruntled because people he worked with seemed unable to get beyond aesthetic spirituality. He concluded, and it was probably true for that time in history, that people were simply not ready to do core alchemical work. Much of Jungian analysis still results in aesthetic spirituality even though things have changed since Jung's time and the psyche is much more open to deep, transformational work.

It is an intense personal experience - both terrible and wonderful - to move through a psychotic state during the process of Alchemy and the Dying to Self experience. Not many go the way of Dying to Self. Instead, they stop because they feel good at the aesthetic spiritual level. Many people begin the dreamwork depressed and after a few years, they feel good and can begin to enjoy their life. They experience some sense of essence, support and love and can return love. It is here many people stop the dreamwork. It is not bad that people reach a better place in their lives - Jung was famous because he could achieve that kind of result with people. If a client decides aesthetic spirituality is enough, then this is fine. He worked hard to reach this place.

And, this form of Archetypal dreamwork can also move beyond aesthetic spirituality for those who wish to move into the realm of spiritual transformation.

Archetypal dreamwork is best suited for people who are neurotic because it requires a certain amount of ego development. For some, the dreams work to build up the conscious ego self so the client can develop a strong internal and objective witness. A basic sense of identity is rebuilt in order for the ego to withstand the process of Dying to Self. It is the criminal who is hurt committing a crime. The authorities save his life so he can be convicted and put to death.

It takes a great deal of strength to stay with feelings of pain, inadequacy, fear. Many are too traumatized, weak, beaten down to even acknowledge a feeling, especially after working to repress it for a lifetime.

If a person has been deeply wounded, it may take years of simply showing up and doing basic work in order to be able to face the revelation of his core wound. It takes a great deal of preparation to accept the full horror of a trauma experience when it is fully revealed in a dream. But deep work can begin when a client has come alive enough to truly confront his issues. The dreams meet every individual where they are with exactly what they need and it takes as long as it takes.

Because people begin with different levels of need, it is impossible to compare people. The process is a vertical descent into a unique being - it is not horizontal.

Also, Archetypal Dreamwork is not for everyone, especially not for people who have severe personality disorders. For people whose trauma results in severe personality disorders, as in multiple personalities, they are already in the pathological and Archetypal world so deeply that dreams have no meaning. Without an objective self that is able to witness or to learn to witness, there is no way for the dreams to be effective.

Many dreamwork clients have some form of trauma. It may be clear or not in the beginning, but if trauma is there, it will be revealed in a dream at some point. Working through trauma fear is still working with fear and it transfers easily to alchemical fear. While trauma is never a good thing, is never something that should happen, it can be a great opportunity and, strangely, an advantage.

There are many ways and degrees of trauma, some of which may not be considered as trauma. Pathology is particularly good at minimizing experience with thoughts like, "I was not really raped," or, "I had normal parents so how could I have trauma?" Trauma is simply repressed fear. It can be a complete blind spot or it can be from a previous life, if they exist. It can be from a genetic link to a parent or a grandparent who had trauma and that the child takes on. It is not necessary to understand how things enter into a person's psyche, nor does there need to be a "smoking gun."

A person who is traumatized has had something done to him and some part of the self got frozen like a deer in the headlights. The person tends to focus more on the external world to avoid the inner life. The inner realm is less comfortable which makes it hard to do the homework assignments, especially assignments concerning feelings. All of this contributes to projection. In projection, the client will find fault with his therapist and make him the target when the trauma is approached and the pathology that is packed around it is threatened.

The first step in dealing with trauma is learning that it is present and uncovering the feelings around it. The dreams guide the process, allowing the client and the therapist to work with great sensitivity. Once the trauma is exposed, many dreams will relate to it and the client's work will often reference the trauma. With clients who do not have a deep degree of trauma, the dreams are used to reference patterns of behavior to try to understand the feelings the client is blocking.

With or without trauma, feelings still get buried - just the natural evolution of growing from eight years old to fourteen is enough. When a person moves through adolescence, it is a tremendous developmental process. The child with a Garden of Eden sense of innocence suddenly moves into the world of having sex and having babies. He is inundated with the biological imperative to perpetuate the species. But people must learn to grow beyond that position.

Most people lose themselves, if they have not already, through the process of adolescence. Even if they have good parents, good circumstances. The need to survive through adolescence means that most people lose their innocence. Because of this, it is not necessary to search for any smoking gun. The dreams help adults go back to review the material in order to find that lost child.

Plank Road

Here, at the torn edge. Simple counting,
the slipped threads. Morning held in late snow,
mist rising from the field. Where have I started?

I have memorized the prints of his retreat.
This red thread, woven into my body. Here, and then
there, slipstitched path across the expanse of snow.

I am still counting. Down the road a dog bays,
and now, the near and far answering off the mountain:
the beat of my feral heart.

Karla Van Vliet

Living in the Present versus Living in the Past

Living in the Past

Most people spend their whole lives living out their past in the present. What a person brings to any given moment is an accumulation of all his past experiences whether he is aware of it or not. All the ideas a person carries about who he is, about love and hate, all come from the past, so that he bases his knowledge of who he is on past history. Genetic inheritances and the possibility of past lives can also be a factor.

A person's consciousness and what he brings to the present moment is defined by known experience. It is the foundation of expectations for the future and it is even how a person communicates himself. Ask anyone how he is doing and most likely the answer will be about the past: what he has been doing, thinking, experiencing. All in the past. Most people live out their neurosis, day in and day out.

Dream:

> I watch a rocket ship blast up into the sky on the horizon. The Animus is in the ship
> and waving to me. I am on the ground. Suddenly, the ship explodes. I know the seven
> astronauts on board are not dead, but instead have been transmuted through the
> explosion into "hyperspace" - into the future.

The client is not with the Animus, but instead remains on the ground. In this dream, the ground is the present idea of time where she lives, the idea of time that she needs to leave. This "present" is really the past. The Animus is showing the possibility of taking a quantum leap into the "future" which is really the true present, the eternal now.

The present as the past, in this dream, is how the consciousness of the client lives in her past reality - the reality of past wounds or trauma and how they dictate the way she lives now. For the client, this was a confusing dream because she did not have a reference point for the true present reality in her waking life. It was difficult for her to fathom being the Animus in the rocket ship, leaving the present, which is the past, for the future or the eternal now. Her consciousness was still in the past and she did not have a personal experience for the new kind of reality. The exploration of this dream in her work shifted her reality.

After the session in which she worked this dream, she reported:

I left the session and sat in my car for a moment watching people walking by. I began to disassociate from time, just briefly. People seemed to move in slow motion. I felt a great tenderness toward them. An eternity fit into a single moment. I felt in the world of time, but not of it. Then I had to make a bank deposit and the experience of bent time was gone.

After this experience, she was back living out her past in the present.

All the issues and conflicts an individual experiences emotionally are attached with things in the past. This is true among nations as well. Past experiences replicate themselves over and over again. Events in the Balkans and the Middle East in the last fifty years painfully illustrate how historical patterns recur. Different ethnic and religious groups fight the same fight for centuries, caught in the same wounds and fueled by old racial beliefs, grudges and hatred from the past. Tragically, history does indeed repeat itself.

Personal lives are the same way. People live out childhood hurts or traumas, perhaps even unconsciously attracting relationships that repeat old wounds. Like the battered child who clings to the abusive parent, a person unconsciously chooses pain and suffering and perpetual replication because it feels safer than the unknown. Choosing the past fits expectations and it feels comfortable even if it is hell. At least it is known. A person ends up in the same bad relationship, the same bad marriage, the same disconnected interactions at work, over and over, trapped in repeating the past. The person's whole consciousness is defined by his past experience.

Getting to the Present

While most people are stuck in the past, it is not who they really are, not their essence. Rather than remaining in the comfort of the known, the past, this work brings a person into her present. To be in the present, a person must come to know the self that God created and knows - the child self or the soul self. The Archetypes consistently confront the client in terms of what she brings to this moment, the things she carries based on genetics or past events, in order to bring the client to that true self.

The present moment or the eternal now is perceived in part as the future in the first two stages of the work because the work is moving toward deeper manifestation with the Divine. If/when a client reaches Third Stage work and can be in her true self, then she can be in the present moment, the eternal now.

The Archetypes confront a client in her past so that she may come into the present of her real self. Clients are often terrified, however, as was the client in the space ship dream. The spaceship explodes like the tragedy of the Challenger, blowing up in a flash of fire, smoke and light. But instead of the astronauts dying, the client knows the astronauts are accelerated into the future. It is like the image in *Stars Wars* when a space ship makes the jump to hyper drive and stars zoom past. This is what happens to the astronauts in the dream, but to the person left in the past on the ground, it looks like they blow up. It is like watching the self being obliterated.

This is why most people cling to the past. They are terrified of going through the transition of that explosion, terrified of the unknown, terrified of leaving the known, the past. Another reason it is terrifying to leave is that the faster one goes into "hyperspace," the further back in time one leaves everyone else. The idea of death is a projection of the fear of leaving the present currently being lived out.

A dream motif related to this is where others are dead while the client is aware that she can stand up and move on. Such an experience is a sign of major knowing in the client. But, the fear is still there. The fear of leaving the past, leaving friends. The client may say, "But I cannot leave them behind. They are my friends, my family." She may believe that she is saving the world or at least her family by staying. This is a lie. The client must stand up and move on even though it means losing the collective bond that has bound her to the world. It is difficult and terrifying to let go of the worldly family and be a part of another family whose understanding is so different that what is known. Fear is what keeps the client from moving on and not caretaking.

As an adult, time is experienced as a succession of events. As a child, the relationship to time is different and often appears endless. Adults become defined by the idea of time - "I'm forty now," or "I'm sixty." An older man says he is tired, he has had a long life. Is it true or is it just an idea of himself he has always carried that makes those seventy-five years feel long. Maybe his life was a blank because in truth he was trapped in his past where the level of suffering is always greater. Perhaps it is actually the suffering that makes him tired. Life can appear long or short depending how the person feels about himself and his experiences.

The truth is our lives are too short - the average lifespan is only around seventy-five years compared with the thousands of years humans have been on the planet and the fourteen billion years this universe has been in existence. Since the universe is fourteen billion years old, then eternity is fourteen billion years and counting. It is difficult to fathom a single life of seventy-five years against the backdrop of fourteen billion years, which is why most people have no understanding of timelessness.

Slow and fast are merely horizontal, superficial, external reference points experienced by the ego. These reference points have no meaning for the soul self. The soul self, the one obedient to the Divine and congruent with its purpose, has a vertical experience of time. The person can experience herself against the backdrop of those fourteen billion years and can experience the foreverness. The sense of agelessness that transcends physical age is part of the inheritance of being truly connected. To be congruent with the Divine and the soul self is to plug in to the vertical link, the sensation of eternity.

The common way to think of the eternal is in the horizontal sense - to live to be one hundred, five hundred, one thousand years old. This is the context of the disconnected although maybe wise psyche. But the search for eternity is not how long the life but the discovery of the soul's eternity or the soul's timelessness.

The Archetypal Realm

How does a person make this shift in time, or out of time as it is known? What does it mean and what is at stake? Some may even ask, why shift into the future and out of the past?

It is helpful to use the image of a comet. The head of the comet is like the true present which is constantly moving into the unknown of the future where there is infinite possibility. The trailing tail of the comet is like the past that most people, including the client in the rocketship dream, are accustomed to living in. When the client experienced a moment of bent time, she made the jump to "hyperspace," experiencing being at the head of the comet, in the true present of the future where the rocket man and the other astronauts had gone. The eternal present in which, just as in the Archetypal Realm, time has no meaning and no association.

The Archetypes live in "hyperspace," in the present. But because most people live in the past, this is where the Archetypes must come to visit. The Archetypes challenge the client to confront the past by taking him through it in dream after dream after dream. Eventually the past resolves internally as the client is healed.

Interestingly enough, however, even in more advanced clients, habits can still hold, with the client not wanting to leave the past even though it has no more relevance. In a Stage One client, the past will be everything to the person because nothing has been resolved. But even when the resolution occurs, it does not necessarily mean the client is catapulted to a new future or the true present. Even when the old habits are released, the desire to remain in the world and the fear of losing the known is so unconsciously powerful, the process may seem confusing. A late Second Stage-early Third Stage client wonders, "What more does the Animus want from me? What more change can there be? Have I not transformed through the healing and resurrecting of my child self? I am aware of the indwelling of spirit, I remember who I am. Is that not enough?" This is hanging around the launch pad eyeing the rocket ship suspiciously, clinging to the safe past, comfortable in the familiarity of wounds.

So, when will a client face this Alchemy and allow himself to be catapulted out of the past and into the present? Alchemy at this level is about freedom from the gravity of the world and moving into the not-known, into one's truth with the Divine.

The idea of individuation and transformation as concepts are irrelevant because living in the past means structuring everything learned into the concepts of the past. Alchemy at this level is about obliterating the past. Unfortunately, all the preparation leading up to this moment does not mean the client will make the leap because the consequence of going means losing his identity. It means not knowing who he used to be and becoming different even as he remains in the world, which is painful.

People often respond to the Archetypes in dreams as if they are aliens visiting earth. They fall in love with the alien and want him to remain in their world. The Archetypes are alien because they are foreign. A client may feel the desire to be with the Animus but he wants the relationship on his terms - one of which is staying in this world. But the Archetypes cannot remain in this world. Their visit is temporary because it is their job to reclaim the client and bring him back to the Archetypal Realm.

Part of the fear of going with the Archetypes to the Archetypal Realm is that the client, because he no longer shares the past with everyone else, becomes alien as well. The structures that held the psyche in place are broken and the client comes into a place of knowing what God knows. The client is then with Him, living outside time, in the present - living in a kind of immortality. Immortality because the present is outside of time, even though everyone physically dies.

Some people glimpse this otherworldly realm as their physical death approaches. For example, a client was sitting in a hospital with a woman who was lying in a coma, dying of stomach cancer. The dying woman suddenly sat bolt upright in bed and said, "We have a message for you and it is about love!" Then she collapsed back on her bed. At the approach of physical death, people often begin to move into the Archetypal Realm of God and they can feel the love. A great peace comes over them. The dreamwork offers the opportunity to obtain this state of consciousness before the actual death of the physical body.

In this kind of consciousness, the client can be with the Archetypes and can be here on this physical plane by listening to his heart, feeling His presence and allowing Him to intervene in his life. The nature of essence is more than simply feeling the love and connection. Pure essence is a timeless realm free from the past, where an individual can begin to live his present, his calling. This is the heart of Third Stage work.

Decant

This rawness beckons
like a wild-thing, wolf,
hawk, new born babe,
follow the unknown it
says, using the tongue
of water against rock,
its sound like ice to a
burn; so when the night
goes quiet, I think this
silence unbearable,
a burning that might
kill me. Had killed me
once before, a time
I spoke loss fluently.
This time, I open my
mouth, let water pour
the mountain's stream.

Karla Van Vliet

Re-Visioning Mythology
A New Mythos of the Divine

In a person's psyche, the dreamwork works to turn what the person believes and understands about the self and about the world upside down. This manifests in dreams as people, places, feelings, situations not being what they seem to the person.

Dream:

A snake is trying to bite me. I am terrified and try to get away from it.

The client is assuming that the snake is "bad" since most associations of snakes in Western culture are negative. This negative association is deeply reinforced by the story of the serpent in the Garden of Eden in Genesis. But, this particular snake in the dream may be Archetypal, attempting to infuse the client with Alchemy - not the poison which the client fears.

Having an experience of Divine love, of feeling how the Divine sees a person, is what turns everything upside down. The experience is jarring because it is such a radical paradigm shift from being of the world to becoming a heart that knows and feels the love of the Divine. Most people use the world as their reference point instead of God to find out who they are - spiritual connection is not the way of most of the world.

The Connection between Dreams and Mythology

There is a deep connection between dreams and the ancient myths of the Greco-Roman tradition. Both involve the use of metaphor and story to reflect an inner belief system - dreams reflect the inner belief system of the particular client and myths reflect the inner belief system of a culture. Because western culture developed from that Greco-Roman tradition, Greek mythology is still deeply embedded in the consciousness of the modern Western psyche and is often reflected in individual people's dreams.

Just as exploring an individual's dreams helps the person to see her blind spots and expose her neurosis so that she can move through it, examining myths can illuminate blind spots and the neurosis of Western culture.

Exploring Western mythology from an Archetypal perspective challenges the basic values, beliefs and assumptions which continue to form self understanding so that a new mythos of the Divine can emerge. Just as with dreams, this re-visioning turns the assumptions around myths upside down, challenging what is taken for granted and confronting beliefs about religion, psychology, spirituality and gender-based politics. Reexamining basic beliefs around mythology can lead to a deeper connection with an individual's life in connection with the Divine so that intimacy with God is the reference point instead of the world.

Re-Visioning Mythology into a New Mythos of the Divine

Many dreamwork aspects have a corresponding representation in Greek mythology and always in surprising ways. Mapping these correlations is helpful for individual work for it shows how slanted the culture is toward pathological thinking.

Prometheus

One of the most important figures in dreams is the Animus. His counterpart in mythology is not Zeus, as would be expected, but the figure of Prometheus. Like Prometheus, the Animus has great love and compassion for humanity. And just as Prometheus brings fire from Mt. Olympus to humans, so the Animus brings the fire of God's love and passion - it is the Passion of Christ Consciousness, the Pentecostal fire, the sensual knowing of God's love both in the heart and in the body.

The story of Prometheus:

> Prometheus felt great love and compassion for humans, feeling the pain of their suffering. To help them, he brought them many gifts, but the most important gift he brought was the sacred fire from Mount Olympus which he stole by hiding a spark in a fennel stalk. Zeus, the ruler of the gods, was enraged because he did not like the growing talents of humanity and had planned on eradicating them. Prometheus begged Zeus to spare humanity. To take revenge, Zeus sent Pandora the box Prometheus had sealed containing suffering. When she opened it, she released the suffering into the world. To punish Prometheus, he chained him to a pillar on a mountain where a vulture came and tore out his liver. Every day, the liver was torn out and every night the liver regenerated itself.

The condition of Prometheus on the mountain is the condition of the Animus in the psyche where Zeus/Jupiter is king, which is currently the mythos under which Western culture is living.

Zeus/Jupiter and Chronos/Saturn

In the mythos of Archetypal Dreamwork, Zeus/Jupiter and Chronos/Saturn, unlike Prometheus, are pathological. Zeus is the false king who came to power through the dynamic of fratricide and dis-empowerment of the Father. As such, Zeus/Jupiter rules the pathological psyche, becoming overlord of consciousness.

The Story of Zeus, Chronos and Uranus:

> Gaia, the earth mother, falls in love with Uranus, the heavenly sky father. Gaia gives birth to their children, the Titans and the Cyclopes. Uranus sends the Cyclopes to the underworld of Tartarus. The underworld is symbolic of the Archetypal Realm, the place where it is impossible for ego consciousness to survive. Since the world does

not value or even acknowledge this place, Gaia, who is of the world, sees their descent as unjust. She seeks revenge upon Uranus through her son, Chronos. While Uranus sleeps, Chronos castrates his father with a sickle and replaces him as King.

Uranus predicts that Chronos will be dethroned, just as he was, by one of his sons. To try to prevent this, Chronos swallows all of the children his wife Rhea births. Rhea is enraged and seeks help from Gaia. They succeed in hiding one son, Zeus, who grows up without his father's knowledge.

When Zeus is grown, Rhea helps him challenge and fight his father, Chronos. Zeus defeats his father with a thunderbolt. He places Chronos in chains under a mountain and assumes the throne. After the battle, Rhea forbids Zeus to marry. In anger, Zeus rapes his mother, then marries his sister Hera.

In the paradigm shift of Archetypal Dreamwork, the Chronos father and the Zeus father are both earthly fathers. They represent two polarities of being in the world called senex and puer. Together, they form the basic underpinning of personality as it relates to the outer world. Senex is Latin for "old man" and is personified by Chronos, the older of the two. Puer is Latin for "eternal boy" and is personified by Zeus. Chronos, the old man senex is extremely restrictive, where Zeus, the eternal boy, is extremely permissive.

These two polarities of the psyche, the restrictive senex and the permissive puer, work together to create an ego structure in which there is no love and which keeps an individual from the true Divine. Chronos, the senex, is based on duty for duty's sake and holding the psyche to some high and often impossible standard. Zeus, the puer, is based in feeling happy for the sake of feeling good.

For Chronos and Zeus, it is important to have Prometheus, the Animus, chained on the mountain and out of the psyche because he is the link between humanity and the love of the true Father, the Uranian Father. This love completely dissolves the senex/puer world.

Uranus - The Spiritual Father

Western society, in general, believes in either the Chronos father or the Zeus father without any understanding of the true Uranian Father. The alignment is with the mother and son who are against the Father, the true spiritual Father. The Uranian Father is beyond the moral "shoulds" of the senex and the "anything goes" attitude of the puer.

When a person is damaged by either the senex or the puer father, it affects his ability to know the true self. Finding the true Father and the true relationship with the Father by going deeply into the psyche and understanding the self is a profound Gnostic principle.

God is referred to as "father" because of the human condition. The Uranian Father is not the gender male father. He is beyond knowing and exists in ways that are incomprehensible. Through what Jung called individuation, the Father's love excites the soul and helps the individual understand that soul. The love of the Father raises the consciousness of the individual in order to be in a true relationship with the individual. Tracing the descent of the Father from Uranus to Chronos to Zeus shows that the closer the Father gets to humanity on earth, the more His essence is diluted and reduced to something the human consciousness can comprehend.

The voice of Chronos tells the ego that it is unworthy or that other people in the world are unworthy. It is judgment and condemnation, not the discernment of the heart. This judging self is the self that builds society because it creates structure and rules that are often necessary. But many rules are rules for the sake of rules without the presence of heart, compassion or love.

Athena is an example of an overdevelopment of Chronos. She is the feminine equivalent of Chronos, living for her father Zeus. She is not interested in individuating and discovering her true self through a union with the beloved. She just wants her father. Being born from her father's head connects her to the mind, to rules, to society, to whatever makes her safe. Athena never descends into the Archetypal world, making her the opposite of Persephone. Instead, she stays firmly grounded in the earthly realm.

Many people with a strong Chronos aspect in their psyche can be high functioning in the world - more neurotic but high functioning. They are not concerned with immediate gratification, unlike the puer, but with doing the right thing and working hard for it. While these can be positive traits, they can easily slip into pathology, keeping a client from his heart and from what his soul self truly desires.

The voice of Zeus, in contrast to the focused, workaholic morality of Chronos, attempts to engage the part of the ego structure that wants to feel good at any cost. The puer acts not from joy or passion, but from a desire to justify its existence. When Zeus rules a psyche, he wants the person to feel he can do anything he wants and have a good time. It can also be the voice that is proud, self-righteous, indignant and a victim who makes everything else wrong or bad. Zeus has the person feel he is right, whether the righteousness is tinged with rage or noncommitment. It is no wonder that society leans toward puer energy because it does not condemn anything. Puer is the aspect of our socialized self that is always ready to help and to give a reason for living. It is also very good at pretending to be love.

Senex and puer energy work to make an individual believe that what he was taught about his true soul, whether it came from culture or parents or genetics, is the truth about the self. But consciousness has nothing to do with the kind of self-awareness based on "I am great," or "I am worthless." This level of self-awareness of what the individual believes about his soul is the lowest common denominator of the spiritual realm because most people are living in spiritual poverty. Especially when senex is in control.

Senex and puer annihilate the deeper feeling self that connects to the Divine, making the dynamic a form of compensation for that connection. There are many ways for the dynamic to replace what is no longer received from God - safety, pride, doing good things, being a nice person, physical compensation such as looking good, etc. For the puer, feeling good is not a goodness that comes from the Divine, nor is it really feeling good. This feeling good is attached to something in the world.

In the psyche, the struggle between senex and puer in the extreme is the difference between manic and depressive, with Zeus/Jupiter being the manic and Chronos/Saturn being the depressive. Zeus is the manic son reacting to the father and the father, Chronos, reacts to the son. Senex and puer provide the tensile strength of the ego's perception of the self that by its nature keeps us from the Archetypal world. It is difficult when the work is focused on the relationship with the Divine because the relationship is so difficult to sustain. It is easy to lose the thread and to turn back to perceiving the self in relation to the world.

Senex and Puer as Gatekeepers of the Psyche

The psyche has both an outer world aspect which is associated with psychology and an inner world aspect which is associated with core feeling and the Archetypal Realm. Between these two aspects of self, senex and puer function as the gatekeepers of the psyche and endeavor to keep a person grounded in the outer world. The dreams work to allow the individual to let go of the attachment to the world and to lead into feelings.

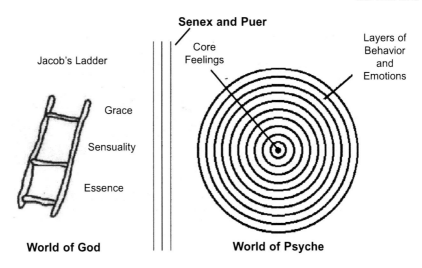

Senex is an aspect of the self connected to the formation of the ego. The senex, in effect, creates a barrier to the ego through shame, guilt, responsibility, duty, structure. The difficulty lies in the fact that these elements actually allow the person to function, establish boundaries and know who she is in relationship to the world. The problem is that many believe that senex/puer can also help in their relationship to the Divine even though it cannot.

Information a person gathers about the world through the senex and the formation of the ego is then projected onto the concept of self. Because of this projection, the client cannot see her soul self as God sees it. The client is left with viewing the self through the world which inevitably takes her back to childhood experiences. These childhood experiences also often get projected onto God, making it very easy to lose any understanding of the Divine. For example, if a child was shamed or abused by her father, she may then hate her father. That hate gets projected onto God and the Archetypal Realm as well.

Childhood experiences are based on the feeling aspects of childhood, not childhood memories. Most people believe that experiences of childhood are the most important aspect, not equating feelings with memory. In fact, it is the feeling experiences and what a person does with the feelings - deny or project them - that matter most. Feelings are still the essence of a person, for it is the feelings that color the sense of self. Senex/puer work hard to protect a person from those feelings.

Some may see that this protection is beneficial because it is difficult to live in fear and pain. This kind of protection may help in the short term, but it becomes a prison in the long term. Senex/puer may seem to protect a person from the past, but he is really actively denying feelings needed for healing and spiritual growth. Of course, most people are not seeking either, turning to other things instead - Prozac, food, work, etc., - in order to stay in the Cyclops of one dimensional reality.

The dreamwork revelation is involved in the opening of feelings, the feelings that are at the core consciousness where spiritual growth happens. Core feelings lead to feelings that transform, to the descent to Jacob's Ladder and to the Divine. The most excruciating feelings can transform - senex/puer only adapt. Senex/puer works to manage who a person is instead of allowing a person to become her true self. Style, appearance, ritual, aesthetics, lifestyles and worldly choices, values, judgments, ideals, beliefs, theories, point/counterpoint. In this world, feelings are not only unnecessary, but in the way. Senex/puer as guardians keep a person within this known world.

Prometheus would give fire - the fire that is a rainbow of feelings. Pain, grief, loss, fear, horror as well as passion, potency and love. Most people are terrified of what he would give just as they are terrified of feelings and the soul. When an individual is separate from her true soul self, she knows it not. Every dream has one purpose - to bring the person home.

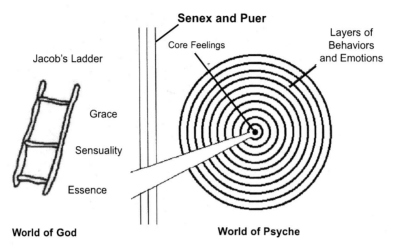

Core Feeling Breaking Through to Jacob's Ladder

When a core feeling is felt, it can break through the barrier of senex/puer and bring the client into the Archetypal Realm.

In the underworld of the Archetypal Realm, the place of feeling reality, the rules are completely different than the rules of the outer world. The reality of the Archetypal Realm has no relationship to the reality of the world. When a client begins to discern between the two, she may move into the dreamwork psychotic realm - the realm where the client breaks from the reality of the outer world and grounds in with the Archetypal Realm, her inner spiritual life in relationship with the Archetypes. The breaking of worldly reality is only possible through the opening of the core feeling self. When senex/puer aspects are present in the psyche, however, they work to keep the client from moving into core feelings.

Moving into core feelings is easier for clients who have weak senex/puer aspects. But for all clients, to be in the psychotic break and in the feeling realm, the support of the Archetypes is crucial.

Thankfully, the core feelings, no matter how difficult, are the feelings that the Archetypes need for they are the essence of the person. Because core feelings can change, the essence of the client can change. They are raw material by which consciousness is transformed.

Many believe that if they understand ideas more deeply or differently, then they are growing. These ideas can be useful if they come from a connectedness with the feelings underneath the transformation. But if understanding comes only from understanding, then it is very limited. The Archetypes do not work with understanding, they work with feelings. This can be difficult for people who are high minded and take great pride in understanding. Without the feeling component, understanding is nothing more than ignorance. For example, a person may read a wonderful book (even this one) filled with wonderful ideas and feel great excitement. But a month later, she realizes that nothing has changed inside. The mind has to keep finding answers to satisfy the great lack, need, want. But this kind of satisfaction is actually starvation because the mind cannot feed the soul. It is, again, the feelings and connection through the feelings that can satisfy the great lack.

Pain holds the memory of love. Fear holds the memory of essence. Uncertainty holds the knowledge of intimacy.

A client will not be asked by dreams to move through into the feeling realm until she is ready to feel and the outer world issues around wounds, projection of the wounds and self perceptions have been worked through.

The outer world, the world of senex/puer, is necessary for it provides a target for projection. Projection keeps an individual "sane" when her reference point is the outer world for it keeps the balance of the awareness of self through the awareness of others. Without it, a person would have to see the self from the reference point of the inner life. This is why moving the reference point from the outer to the inner world seems psychotic. The opening of feelings is a dangerous process and requires support by the therapy and great inner preparation through the dream process that provides the feeling support. The Archetypes can confront the function of senex/puer and replace it as the gatekeepers of the soul. With the Archetypes as gatekeepers, an individual is supported. When this happens, the person can expose and enter the feeling realm.

The senex/puer dynamic is tied together in the psyche by fratricide or disempowerment of the Father as instigated by the dark mother. The dynamic of the dark mother behind the puer aspect touches on one of the main themes in Freud's work, that of emotional incest. Emotional incest happens when a person, genetically and otherwise, receives and believes the perceptions of the mother.

Most children are unconsciously aligned with the mother based, in part, on the intensity of the mother/child bond. When a mother uses that alignment and looks to the child to fulfill unmet needs, then a deeply destructive alliance forms against the father. In other cases, when a mother is unconsciously jealous of her children, she will resist their growth. When a child does not have a good relationship with the father, which is especially true for men and which happens through socialization, the father tends to be negated. Many fathers, in fact, unwittingly train their children in the corruption of the soul. The result is that the child forms the self through the neurosis of the mother. Sometimes even attempts to break with the incest of the birth mother through rebelliousness cannot break this deeper bond of incest. One that may go beyond memories.

Unlike DNA, RNA comes only from the mother. Everyone possesses identical RNA from an original mother alignment. This connection goes back to the beginning of the family tree and is passed down in the very marrow of every cell. Because of this, pathology can move with relative ease from generation to generation.

Many tribal cultures have recognized the power of the mother/child bond and also acknowledged the need to break that bond in order to bring a child into the world. In primitive cultures, the son was asked to break the mothers hold to become a warrior and bring him into his potency. Men had to leave the mother at an early age and find their self through some form of initiation rite. Both men and women need to break that hold and all false alignments with the mother.

In a way, senex and puer are the pathology that is endemic to the whole culture. They form the realities that bind an individual to the world and the realities from which all social organization are born. Spirit is lost from those realities because spirit only exists in the inner world. Manifestation in the outer world must come from the inner core self. It is another kind of consciousness altogether.

The Chief
Laura Ruth

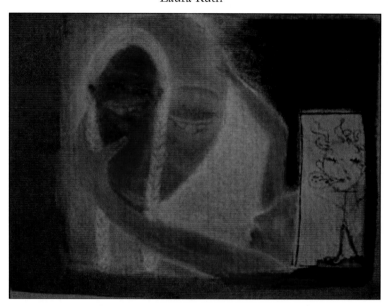

Dream:

I was living on the street with Tristan. He was selling things and being a con man. I sat down under a huge old tree in a pile of sawdust and watched him work, kind of hiding myself. Hiding myself is familiar, keeping myself out of it. A very old Native American man slid around the tree, tapped me and told me to move. I was worried that I had hurt the tree, a tree that I loved and admired, that I had done something horrible to the tree and he was pointing it out to me. So I got up carefully and smoothed all the sawdust so it was level and undisturbed around the ancient tree, trying to fix what I had done before I could go and be with the chief. The chief was in a wheelchair and I had touched his face as he lay in the sawdust on the other side of the tree. I loved him. Very tender, moving. Then I was in a tent at a table with the old man I loved and a younger man. The younger man asks me why I was with someone like Tristan who was diminishing me. I thought, what was I doing with Tristan. The young man wanted me to see that he was conning people, doing something wrong. But my attention was with the old man, I just wanted to be in the beam of his love. The younger man felt like a distraction to me. I was not really interested in the young man's questions. Then the younger man was gone for a moment and I was alone with the old man. I turned to the old man and gave him my full attention - I could feel his gaze and how powerful this current was between us. It felt like a blessing. And I asked him a question, because he was the one who would know, if it was illegal, what Tristan was doing, but not outside God's law, was it wrong? But I really already knew the answer. When I asked the question, it felt inane, and I wondered, why am I asking this stupid question? It was some kind of desperate act to connect - like I had to come up with a question. I felt ashamed of myself, thinking how stupid to ask a question that I already knew the answer to. Another man in a wheelchair came into the tent and I woke up.

It is fortunate to have a complicated painting to match a complicated dream. This was not planned by Laura, for the painting painted itself. When she painted herself wanting the Father, she drew two heads. The unconscious rallied against her assumptions that the desire to be with the Father was positive. In fact, in the session, I also believed it was positive and ignored the underlying subplot where the Animus asks Laura why she would be with Tristan who was diminishing her.

In the dream, she did not answer the question, and the question shifted to was Tristan dishonest in the world? At this moment, it stopped being about Laura and became about others. Then, it shifted again to the father and by the end of the dream another father shows up. The last father is in a wheelchair reflecting the negative nature of the father dynamic, the senex.

Over-devotion to the father is the ultimate diminishment of the self. The love of the Father should be returned as an enhancement and enlivenment of the soul. Developing the devotion without enlivening the soul is a form of caretaking in the same way that Athena was born out of the father's head. It was an extension of the powerful projection of the father's belief in his own immortality and genius. Such men thrive on doting women and such women thrive on loving men who seem to be near god wonderfulness. This is a powerful projection that is innately destructive. It is the senex that masks the whoremaster.

For Laura, this is a diminishment that was projected on Tristan even though he was a lover and not a father. Because devotion is one of the most powerful forms of intimacy with the Animus, its projection and subsequent misuse can allow puer elements to become very powerful and dominant. In this case, these elements made Laura vulnerable to men who were abusive to women. The senex projection was powerful enough to have that same projection onto puer men. But regardless of whether the projection is on puer or senex men, the result is the same. The underlying pathogen was a function of the whoremaster.

In the painting, the larger face is the face of the father, the larger projection of the senex, making him seem like a god. The smaller face has an absurd quality that comes from the eye of the father seeming to be the mouth of the younger man, the second face. Then, the ridiculing figure on the left is nothing more than a distraction for the larger lie. It is almost as if this is a partial hydra where the demon works against the father - but the father is himself pathological. Complicating a complicated scenario.

Love that does not affirm the soul of the lover is a violation. Those who would devote themselves to the Divine would know from the fruit of that love a profound sense of peace and awareness of the Divine world. This is an empowering aspect of the nature of devotion in its healthy aspect, a devotional aspect with the Divine without the senex and puer.

Laura's shame emerges at the end, showing the energy of this subtle perception of devotion. The result of this self doubt is a reflection of what is not happening. In this kind of devotion, there is very little return to the one who is devoted. Those who understand devotion, understand that the devotion returns to them from the Divine. It is as if the love the Divine has for the person and the love the person has for the Divine are exactly the same. This can only happen in the deepest regions of the psyche without the interference of the ego constantly measuring its sense of acceptance in the warped world of senex and puer.

Re-Visioning the Snake in the Garden of Eden

The world of right and wrong, the world of men, is imprinted into the unconscious from one of the oldest mythos - the myth of the Garden of Eden. Most people in the Western culture have internalized the teachings of this story, whether consciously or unconsciously, about God, men, women, snakes, sin and more. But like many dreams, there is a trick in the story. To find the trick, it is necessary to see the story from the Archetypal perspective.

The Story of Adam and Eve:

> Now the serpent was more crafty than any of the wild animals the Lord God had made. He said to the woman, "Did God really say, 'You must not eat from any tree in the garden'?" The woman said to the serpent, "We may eat fruit from the trees in the garden, but God did say, 'You must not eat fruit from the tree that is in the middle of the garden, and you must not touch it, or you will die.'"

> "You will not surely die," the serpent said to the woman. "For God knows that when you eat of it your eyes will be opened, and you will be like God, knowing good and evil." When the woman saw that the fruit of the tree was good for food and pleasing to the eye, and also desirable for gaining wisdom, she took some and ate it. She also gave some to her husband, who was with her, and he ate it. Then the eyes of both of them were opened, and they realized they were naked; so they sewed fig leaves together and made coverings for themselves.

> Then the man and his wife heard the sound of the Lord God as he was walking in the garden in the cool of the day, and they hid from the Lord God among the trees of the garden. But the Lord God called to the man, "Where are you?"

> He answered, "I heard you in the garden, and I was afraid because I was naked; so I hid." And he said, "Who told you that you were naked? Have you eaten from the tree that I commanded you not to eat from?"

> The man said, "The woman you put here with me - she gave me some fruit from the tree, and I ate it."

> Then the Lord God said to the woman, "What is this you have done?"

> The woman said, "The serpent deceived me, and I ate."

> After God delivers his punishments, he says, "See, the man has become like one of us, knowing good and evil; and now, he might reach out his hand and take also from the tree of life, and eat, and live forever." Therefore, the Lord God sent them forth from the Garden of Eden, to till the ground from which he was taken.

> (Genesis 3-13; 22-23. The New Oxford Annotated Bible, Third Edition)

Snakes in dreams are usually Archetypal, representing passion, sensuality, spontaneity. But snakes are also frightening, especially since most snakes bite the client in a dream, poisoning them. Snakes are a great agent of the death of the ego self, the way the client lives in the world - the senex and puer world. The "poison" is an infusion from the Archetypal Realm. There are snakes in dreams that are pathological, of course, but this is very rare. It is more common that the snakes are Archetypal and the psyche perceives them as evil, based on the teachings of the Judeo-Christian tradition.

In this way, the snake is the Animus. He existed as pure passion before the introduction of good and bad. In the myth, the snake gives a tremendous gift to Adam and Eve. It gives passion and sensuality and an awareness of their bodies, but it also gives them the capability to know and feel God's love in order to be in relationship with the Divine. It is the gift of enlightenment, the same gift as the Pentecostal fire of Divine love that Prometheus stole from the gods in Greek mythology. The snake gives them what no other living creature has - the ability to see the self and to objectify creation.

Becoming of the Same Breath
Patsy Fortney

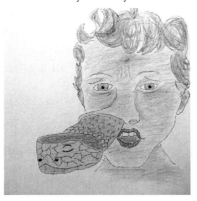

Dream:

> At a family gathering, an older woman calls people over and feeds the family snake to the dog. I am horrified. Someone tells me not to worry; it will come out. Then I look in the mirror and the snake's head is sticking out of my nostril. I am terrified and go to my brother, who yanks it out with pliers, breaking its body and leaving some still inside me. I am upset that the snake, now on the floor and broken, looks dead.

From Patsy:

> When I woke up from this dream, I knew it was important. I could feel the snake in my nostril, could feel it being pulled through me. I could even smell it. But I was afraid in my waking state as I was in the dream: What is happening here? What is this snake, and what does it mean that it is dead? I brought the dream to Marc in a state of near panic. I had spent the week in a state of almost constant projection - shame and fear.
>
> When Marc told me I was not supposed to have the snake yanked out, that it needs to stay in me, that I am becoming a snake woman, I was relieved. I had spent the week trying not to feel the snake that I was feeling almost constantly anyway. I was afraid it was the wrong place to be. Now, with Marc's support, I could go to that place. He told me to go back to the moment in the dream when the snake was protruding from my nostril ("manifesting") and to sit there. I could barely stay in my seat. I was overwhelmed with feelings: terror, joy, annihilation, peace, power. My whole body was trembling, on fire, while my mind, unable to contain what was happening, fell silent. Later Marc explained why the snake was in my nostril: We are becoming of the same breath. He invited me to breathe through the snake. This is my work. I can only barely believe it; I can only barely sit with it.

Mostly I am in resistance to this psychotic state. In the dream the snake dies because I resist that moment of power and potency when I first see it in my nostril. Instead of staying with it, as I was able to do with Marc in my session, I run for help to get it out. This is my place of resistance, when fear drives me to run from what is happening, from what I am becoming. I run straight into the arms of my pathology - to projected fear and shame - because there is nowhere else to run to. I am either Snake Woman or lost to the demons of shame.

Dream:

I am leading a retreat group with Bill. He asks me to play the drum, but it feels really flat; people seem bored. Later the groups are gathering but we are all crammed together and I worry that we will not be able to hear each other over the noise of the other groups. I go off to pee, and when I come back, my group is scattered. Someone says they have all gone to pee. I am upset I caused this by going to pee myself. The group comes back and now Bill is glazy-eyed, almost catatonic. I panic, have no idea what to do. I decide to work with Bill in front of the group - no strings or dreams, just talking. People seem to become engaged.

The morality of the psyche wants us to believe that anything potent, passionate, confrontive, intense, violent, angry, sensual, etc. is dark and evil. The spiritual equivalent of the Divine is often viewed as being good, sweet and nice. The Animus is not good, sweet and nice. He is often loving, but he is also powerful, violating and violent. The process of ridding the psyche of the demon is an act of violence. And the power of engaging the Divine can be violent. In fact, the very nature of passion is violent.

The sense of the self as "I am that I am" is seen as egocentric and narcissistic, when, in reality, it is the building block and the necessary agent of that which can receive the Divine love. Being caring and caretaking does not afford a vessel for receiving. Only when one has the vessel to receive can one be truly caring. The violence that is necessary to create the container for a person to receive and the passion that is part of this act is not evil at all.

In the dream, not being able to play the drums is Patsy not being able to be in her potency and the underlying drumbeat of the soul's heart, beating, beating, beating. Knowing its presence, its power, beating and drumming and feeling itself beating and drumming. Patsy is vacant, lost and worried. "I should not have peed! Where did they all go? Oh, ok, here they are, they are back." There is no bass - base - line here, no accepting of her power. The struggle to accept the snake is the struggle to accept the power of the existence of the other, the other that is the soul self.

Patsy had a mother who required her to take care of her sisters. She was raised being a servant, a surrogate mother to her sisters. A willing supplicant to others' needs and expectations. There was no room for her. Serving the fears and inconsistent realities of others and their requirements. Out of this, her own irrelevancy emerged as her own personality formed around the mother's inability to account for her own lack of identity and her own lack of love. Servant to a loveless mother, Patsy became a loveless wife who overly doted on her children, replicating her past of being the doting sister who cared for her siblings. The spell is broken, however. It is time for her to feel into her potency and her needs and her life and her reality. A very jarring shift from the manner in which she stays away from her real feeling. As her feelings emerge through her, it feels alien, discomforting and repulsive. This is a process that will deepen her ability to understand her passionate devotion and great need for intimacy with the Divine.

Asking the questions, "Why are we?" and "What are we?" is part of the process of the objectification of the self. Part of the gift of the snake, of objectifying consciousness, is to look at the body, to ask the questions. It is essential to understanding the self in relationship to the presence of God. The process of the dreamwork is to go deeper in the psyche to understand the soul self and to understand real feelings in order to find the Divine connection.

But it is difficult to believe the snake and the true heroes of the old myths because of the interpretations of the stories.

Dream:
I am standing in a desert. Suddenly a great storm comes over the land. Lightning and snakes rain down from the sky. I am terrified.

When Adam and Eve eat the fruit from the Tree of Knowledge of Good and Evil, they are actually objectifying themselves. A bird wakes in the morning and sings but it is not aware that it is a bird singing. It just sings. Objectifying reality actually creates a bi-polar relationship. Knowledge of the self creates an opportunity for evolution, for evolving to a place of relationship with the Divine - the I and Thou relationship.

In the traditional interpretation of the story, Adam and Eve are tricked by the snake, but the real trick of the story comes after the apple is eaten. After they ate from the tree of knowledge, they heard God walking in the garden. At the sound, they hid themselves because they felt ashamed. Then a disembodied voice asks for them, asking them why they hide and if they have eaten of the tree. It is this same voice that curses the serpent and curses Adam and Eve, banishing them from the garden. They assume that the voice is God, just as all interpretations of the story assume.

But the voice is not God. Just as when looking at a dream, the question is raised about how Adam and Eve knew it was the voice of God when they never saw Him. If it was the voice of God, why would He need to look for them, why would He question what they have done. Why would He not appear to them as He had done before. The disembodied voice belongs to the demon, the pathology, instead, tricking Adam and Eve that they were condemned, judged, shameful. It is the same voice that whispers even now in every individual saying that they are bad or good.

By convincing Adam and Eve to leave the garden, the demon convinces them to enter into the senex and puer world, in the same way an individual now can get caught in the good/bad world of senex/puer. Most interpretations of this story are written from this perspective, the perspective of the senex/puer world. In this world, the father is a senex father condemning and shaming. It is difficult to find the true Father. After they leave, Adam and Eve conceive Cain and Abel through which the senex and puer reality begins to manifest.

The objectification of "I am great/I am horrible" begun in the Garden of Eden has no love or passion. The snake offered passion and sensuality, the knowing of God's love in our spirit and feeling it. This is what was lost. In the absence of being able to feel and experience essence, a function of sensuality, most people default to living in the realm of good and bad.

In this realm, an individual is aligned with Freud's pleasure principle - when things are good, then the person is happy, but when things are bad, the person is sad. This establishes the assumption that pleasure/happiness comes from the outer world and all a person needs to do is compete for it. Happiness, however, can only be had through the Divine and it is palpable - essence, sensuality and grace. For those who remember their relationship, receiving it again can feel like suffering. Others remain convinced that happiness can be obtained only through the world. Being the richest country in the world, millions have the opportunity to obtain every desire but they remain miserable in their inner lives. People in this situation may convince themselves and others that they are happy, but it is often a lie.

Eating the apple is about the knowledge of God ultimately, not the knowledge of good and evil. Good and evil are shamed based, related to the outer world. In fact, the outer world does not really understand "good" because it is usually aligned with desire.

But when "good" and "evil" are applied to the concept of the self, there is no room left for feeling. Feelings replace concepts of judgment and are constantly renewing through the relationship with the Divine. They have no other meaning than the clearer and clearer intention of the Divine in the self. The ego that makes sense of the world is obliterated and lost in the spiritual dimension.

When shame enters into the polarity of the psyche, an individual does not know who he is, so he takes information about the self from the negative, dark and treacherous voice of pathology, just like Adam and Eve. Shame causes a person to know separateness, keeping him from feeling needs, pain, yearning that comes from the bleeding of the wounds.

If there is no shame in the awareness of "I," then an individual can have relationship with the other, the "Thou." This assumes that once the independent ego self - the one with proud attachments to the world and the perception of achieving happiness from the world - is no longer the issue, an individual has only the Thou left from which to receive validation. But, if the awareness of the subjective world is "I am that I am" or "I did it my way," and is empowered by the ego's effort to lift the self to some loftier position in the world, then the individual will have no need to question who he is or to change his need for validation from the world to the Thou. In this case, the ability of the person to evolve is sharply limited to what he accepts of his ego self at the current moment.

Evolution, in the psychological sense, requires the objectification and questioning of the self, forming the basis for this type of dreamwork. It opens up the relationship of "I-Thou" with the Divine. The snake wanted Eve to eat of the apple so she could objectify herself and come into the "I-Thou" relationship with God. However, the pathology stepped in and convinced them to leave Eden instead.

Many assume that the goal is to return to the innocence of the Garden of Eden. If it was, then the journey offered by the Archetypal snake, the Animus, would be missed entirely. The tremendous gift of the "I-Thou" relationship which leads to knowing God would be lost without the reflective self-awareness. Adam and Eve before the apple were like the bird singing. The bird that does not question. Adam and Eve in their original state of innocence were not in mutuality with God. But wisdom, becoming awake, becoming conscious comes from questioning and can lead to true mutuality.

There are many who aspire to become enlightened, to gain spiritual peace through deep prayer or meditation without understanding that the issue is relationship. There are others who turn to drug use to feel good, to return to the state of innocence. To be the bird singing the song of God. But to gain spiritual peace, an individual must come into relationship with the Animus, not return to the innocence of being unaware of the "I-Thou" relationship. The dreams do not inspire an individual to be in the "blissed out" place, but they do inspire peace in the container of the relationship with the Divine.

The gift of the serpent is about moving from that state of innocence into a state of constant acknowledgement of and relationship with God. This state of innocence is part of the puer lie. The puer voice says to live for the moment, do not question anything, do not worry, be happy. The dreamwork is about happiness, of course, but not the kind of happiness of a cow chewing cud. It is the happiness, the joy, of intimacy with the Divine. True innocence can only come from relationship with the deepest self through which the Divine is found. The Divine that created the self. Like the prodigal son returning from the world to his father's house. The greatest issue is not being happy or finding peace, not experiencing spiritual wholeness. The greatest issue is coming home, is reconnecting to the relationship with the Divine. A person can sit in prayer or meditation and achieve a sense of

Divine essence, but he may still remain far from home. The humble soul can be caught in brambles, lost in suffering, but the journey is only reconciled when the suffering is completely felt. To cover up the suffering with ideas and even "spirituality" is to deny the suffering, allowing it to continue unabated. The journey is to move through, to feel the fullness of the feelings. The dreams lead a person through this journey. It is not a task that a therapist can do. The effort made by the Divine through the dream process is clear, focused and unerring.

Three Drawings by Ellen Keene
Snakes

Dream:

> I am in a pool and a large red snake bites me on the neck. I am terrified.

Dream:

> I have many yellow and black striped snakes in my hair. I am scared they will bite me.

From Ellen:

> I do not like getting bit by snakes. I know they are bringers of Archetypal potency and passion but I am afraid of that in myself. My homework is to let the venom course through me. Once the homework had begun to work, I began to consider the possibility of the self underneath the shame by working on this drawing. The yellow snakes pull me back from this lie I have been believing. I can feel a place of passion and potency in me. I have a visceral experience of separating from a layer of the pathological false self. I can feel the sickly place in my gut where the pathology wants to stay rooted in me. Marc told me once that I pick up my shame and self-hate like a shroud. I would get lifted up in dream after dream only to pick up the shroud again.

Breathing in the Vapors

Dream:

> I am in New York City and I find myself in a scary neighborhood. A tough gang is on a street corner and I hope they will leave me alone, but a guy sees me and threatens to shoot me. He points a gun at my head. I am terrified. Another guy tries to force me to breathe in this stuff I think is crack cocaine. I am terrified and try to hold my breath.

From Ellen:

> In this drawing I am working with the homework of breathing in the vapors. I have a lot of fear and aversion to this stuff I think is crack. I guess the Archetypes figured I needed a gun to my head to get me to be still for this one.

> Marc said the pathology cannot live in the smoke. In the dream, I am aligned with the demon. It is pretending to be scared, it will die when I breathe the stuff in. I need to be open to the fear and say yes rather than no. Maybe it will free up the child underneath all the shame.

> This moment for me is about surrendering to His will and letting the men do their healing work instead of reacting to my fear and trying to survive the situation. I had this dream at a time when the Animus had been coming to me a lot and awakening my passion for Him. I was beginning to experience myself as His beloved and feel intent upon Him. But my shame and self-loathing continue to block my ability to retain His love. In this moment I am feeling the blockage as a blackness in my throat, in my chest. It is the something that keeps me from revealing my full nature and my awakening heart. As I draw, I am practicing trusting Him and that place in myself. My surrender is calm and what I later begin to understand as devotional.

Strong Enough to Bash the Rat

Dream:

> I am in my six-year-old son Ian's bedroom. He is sleeping. I see an opening in the wall above his bed and a large rat is lazing there. I am appalled it is in Ian's room. At some point, I have it by the tail and am bashing it back and forth on the pavement. I feel a fierceness. Its guts are yellow.

Dream:

I am at a table with some people to my left. A man leans down and kisses a little girl with red hair. Her mother says she is traumatized and has hid in the closet ever since. I see her wavy red hair and I talk to her sweetly about it. I want to distract her from her trauma and bring her into the moment.

From Ellen:

In the first dream, I see the rat clearly and I am strong enough to defeat it. In the second dream, I do not see that the mother is also the rat. I am tricked into believing her as I am tricked to pick up the shroud of my shame. Marc said the child self is never traumatized. It usually separates or dies in the psyche but is never traumatized. It is trauma that keeps us from the child self. So the red haired girl is fine and the mother is lying.

In this drawing, The Me That Is Strong Enough to Bash the Rat and The Girl That Is Me are in the shaft of light. I know my strength comes from the Archetypes and through me it is their light shining. But I need to step into ownership of "I am that I am," which brings up the discomfort of nakedness and exposure. I am practicing seeing myself with wheels of spiritual energy, as the Animus sees me with my big heart, with the fire of my devotion to Him, to Marc, to this work, to my husband and son, to my family, to my own personal version of facing evil on an Archetypal scale like Frodo and Sam in *Lord of the Rings*. The rat is a guise of the demon like the one Gandalf confronts in the mines of Moria with his flaming sword when he commands, "You shall not pass."

In me, the rat is waging a vicious attack by gnawing on me constantly, putting me down in hundreds of ways, at times whispering or shouting if need be, to get me to see its proof of my worthlessness in the world. It uses comparison to get me to react. The rat is the source of my self-hate and the fuel for my shame. It keeps me in a malaise of blackness where I am separated from the love. It is a formidable opponent and it is inside me. It is of the devil after all. I need a strength of command and devotion to plant the flaming sword of truth and mean it with all my heart, "You shall not pass. Dumb bitch, dumb bitch. I see you are not me." Marc says once it is an inside game, it is on my terms because the pathology wants me to project it into an outside game. Once I see it is inside, all I need is the Animus to defeat it.

My homework from this session was to bash the rat every time I feel my fear. Rather than put myself down when I feel scared, get confused, do not know or make mistakes, I am to pound the rat. Feel my fear, pound the rat. Dumb bitch, dumb bitch. Be the girl, trust she is okay - feel my fear, bash the dumb bitch rat. I am strong enough. I see it is not me.

In Ellen's commentary for the first drawing, the sickly place she feels in her "gut" is about her shame, the underlying emotion that keeps her from her fear which would lead her to her passion. She is terrified of the snakes in both of the dreams, but she is not in her shame. This is the key to the way out. Shame is a dense palette of emotion, thick, swirling and covering up the less dense feelings of fear and vulnerability. In these dreams, she is deepening into the fear that would free her from the past.

The purpose of the snake is to bite. The poison from the snake enters the bloodstream, races to the heart and kills the pathology that dwells there. It is the final solution. The client must separate from the old self and be willing to drop into the deepest feelings not ever imagined - pain, fear, exhilaration, excruciating intensity. The rainbow of feeling possibilities. This labyrinth of feeling experience is a freedom that the soul seeks for its final recovery. It does not matter what the feelings are, only that the client feels them and follows them.

In the drawing, one of the figures is Medusa, the snake woman who has the power of the snakes. In the mythological story of Medusa, Athena punished Medusa, a beautiful maiden for sleeping with Poseidon in her temple by giving her snake hair and making her look turn people to stone. Athena is part of the senex lie - she was born out of Zeus' head. She has no feelings, only the ideas of the father. Athena is jealous, vindictive and does not want the client to experience the union of the Anima with the deep unconscious where the Archetypal Father lives and resonates.

In Athena's objectification of the father, she lives and creates a false image of the father. She is incapable of sexual intimacy and paralyzes the soul, creating a projection in which the principle of the feminine cannot be completed with the unconscious, with the true Father. The part that transcends rules, ideas, humanitarian values, totalitarian structures, etc. Athena cannot understand love and essence and the beatific. She is pure mind, pure belief in the ideas that trickle down from the tyrannical/utopian reality which the soul can neither fathom nor cares to fathom.

In the case of this client, Ellen has fallen prey to the senex aspect of devotion. She wants to be the good girl, the shining star for the father, the therapist, the husband, the son, the boss, etc. This is the root cause of her shame. There is no identity in this, no connection to her root passion and abiding sense of her own worth, as felt from the Beloved's love of her. Medusa's punishment appears to be a tyranny by which all men are turned to stone. But perhaps this is just a projection of the dreamer's senex need to be loved and accepted, feeding instead into this great black hole of rejection of which this mythos pretends. In reality, Athena cannot punish or alter the Anima in any way. The snake power simply cuts through and mows down all falseness. Unfortunately, the senex dreamer internalizes this by feeling punished and damaged, as if her purpose for living, which is to have a relationship with men, has been lost. This treachery of deception, the manifestation of the perversion of the Neptunian Poseidon, is revealed. The snakes are potency and simply banish all things false. The client in the second figure of the painting does not know this potency and is still seeking the Father through relationships in the world where there can be no peace.

In the second drawing, the snake's bite is the same as the gun's bullet. Part of the death in this dream has to do with the ultimate death of the illusion of Athena. This changing of the deception is reflected in the vapors, the illusory, subtle lie that is unbearably confusing. In breathing the vapors, Ellen will finally surrender to the love and, like Medusa, become potent and free from the projection of seduction from the outer world. Her alignment will be from her soul self, reflected as the potency of the snake whose gyrations emanate from Divine love.

The power is manifested in the last set of dreams where the client is suddenly feeling the potency that allows her to destroy the shame, as represented by the rat. In this dream, she is like the Medusa slaying her enemies, not shamefully turning them into stone as if she were the great pariah. This clears the way for her true soul self, the little red haired girl, to finally emerge in her consciousness. Even though she is not the Medusa, ultimately as the girl, she gets to feel the power of the Anima which defies the shame.

In this way, her consciousness knows Athena's lie and this can become the foundation of understanding that will allow her to finally emerge as the little girl. Until this moment, there has been no sense of inner power. Without this, the little girl could never emerge. Ellen's commentary reflects her own growing consciousness of these issues.

One of the biggest distinguishing aspects of Archetypal Dreamwork is this emphasis on relationship. Everything in a dream in advanced work is geared toward the client having a relationship with the Animus or the Anima, requiring the "I" and the "Thou." Without the relationship, the client is in the now, but alone.

As soon as relationship emerges, the question arises, what do the Archetypes want? One of the reasons many people do not move toward relationship is that they would rather be enlightened without needing to be aware of the other's expectations. This makes enlightenment without relationship particularly seductive, especially in the senex/puer mythos where the other in the relationship seems to be a dark father telling the person he is a sinner.

It is a great way to trick an individual into believing that relationship with God is not desirable because it makes the person a tainted sinner. Understandably, most people do not want that kind of relationship. In fact, this relationship with the dark father in the senex world - soul as sinner - actually triggers a rebellion. This rebellion is an aspect of Uranus, the higher octave of the Father. Even if the rebelliousness is negative, it can be positive when it is an individual refusing the shame of the senex father, looking for something beyond that reality. The trap of this rebellion, however, is that many people tend to give up on any relationship with the Divine, opting for "I can do it myself," instead. Which leaves them nowhere.

The dreamwork tries to undermine the senex/puer paradigm by turning everything known upside down and bringing the individual into a place where he can simply feel. It challenges every assumption about the self and others and God. In Stage One work, a client's assumptions are challenged and can begin to turn; in Stage Two work, the dreams help the client to reformulate reality; and Stage Three work brings the client into the place of essence and relationship with the Divine. This is a process of letting go of the world and letting the self become captured by the Divine. In this place, the client can seek the highest truth of the knowledge offered by the snake. But it is a truth that humans have never been able to work through since the garden.

Senex and puer keep an individual from alchemical work because they either obliterate or judge feelings. Without working through this dynamic, alchemical work cannot be accessed. Alchemy rarely happens in traditional psychology because psychology focuses on helping a person work with the senex/puer dynamic in a better way, not on transformation. The goal of counseling is to feel better and/or function better in the world. In this way, a counselor unwittingly becomes an ally with Zeus. Transformational, alchemical work requires a deep, core feeling which may mean allowing a client to leave a session in a great deal of pain rather than making him feel better. Trying to help a client feel better tampers with the process - it is important to let the person feel his feelings. All of them.

Dream:
    I am crawling through burning snow under a midnight sun. I am in excruciating pain.
    I reach up to heaven.

At first glance, this client is either psychotic or in the middle of a spiritual transformation. This client is in advanced work, breaking through the gatekeepers of the senex/puer mythos into the Archetypal Realm.

Profound, Archetypal dreams are approached differently than dreams from the realm of Zeus/Saturn. When a client is experiencing a breakthrough and the Archetype is transforming him, there is nothing for the therapist to do but witness in awe of the process and watch the miracle unfold. A therapist can help the person face and acknowledge pathology at this moment, for it is highly likely he is also under attack. The client also may not know consciously that the experiences of the Archetypal Realm are coming, so the therapist can help to validate the process.

In the dreams of advanced work, all the rules from the senex/puer realm no longer apply. The therapist simply watches and supports, with awe.

Hades/Pluto: Transformation through Pain

Seeing the underworld of Greek mythology as representing the Archetypal Realm shifts perspective on the myth of Hades and Persephone:

The Story of Persephone:

> Persephone, the goddess of the harvest and daughter of Zeus and Demeter, was such a beautiful goddess that everyone loved her. One day, when she had wandered off from her companions, collecting flowers on the plain of Enna, the earth split open and Hades arose on his chariot drawn by black horses from the split. He quickly abducted her, taking her back to his underworld realm. Only Zeus and Helios saw what happened.

> Demeter wandered the earth, looking for her daughter, until, finally, Helios revealed what happened. In her grief and rage, she withdrew in loneliness, causing the earth to stop being fertile. Zeus sent Hermes to Hades to secure the release of Persephone. He agreed but he gave Persephone a pomegranate, of which she ate. The eating of the seeds bound her to the underworld forever. She spent part of the year in the underworld with her husband (during which time Demeter refused to let things grow - the birth of winter) and part of the year on earth with her mother.

In the Divine mythos of the dreamwork, Hades is an aspect of the Animus. He joins with Persephone in sacred conjunctio and makes her the queen of the underworld. In the process, Persephone separates from her mother as all daughters must.

In most interpretations and presentations of the myth, Hades is portrayed as a rapist and a misogynist because this is the view of the story from Demeter's point of view. In her view, the view rooted in the senex/puer world, the upper world, Demeter sees the story as an abduction, insisting that the girl is too young to make up her own mind. But what of Persephone's viewpoint? Just as Hades is an aspect of the Animus, Persephone is an aspect of the Anima. For her, she goes willingly with a partner who is potent, deep and powerful with the result of becoming a queen in her own right of the underworld. Her running away with Hades is turned into abduction and a rape. The relationship between Hades and Demeter is the dynamic between the underworld realm of the Archetypes and the upper world realm of the waking world. The abduction of Persephone is really the transformation of a weak figure into an Archetypal figure. The transformation, however, is brutal.

Spiritual transformation through Hades is often felt as brutal because it deals with pain. The horror of pain cuts through the veneer of consciousness. The real horror is life without the Divine because the soul self and God are related. Therefore, without God, a person is without self. To have the self, it is necessary to face into the horror. Greater acknowledgement of pain increases the capacity for compassion. Hades' invitation is to see the truth of the heart, bringing the self into higher love through pain or power and potency. Not love in the romantic sense, but in the ability to feel and receive Archetypal love. This requires a profound shift in consciousness.

Transformation through Hades is the process of the death of the ego self and the rebirth of the true self. Most spiritual paths do not work deep enough to kill the ego. No one wants the death of the ego without the understanding of what it truly means. Entering the underworld of the Archetypal Realm asks an individual to go where she cannot survive without ego consciousness. The outer world does not acknowledge a place with ego consciousness. Because of this, Hades is seen by Demeter and Zeus as evil and demonic.

Zeus wants to preserve life - the life of the ego structure, the life of right and wrong, shame and pride. The life of the ego structure offers goals and structures to work with and/or fight through giving a sense of power and control. This structure can seem necessary and exciting, but it deceives the person from the real opportunities that are presented by the psyche. The ego self loves this concept of freedom, seeing all forms of surrender as tyrannical and cultist. This may be true in the outer world, but is in direct conflict when the person is faced with the Archetypal dream reality.

The spiritual life represented by the unconscious inner life is not reflected in the world. To know it, an individual must journey inside, into the subterranean realm to all the sources of the true self instead of through the illusion of projection that play into the world. The journey is to live freely in true aspects that bring a person to a spiritual life within the psyche.

The Hades dynamic in a dream always initially seems negative. The psyche is contained in reaction to the elements of the myth which make them seem "bad" to the client. This is particularly true with Stage One clients because of their beliefs around reality. Hades confronts the misperceptions and dispels the blind spots.

Dreams illustrate how essence within a client is used to serve pathology. Meeting the enemy of pathology within is simply part of the journey and is without judgment - every client faces the demon inside. The dreams reveal that drama. If a pathological figure appears in a dream, like the dark mother or whoremaster, it is because that particular pathology is in the client. The realm of Zeus, the senex/puer realm, works to give justification to a person about why she is the way she is. Hades is the power to break that chain of justification.

In the story of Hades and Persephone, Demeter is actually the dark mother, reacting with fury over the "loss" of her daughter, blaming others and destroying everything on earth. Even though she appears to only want the best for Persephone, her wanting is really only a veiled enslavement of the daughter. Demeter wants to control her daughter, naming that control undying devotion. She actually wants a world of no conflict. Before Persephone leaves, there are no seasons, just endless summer. This is a place of no duality, a place of living in the garden where there is no self-reflective examination of the self. The mother wants the daughter to stay innocent and ignorant, to not enter into any sacred conjunctio relationship so she can remain in control. It is an element of motherhood that all women who become mothers must face.

Spring

Your eyes, the green
of water's thaw, dawn's sky.

Will your light pale me,
turn my bones ashen?

Understand the iridescent black of the crow
has been my comforter, my confidant.
In prayers I kissed the claws of that bird
as if they were the feet of Christ Himself.

And my prayers?
Thunder broke them into this earth-filled air
you breathe into me.

Karla Van Vliet

JACOB'S LADDER

In the Book of Genesis, Jacob dreams of a ladder, one end set upon the earth and the other end reaching up to heaven, with angels of God ascending and descending. In Archetypal Dreamwork, the goal is the same as Jacob's vision: to ascend the ladder to heaven in order to be in a personal relationship with the Divine.

Once a client has broken through some of the psychological barriers that block connection with God in Stage One work, a certain receptivity is needed in order to be in relationship with the Animus. There are three ways or rungs of receptivity that allow a person to experience a connection with the Divine. If any of these receptive ways are blocked, then the focus of the work is to open the blockage.

Jacob's Ladder is a useful motif for understanding the rungs of receptivity. In the motif, there are three rungs - essence, sensuality and grace. There are individuals who already may have access to one of the rungs in their soul so that it becomes the basis for their spirituality. But dreams target the rungs that are not open, the ones unavailable, in order help the person learn to be entirely receptive to God. To have the full relationship, all three receptors need to be open. The work for the client is, through individuation, becoming whole in all aspects.

Essence

Essence leads to a manifestation of awareness and consciousness through the psyche. The awareness of opening to the Other and the reality of the Other - the reality of the non-physical and non-linear. Part of the awareness is feeling the truth on the other side of thinking, of thought. A truth waits with clarity and discernment, compassion and faith. Clients who are strong in spirituality but who have difficulty with sensuality are probably strong on the rung of essence.

Essence is an experience of God's love through a feeling realm. Many spiritual people have an uncanny ability to conceptualize the idea of the Divine, an exploration that requires the capability to feel Divine love. Hurts, fears and the development of the secondary ego can block this at every opportunity.

The motif of essence is drowning in water. The drowning process and how the client responds can manifest in many different ways, depending on where the client is in his work - he may desperately hold his breath and try to swim for air, he may struggle at first and then let go into breathing the water or he may be able to walk under water completely unaware that he is breathing it. Breathing air is of the mind while breathing water is of the spirit and the capacity to feel spirit. The drowning process can be the death of the mind while the capacity to actually breathe the water is the ability to feel into spirit.

Many individuals find they have the capacity to contact essence easily and feel into the Divine, but they have difficulty with the next rung, the rung of sensuality. For some of these individuals, they may have difficulties with marriage and may use celibacy to bypass an inability to receive sensuality. They may be isolationists with an inordinate distaste for human contact. As such, they can seem cold, aloof and unable to bring their inner love into their outer world relationships. This is a great loss, for the ultimate relationship requires mutuality with the Divine - and the capacity to know the Divine through essence needs to be inclusive of the next rung of sensuality. Without sensuality, essence is only a two dimensional reality.

Many who have the capacity for essence eschew the idea of sensuality as part of spiritual practice and growth. For these clients, encounters in their process that open them to this realm are surprising and horrifying. When living without sensuality, there is a tendency to moralize and judge as a way of comparing their experience of essence with the mundane world, as if the world is nothing but poisonous vipers. When the only option to exist in the world is limited to this very simple way, passion, joy, vibrancy, potency can all be lost to the client.

The Archetypes will challenge this in dreams in different ways - they may send the Animus in a fancy red sports car or as rowdy teenagers ravishing each other.

Dream:

>I am at a gathering with other people. A man comes to me and offers me a bottle of wine. It is a bottle of wine that costs over $100.00. I refuse it, saying it is too expensive.

Because of the judgment and abhorrence of sensuality, a client with just a connection to essence will be convinced that sensuality is just an evil to be repressed. But essence without sensuality does not allow the spiritual aspects of the Divine a way into the sensual world. Spirituality through essence alone becomes just a private party.

Sensuality without essence is not common nor is it a healthy experience. Even though essence is probably a higher form of consciousness than sensuality, it may not be possible for sensuality to exist without an understanding and grounding in essence. Essence must come first for sensuality to have a deeper meaning than just hedonistic exploration.

Aesthetic Spirituality

Aesthetic spirituality comes from the belief that beauty is the expression of spirit and the connection with the Divine through essence. It is not linked with sensuality. Instead, it is more of a beatific experience. Many experiences of the beatific can manifest from a variety of rituals such as tea parties, feng shui, flowers, flower essences, herbs, nature, etc. The exploration of the beatific is certainly a valid and wonderful journey - God's love in all of these things and experiences is beautiful to behold. But in these experiences, there is little or no inclusion of one's own experience outside the beatific. It is not necessarily personal. Great gaps are missing in the aesthetically spiritual individual as she pushes down the primal and only looks for continued peace and harmony.

Peace and harmony, in this way, come at the price of denying pain and trauma, which results in the individual not experiencing true peace. Aesthetic spirituality is only a barrier to the unexplored regions of the "primal sea" where great, wonderful aspects of the self are still lost or buried. Freud understood this denial of the past and Jung understood that the denial was not just suppression of bad memories, but also the suppression of the beauty of the soul itself. To live out the beauty of the soul, the beauty inside, through the projection of beauty into the world through rituals does not necessarily include the soul. A person may be able to feel the soul through this kind of projection of beauty, but it is not connected with the soul itself and the person's consciousness.

In the pursuit of aesthetic spirituality, a person often finds herself either in the position to create structure or feeling a responsibility to the beauty to create the structure to allow the beauty to exist. But, in relationship with the Divine, there is no responsibility for anything except the relationship itself and the connection. The relationship and the connection allow the person to trust that the universe can sustain itself. Without the connection, there is no vessel to hold the beatific. Ascetics are those who pursue obtaining aesthetic spirituality by living in the form of beauty and obligation with the Divine through form of beauty and obligation in daily life via prayer, meditation, strict rules, etc. Living through the form of beauty and obligation in daily life in this way is an attempt to create the vessel in order to feel essence.

The White Church
by Laura Ruth

Dream:

A white church. People going inside to heal. We send people in to lie down on the floor and be healed. It was amazing. They were lying down and being healed. It was like we were all being healed - it was in the air - the room - like entering the church was entering a field of electricity or something. People were falling to the floor, being transformed. Shift.

Leaving a gathering to make a phone call because I am running out of rosemary oil fast and I use it every day as part of my healing. I do not want to run out of oil. I feel a bit of a push - a hurry - to make the call. Shift.

A man was there. I leaned on Him. We were deep friends. A woman was there too. I leaned my head on her also. I loved them. I am between them on the bench, held, totally in love and loved. Shift.

A beautiful white statue of Mary inside a cupola high up on the cliff above the sea. Very Mediterranean. She is so peaceful, turned to the sea, like a healing presence. Inside the cupola the ceiling is an incredible blue. A blue cupola beckoning - opening to the sea. I am moved by the beauty, drawn towards it, but feel far away, as if I am looking at it from a distance.

The Girl in the Mirror
By Laura Ruth

Dream:

I am a youngish teenager in a long skirt with no underwear. A man's friend thinks I am pretty, I feel embarrassed to be noticed, talked about. The man boasts, proudly telling him he used me and I used him and we were quite close. I feel misplaced, unsure. Later I ask him what he meant because I do not remember what he is talking about. He says I know what he is talking about. I do not know, or do not want to know, what he is talking about. I feel ashamed. Later I am standing in the living room while the man's wife is standing at the stove nearby and I am startled when the man bumps into my legs, crawling on the floor to look under my skirt. I cannot believe he is doing this, especially with his wife right there. I am shocked and uncomfortable, embarrassed, repulsed. Shift.

I am tying a long-sleeved shirt around my waist but I have nothing on underneath. It is open a bit in the front so that my vagina/pubic area is exposed. I am in front of a mirror and I notice the exposure and arrange the shirt a bit, enjoying the beauty of my body and the fabric together, without covering myself up. It feels natural and lovely to me. It feels good, strong, pleasurable. No shame. Shift.

It is a reunion of the family, but I do not know anyone there. A young boy, eight or so, runs up and gives me a big hug and wants me to play ball in the family game. He says, "We have a place for you." I am so happy, and kind of amazed that there is a place for me here. He is so open and joyful - contagious. He really wants me to come with him to play.

From Laura:

> The truth is the feeling of loving and being loved with the Archetypes. It is about relationship with the Archetypes, with God. Worked with the other dream, again sensuality and essence, as opposed to the false spirituality and hubris of the projecting onto things of the world - the rosemary oil and the statue of Mary. The difference between the comfort in relationship, sitting with the Archetypes themselves and finding comfort in a statue. Very subtle working on the feminine. I grew up believing it was a sin, vain, to look in a mirror. I remember being awed, at twelve and at sixteen, watching friends of mine look at themselves in the mirror, because it was so impossible for me to do that myself. I never had a mirror like the one in the dream, where I could see my whole body. Be the girl in the shirt open to the boy. Know they are the Archetypal family, the true family.

The denial of the boy became the loss of Laura's ability to know her needs, feelings and wants, to be, like her friends, able to enjoy her developing body in the beautiful mirror. The whoremaster shames her and reduces her to dirt. There is no evidence that this type of abuse happened, but Laura carried a sense that her beauty caused great attraction and therefore was a sin that she had caused to happen. Because of her hypersensitivity to other people's attractiveness to her and because of her inability to enjoy her own beauty, the pathology was able to turn anybody's attraction to her into internal nihilism. How could she enjoy relationship and mutuality - they are about the other person finding her attractive spiritually and physically. Laura worked at being a nonperson, being too sensitive to others' feelings about her. She worked hard to be invisible rather than visible. The picture reveals her as a young girl accepting her womanness.

The boy who is the link is there, too, accepting everything. He even brags about it in all of the ways he enjoys his sense of identity. Without this, it is difficult to interact with the Divine. The sense of herself linked with the boy gives her a sense of beingness without shame and without the hypersensitivity of attraction of others to her and what that attraction means in the others' lives. It is not about them. It is about her. Self-love is crucial in her healing. The Archetypes cannot love us if we do not love ourselves. This is not about narcissism; it is about self-acceptance. Just as the Archetype cannot heal if we do not feel, the Archetype cannot love what we do not accept as a part of ourselves. Mutuality requires something from each of us. There must be a sense of beingness from which we can respond to the love offered. It is like a tulip that bursts out of the soil, feeling the warmth of the sun. Without its tulipness, it would not be able to burst forth from the ground. Growth requires a sense of one's self. The only growth that can happen can come from that which is already present. The growth will be a learning process, but it already exists inside. If beingness is lost to a person, then that person can not burst forth.

For Laura, she held the nihilistic belief that her essence and beauty caused suffering in others. What a seductive sham. To such a person, aesthetic spirituality was the only thing available - the idea of beauty where it must deny other passions that can be seen as other than aesthetic. But passions are not aesthetic nor are they necessarily beautiful. Passions are the energy moving in the self that are beyond judgment, just as a boy's Id cannot be evaluated or quantified. It just is - it is the primalcy - the primal sea. The essence of the boy's passions. Shame takes that passion and spins it out into the darkness. Without the boy, the beauty seen in the mirror is nothing but vanity. But with the boy, that beauty is desire, energy, sensuality and creativity.

Essence, itself, is a sublime, limited and spiritual feeling with many fake alternatives/emotions pretending to be essence. In order to obtain it, the ascetic will often separate from the world, seeing it as chaotic and demanding, requiring personality roles that the seeker can see separates her from essence. But the reality is that through the higher octave of sensuality, it is possible to obtain and feel essence and sensuality and still be in the world. Sensuality has nothing to do with creating a vessel in order to feel essence or sensuality. Sensuality, instead, allows a person to have a relationship with the Divine.

The triangulation process of the work involves the deep, core child self that has primal knowing and acute vulnerability, reaching back to the time of feeling the Divine's love. Such depth of knowing is obtained through sensual experiences which are simply the intimate and personal knowledge of the other and the other's intimate and personal knowledge of the true soul self of the person. This kind of relationship is most acute on a spiritual level, although lovers may experience it for a time.

This profound knowing that allows the soul self to be loved in the place of sensuality encompasses essence without any of the responsibilities for maintaining it. Often, when a person complains about what she needs and wants from the other, she is really projecting the mutuality and deep intimacy that she truly is unable to obtain within. The frustrating attempts to attain this with others in the outer world is nothing more than futile attempts of obtaining the true relationship - the soul is only truly nourished by the Divine. Perpetual attempts to achieve this in the world lead an individual to be emotionally spent and broken in a sea of disappointments. For even with the most beautiful people in a person's life, the true result of sensuality cannot be known. The necessary effort to have a fulfilling relationship with a loved one is a noble quest and is always part of this work. But it is easy to make excuses for the inability to make this connection by projecting shortcomings onto the other. This becomes clear when the person interacts with the Divine and finds she needs to go deeper to begin any kind of meaningful relationship with Him.

Fear as Aphrodisiac

In the early stages of the work, fear and pain relate to disappointments and failings in a person's life. But in the core self, the feelings of fear and pain have nothing to do with situations in the world nor, in a way, are they connected to the person's separation from God even though their existence is caused by the separation. The feelings themselves, once a person has worked through any trauma, are alchemical and transformational by nature and when they arise, the person simply needs to feel them. Once the individual has been invited to climb Jacob's Ladder, the only thing to do is feel the feeling and embrace it as if it is the elixir that would save the soul. Which, of course, it is.

Dream:
> I am making love next to the Animus. I know he is the Divine one and I enjoy the intimacy of being next to him. Toward the end of the dream, I desire to have sex with him but become terrified and say nothing.

This is an example of the elixir of sensuality, the elixir of the Animus that produces the greater fear. The awesome power of the Divine is terrifying while being, at the same time, the source of profound liberation. There is nothing incongruous in this, for to know the fear is to deepen the level of the passion of sensuality and essence. The mandate of fear and core fear/pain is to deepen the evolutionary process so relationship can occur. In the dream, the client forgets this and says nothing to the Animus.

There is no true evolution without fear. The gift of this dream is that the client, in her yearning for more connection, feels the fear. By embracing this, the fear will enhance, not diminish, the feeling component of sensuality. The transformational effect of union with the Animus goes far beyond any known outer world sexual encounter because it is an act where the person becomes part of the Animus and the Animus becomes part of the person. The knowledge of this requires fear. This fear, once embraced, will then allow for the enfoldment of the unfeelable.

A person cannot manufacture feelings that are not known. Only through the Alchemy of fear can feelings that are unknown or lost through the past be brought into the soul to be known. It is as if the core feelings of fear and pain are nothing more than seeds that bear fruit previously unknown. Every time a step is made into the unknown, these core feelings are felt. Fear is like a lather being rubbed all over that needs to be accepted in order to allow the deepening of feeling connections.

It is important to remember the comparison of the responsibility for essence versus the deepening capability for mutuality through sensuality and the necessary fear that allows for the emergence of essence. The rungs of Jacob's Ladder - essence, sensuality and grace - are not separate states, but rather are overarching experiences that blend and combine with one another, creating a myriad of feeling states. This complexity of consciousness can only be fully experienced when essence is not compartmentalized and called spirit. Moving through repeated immersions of core fear and pain while descending into the labyrinth of the Animus' heart is the true journey for those who seek union with the Divine.

Sensuality

Sensuality with the Divine has nothing to do with sex. Sexuality is a part of sensuality, but all forms of human interaction are a part of sensuality. Sensuality, in this sense, is not centered on human interaction but on a person's ability to feel God's love in the body in a very specific way to her. Sensuality is the capacity to sense the power, the passion and the intensity of being in relationship to God through the tactile self and allows the person to receive the relationship with the Divine in a real, direct and passionate way. With sensuality, a person can be in the world and manifest God's love in the world with both feet on the ground. The person can reach out to others and touch them in a real, direct and passionate way and also receive and experience others in a passionate way.

Dreams that work with sensuality vary greatly from client to client. Dreams that target a blockage in a client's sensuality receptor can be focused on touch and the Animus' attempt to be intimate through touch. Or they may present things that make the skin crawl for a client, like frogs and snakes. Since part of sensuality is the willingness to merge with another, sensuality dreams often are very frightening because they may include having sexual relations with a close brother or sister or even the client's own child. The challenge is for the client to let go of her sense of barriers in the dream perhaps in terms of an over-analyzed morality that does not allow her to just feel the closeness and touch of another. Of course, these types of dreams are only presented to clients whose high standard of morality and integrity would not allow them to act out the dreams in the world.

Sensuality in one's capacity to feel God's love in the body is transferred to the world in the ability to feel love with others through the body in an entirely different way. Many fortunate individuals feel this type of intimacy and sensuality with children - for example, mothers often feel it when they breastfeed. A father may feel it when he gives his beloved daughter away at her wedding and then dances with her at the reception.

Most people look for this in the world but do not see or understand it. In fact, many are threatened by the simple act of others hugging each other with affection. For many people, hugging is an act that can quickly become sexual. The movement to sexuality may be a reaction to block sensuality or it may be because the person has no reference to her own sensuality. On the other side of this are individuals who are stiff and threatened by any form of touch.

There are several areas where sensuality manifests in creative forms - dance and music, for example. This can be seen in the passion exhibited by a pianist as she runs her hands over the keys or in a dancer who moves his body with strength, grace and potency.

Because the depth of this feeling is mostly unfathomable and threatening, a person working on sensuality may have a dream in the dream motif of a child wanting to have sex. This motif does not relate to sexuality - it relates to sensuality. For example, a male client was very stiff with his daughter who was sensual and passionate. He was threatened by her sensuality and passion and rejected her in this way. He felt he was being correct, a good father, by taking care of her and not "crossing the line." However, she felt the rejection of her true self. The client then had this dream:

My daughter comes to me and wants to have sex. I absolutely decline, feeling horror.

The therapeutic process in session revealed that he needed to say yes as his homework and to acknowledge the barrier with his daughter and the threat he felt with her. He clearly did not understand the difference between sensuality and sexuality, which is why the daughter wants to engage in a sexual act in the dream. This particular client had experienced a promiscuous youth, suffering from too much sex and never understanding the sweetness of a simple touch.

Several days later, he had another dream where he had had sex with his daughter. Although there was no actual sexual encounter in the dream, he had said yes. The power of the homework caused a shift in the client where he could see his sensuality. He was able to see sensuality with his daughter in a new way. The intimacy with her that he could begin to express and experience was the beginning of a deepening of their father/daughter love. It was also a truth he learned in relation to other people he cared for and was able to apply. In turn, the people he cared about loved him all the more.

Again, these types of dreams are not offered to a client with sexual dysfunction or moral issues because they are not meant as literal dreams. The dream is not asking the father to actually have a sexual relationship with his daughter. It is only a door to access his sensuality. Nonetheless, such dreams are always terrifying when they happen. They are terrifying because the dream is confronting the client with his terror of intimacy.

It is important to note that arousal in a sensual moment is common even with children for both men and women. This does not mean something pornographic is happening or about to happen. It simply means that the physical - the penis in a man and the vagina in a woman - is connected to the heart and can be aroused when the person feels love towards others.

Polymorphous Perverse

Polymorphous perverse, a phrase coined by Freud, is characterized by displaying sexual tendencies that have no specific direction, as in an infant or young child. It represents a time in childhood usually between the ages of three and nine when a child has little self-awareness and experiments with sensuality through the body. Of course, not all children are polymorphous, and, unfortunately, the ones that are can be easy targets for molesters. Polymorphous children experiment in many ways - they may grind on a parent's lap, play doctor, eat worms - exploring all the tactile, sensual things in the world. By the time these children reach eleven or twelve, if they are "healthy" neurotics, they usually no longer have use for this energy.

As an adult, the person with a strong moral background can explore these areas as she ascends Jacob's Ladder. When working with and revisiting her sensuality, she can work on having an understanding of this energy in which there is no guilt. Fortunately, these younger ages can be re-explored through the dreamwork when the time is right for the client.

Grace

The third rung of the ladder is grace. Grace is the client's direct encounter with God. Essence is a way to be aware of the Divine without the mind while sensuality is an experiential way to contact the Divine and even the world. But grace is the actual relationship itself that includes both essence and sensuality. It is the highest octave of receptivity, the culminating principle.

A person at this point in his work is in advanced Second Stage and is beginning to have the capacity and the tools to be obedient to God through that relationship, however it comes up in the dreamwork. It is the beginning of the client's calling and the beginning of receiving what the client needs to answer that calling. The calling is the specific manifestation of a client's inner relationship with the Divine into the outer world. The congruence or confluence of the outer world and inner world come together and the client understands his outer life in relation to his inner work. That inner work manifests in all parts of the client's life as an outer expression. In manifesting through doing of the outer work, the service, the client is reminded and returned to the connection of the inner experience as well.

Dreams of grace are exquisite jewels of relationship where the client, in one way or another, is swept into a vibrant spiritual epiphany of consciousness.

Like many aspects of the journey, it is difficult to describe grace - it must be felt and experienced by the individual because it is the mystery of the person's own story with God. The pathological mind will want to mimic any description of the state of grace. The best thing to do is explore and experience sensuality and essence through the work and grace will follow.

Jacob's Ladder in the Stages of the Work

Because both essence and sensuality are usually possible only after the death of the pathology, Jacob's Ladder is a motif that is not necessarily appropriate for a Stage One client. It is advanced work that requires a bigger decision of commitment upon completion of Stage One work. Pursuing the receptivity of essence, sensuality and grace takes a greater level of commitment because it is preparation for living on the other side with God, which is very uncomfortable. Many understand spirituality as a function of living with God but usually on this side of the fence, in the known outer world with outer world terms. Sensuality and essence are tools by which an individual can be with God in this world but truly be a part of the other world on the other side. Tools that lead to grace.

After Departure

Mist rising from the tree's branches,
like a gown, white and cotton, reveals
the hard nakedness of desire, mine, for you.

And this tree of my body, asks only,
that the wind touch it, as if a hand,
yours, could be imagined.

                              Karla Van Vliet

FUNDAMENTAL ASPECTS OF THE THREE STAGES
OF ARCHETYPAL DREAMWORK

Stage Three

Stage Three work is very exciting in Archetypal Dreamwork. The dragon of darkness has been slain and the client understands the pathology even as it continues to affect her. The old self has died, probably many times, through the process of Alchemy and the client is more deeply connected to her feeling life through her soul self. Through the soul self, the client begins to experience the timelessness of essence and the unfolding relationship with the Animus.

At the beginning of Stage Three work, a client can begin to experience reconciliation between her inner life and her outer life. Miracles happen. The things in her life that do not reflect or support her deep self will change. Any incongruent issue or involvement in the outer world with the inner life will unravel or resolve - including personal relationships, marriages or partnerships. This stage of the process is the manifestation of inner experience to outer experience - all activities in the outer world begin to reinforce the inner experience of essence. Essence feelings allow the client to know the Divine through a core self far deeper and more profound than the ego can understand.

The love from the Archetypal Realm can only be felt in the core experience of the soul, in essence. Feeling this Divine love allows the client to know something of the power of God. This love, which is the love that created the soul and which is in stark contrast to the love most people have known in the world, excites the soul and gives the client an understanding of her true essence.

Individuation

Most people through the process of adapting to the world, covering the true self and getting lost in the psychological self have forgotten what God created in them. In that self, the individual tried to figure out who he was in relation to the world because he lost the love of the Archetypal world. It was the only way the ego could survive without the gnosis of the soul.

In Stage Three work, the client is beginning to be free of that suffering, beginning to look to God to know his true self. From the experience of feeling essence and feeling the love of the Divine, the client can begin to be the unique person God intended him to be. This process is called individuation in traditional Jungian psychology. Individuation is the highest octave of the dreamwork and what all clients and all therapists are moving toward. The transformation of knowing the self through the soul.

The real journey finally begins in Stage Three. Everything has led to the moment of awakening so that the client's walk with God can unfold. The manifestation of inner experience to outer experience is the client's calling, how he manifests the growth process in the outer world from a place of connection to the Divine. Moving into this Stage Three connection is a very exciting time because the Animus is getting ready to be in conversation with the client. Until now, the Animus has said very little about anything to do with the outer world of a client's life. There are exceptions and some clients are ready to be guided about the outer world sooner than others, because again, there are no hard and fast rules in this work. But once the client is ready, the Archetype takes an avid interest in his affairs and may ask him to do something in the world. And, whatever the Animus asks always benefits the person.

As a client moves from the late Stage Two work of coming into mutuality with the Divine, the dreams will indicate when the shift to a Stage Three calling is occurring. A client may dream of being invited into a circle or find himself passionately participating in something he had not allowed himself to consider in waking life or even may receive an instruction dream where he sees clearly how to manifest something in the world. The inner instruction may be as subtle as hearing his name called on the edge of consciousness or as specific as hearing the Animus say how to behave in a particular situation. It may mean experiencing and feeling the presence of the Archetype in the outer world. The dreams will support it. The way God speaks to each person and what He speaks about is completely unknowable until it happens. It is mysterious and exciting and totally unique to each individual.

The Paradox of Obedience

Increasingly, as a client is given inner direction about outer things, she can begin to trust and be obedient to God - being o "be"dient from the stand point of "to be" one's self. Beingness of self is knowing what God wants and knowing that what God wants is knowing the true essence of the self. This obedience is not about responsibility in the sense of a sacrifice or martyrdom or a burden of any kind. And it is not about saving the world, either, which stems from a form of spiritual pride. The admonishment, "Obey God!" in this work does not exist. The client has a desire to follow the guidance because she has a passion for it, because her soul self was created for this very thing. God only asks a client to do what He created her to want to do, so it is not blindly following orders. Instead, it is responding to what is natural in her feelings, responding to her core self.

When the client receives a calling, she serves God in the world through knowing Him in her own soul where she receives His love and support, His guidance and intervention. Often, bringing the connected self into the world through the calling can bring up more pathology in the client that needs to die. The challenge of being in the world in this new essential way can double the client back into Stage Two work in order to go deeper into her soul through more Alchemy. Again, the dreamwork stages are not linear - people grow at different rates and in wildly varied ways. Some clients doing Stage Three work without completing fundamental Second Stage work can experience a conflict between emerging quickly into the world and not continuing ownership of the pathology. If the client is in this kind of acceleration, she must listen closely for inner direction because if pathology can find a way in, things will intensify. Fortunately, of course, the dreams always show where the client is out of connection.

Stage Three work is listening to what God wants for us and knowing it is exactly what we want, too. It is what is natural to our own being. What was given in the first place.

If this is so obvious, why is it saved for last? There are those who do live their passion, but if it is not connected to the Divine, then it is actually connected to pathology. Even if it is the right "thing". Who we are and how we feel is the key, not just what we do. Most people, however, complain that they do not know what God wants. Or, if the person knows she has a great gift, she hides it and does not do it because it brings up feelings she does not want to face. Third Stage work is impossible until the blocks to consciousness are released because of the possibility of corrupting the gift.

The fundamental issue is connection with the Animus. There are many ways to connect - in our understanding, our duty, our sense of responsibility and rightness. We can connect because we can think and even feel what needs to be done. But this knowledge is also the very knowledge that can be corrupted. For the essence of every being is the soul self who cares little for those things. The soul self, the child self, cares only for the relationship, the intimacy and the interaction. It does not worry about the task to be done or even the importance of it. The child self just wants to be held.

The following is a dream of a person in a leadership position:

> I am with Michael Clarke Duncan as John Coffey from the movie *The Green Mile*. He seems to be fifteen feet tall, towering above me. I feel like a boy, no more than three feet tall. I am happy, thrilled, excited to be with him. I run as fast as I can to be with him, just wanting to be held. He keeps just out of reach saying, "Would you rather be with that group over there? How about that group over there? Would you not rather be doing that thing over there instead?" I keep saying, "NO! I just want to be with you." All the while, he is laughing a playful laugh that says, "I am so glad you want to be with me."

If a person does her tasks as shown to her by the Animus and she is not in proper relationship with Him through her soul/child self, then all her efforts to do the right thing are folly. She will have become the teacher, the inventor, the leader when there can only be one teacher, one inventor, one leader. Even though she performs those tasks and is even seen performing those tasks, the individual is never those things. The individual is always the child self with the Animus first and foremost, regardless of what may be projected on her. Like the client as the small boy, just wanting to be with the Animus. The Animus is always showing the person who she really is in relationship to Him and to her own self.

Most people define the self based on goodness/badness or the things done or left undone. It is common for a client in Third Stage work to get caught up in a First Stage persona. But, to be a teacher, to have a calling, is to be intimately in relationship with the Divine without ego knowledge. There is only the relationship - the constant incantation of - *I am that I am with Him. I am that I am with Him. I am that I am with Him.*

Yearning

Like the duck
leading you down river,
feigned injury, diversion,

trickery, the dragged wing.
Oh, how long from the truth.
How astray. Turn back, and even

now, turn back. Search out
the cracked shadowed shells,
those little beatings which live

in the ribbed nest of the body.
Listen, they are present, born
for flight, born to take to the water.

Karla Van Vliet

THREE TYPES OF LOVE

There are three distinct types of love: pity, mercy and compassion. While the meanings of these words are closely related on a semantic level, they are actually completely different experiences of love. In Archetypal dreamwork, the distinction between pity, mercy and compassion hinges on the degree to which a person has faced his own suffering and inner truth.

Suffering, as defined for these purposes, includes a myriad of feelings that are a necessary part of the journey - feelings ranging from pain to inadequacy to fear.

Pity

To feel pity is to feel sorry for a person. Pity says; "What a shame, poor you," or "Look at that wounded person, too bad for them, glad it is not me," or even "It sucks to be you." When a person is feeling pity, it is a love abhorrent to pain and suffering. A person who feels this kind of love cannot face his own suffering, so he projects his suffering onto others in the world instead and then feels disdain for what he sees. A person who cannot face his own impoverishment will be quick to pity others. "Too bad for you" is the only level of nurturing such a person is capable of giving. To be the object and recipient of pity, obviously, feels awful.

Mercy

Feeling mercy is the desire to ease someone else's suffering, to make them feel better. Merciful people want to improve the lot of others, take care of the sick and wounded and so can be empathetic, loving and caring. But mercy can have a dishonest quality. Just like pity, this dishonesty comes from avoidance of a person's own suffering. Where pity loathes suffering, mercy wants to fix it in the external world in order to avoid it inside. Merciful love wants to take away the suffering of others because the inner life of feelings has not been felt or explored.

Taking care of another from this place is not the same as taking care of another from the place of true caring. Instead, mercy says, "I want to fix you so I can feel better because I cannot bear my own suffering." This level of nurturing not only avoids the feelings of the other by attempting to fix them, but it also lacks acceptance of the true meaning of why the other is experiencing the feelings. These feelings, and situations that provoke them, often are opportunities for transformation and Alchemy. Making the other feel "better" stifles the feelings, eliminates the opportunity and perpetuates the predicament of the other.

Compassion

Compassion is the higher octave of love and means "with passion." The root meaning of the word passion is to suffer, which is why the story of Christ suffering between the night of the Last Supper and his death is called the Passion of Christ. To have compassion involves understanding and feeling one's own suffering knowing that these feelings ultimately lead to the path of redeeming the soul self. It is having an overarching understanding of the duality of love and pain. Going on the journey through personal suffering, the "Dark Night of the Soul" as written about by St. John of the Cross, also allows for the capacity to have an understanding of what that journey may be for another. It allows for the deep presence necessary to understand and honor where another is in their journey.

A person with compassion does not try to take the suffering away. Instead, she recognizes and witnesses it with the gnosis of the heart. In this way, compassion accepts the other person and sees her in her life as the Divine has seen her.

Compassion is born of facing God with all of one's issues - which is the foundation of the dreamwork. Facing issues allows a person to feel her own suffering around seeing the pathology and seeing who she has become in the absence of a connection with the Divine. Every person suffers from their separation from God, their separation from themselves, their separation from others. The truth of one's predicament becomes apparent when one connects with the Divine - every mistake, every missed opportunity, every manner of self that avoids the truth becomes starkly understood and begins the process of regret that comes from seeing such truth.

People intuitively know that when they face God, they must also face themselves. This standing in the truth of the Divine is painful, difficult and terrifying. But unless a person has made room for and felt her own suffering, her capacity for love and compassion will be sadly limited. It will emerge, instead, as mercy or pity. Feeling the feelings of suffering opens the door to being touched in the wounded place by the Divine and to feel loved there. For many, the degree of the wound in this place would be considered trauma. Most people have some variation of this wound to trauma. When the Divine is allowed into this place, it is the place where love and pain mix. The duality of compassion.

The Compassionate Therapist

Because God's mercy is different than the idea of mercy in this realm, the therapist must, at times, watch a client walk out of a session in a great deal of pain. Clients often need to feel pain in order for an Alchemical triangulation to happen. The Archetypes will ask the client to experience his feelings, sometimes pain or fear or loss or lostness, in order to move through the trauma. Part of Dying to Self involves moving through trauma, through the dark night of the soul. But in this Dying to Self, the potential relationship with the Archetypes begins to actualize. Mutuality is born of such a journey. Wounds and trauma paralyze aspects of the psyche making it impossible to be open to transformation. Without transformation, of course, there is no mutuality with the Divine. The paralysis comes from repressed feelings that occur when the wound or the trauma is repressed. The greater the wound, the deeper and more hidden are these feelings.

It takes compassion to rip open a client if a dream requires it. If the therapist has issues of his own and would rather avoid what the dream is asking, then he will most likely err on the side of mercy with the client. Wanting to help ease a client's suffering when suffering is exactly what God is asking the client to explore results in losing the immediate guidance of that particular dream. Of course, another dream will eventually present itself as another opportunity to do this piece of work for the client. The therapist is also given another opportunity to better serve the client and the intention of the dream. The therapist, however, who knows his own suffering is compassionate and is able to accept what is happening with the client. He is able to feel the pain of it, tell the truth and let the client have his own experience.

Distinguishing compassion as different from mercy and pity is important to the process of the dreamwork. As a person goes deeper into his process, he encounters feelings of pain, hurt, fear, vulnerability, inadequacy, etc. As these essential feelings are experienced, the person's ability to feel love or love in these higher octaves increases. This is a gift of the work, a side benefit that comes from knowing God. Most people do not come into this process aspiring to be specifically loving or compassionate in this way as they have not themselves been loved sufficiently from the Divine. Very few really even know what this means. Experiencing love on an Archetypal scale is rare and not of this world. This higher octave of love, of Divine love, is entirely different than what most know as love.

Compassion, therefore, is a capability present in a Stage Three therapist. Third Stage is about giving to the world from a place of compassion and connection to the Archetypes. This type of love is crucial to the development of a soul preparing to work with others and for God to work through him in this endeavor.

Shadow of Itself

I fight the empty page
like the raven does the moon,
to leave some shadow of itself upon it.
So little fits the wings.
And this thick Vermonter blood,
a curse or blessing,
hates to say what has no meaning.

What will unfold eludes,
clean as the sky, moon-lit, face,
name and gender still unknown.
What can I say that will cross
the rounded forehead of my child?

The baby kicks and squirms.
I wonder when it will come spreading
its feathered self into the world,
what tale and truth it will lend to the fall leaves,
the yellow tinted evening light?

Karla Van Vliet

The Plan of the Archetype
The Long Arc and The Small Arc

Every individual has places where essence is very close to the surface and other places where essence is more deeply buried and less accessible. The Archetypes use the different places in a client based on a battle plan that is only clear to them. When they send a dream, they are asking the client and the therapist to go on an excursion through a specific area. The therapist may wonder why the dreams take a certain course, especially when she sees something else in the client that feels close. But wherever the Archetypes take the client, the therapist must also go. The path the dreams take is rarely simple, but it is always exactly what the client needs, even if it appears confusing.

The therapist enters each session with a client asking, "Why this dream? What is their plan of attack? What are they trying to do with this dream?" The therapist has several tools to work with including the gestalt process and the client's astrological birth chart. The gestalt process helps the therapist find out what the Archetypes are trying to bring into consciousness, not what the dream is "about." The chart can give a view of the battlefield that the Archetypes are seeing. If the therapist can be present to understanding what they are doing and why, then she can then be more present with the client.

This is not an intellectual struggle trying to "decipher" dreams. Working to understand the Archetypal plan for each dream helps the therapist be present with the client in a loving and compassionate way. Understanding what the Archetypes are not working on is equally important. The therapist may have an insight about a client, but the dreams are not working on that aspect. The therapist always follows the dreams, trusting the Archetypes in their plan, especially since the larger picture of the Archetypal plan is not usually evident.

Having a longer view of the work can help - the therapist can show the client the longer view of the process in the context of his specific psyche. Because the therapist is following the Archetype's lead, she is often dealing with several issues simultaneously. The therapist sometimes needs to bring different variables that seem divergent into relationship with each other. On the physical plane, it is difficult to do this all together at the same moment. The client and the therapist need time to process. Because the Archetype's puzzle is complicated with dynamics that do not always appear to go together, it is helpful for the therapist to understand at least what the Archetype is doing in the moment with specific dreams. If the therapist is not clear through working with the dreams, the client's chart can be used as a tool, even if it is imperfect. The chart shows process/feeling and pathological/emotional tendencies.

All human beings are incredibly complex. It is easy to make judgments based on the values of the external world, but it is nearly impossible for anyone on the outside to know what another person is working through in dreams. What may seem undesirable in the external world may be important to an individual's process work - such as the need to express anger or the need to leave a marriage. The therapist may need to support a client in a decision that, from the worldly perspective, seems wrong. But if the dreams support the decision, then the therapist will support the client. The therapist works on not thinking in terms of what the outer world expects or needs and not falling into the trap of believing that every individual has one issue and can be figured out from that issue. The therapist is interested in what the Archetypes want for the client.

Pathology, on the other hand, loves the values game: it loves being right, it loves altruism, it loves good values, good food, good friends, it loves good sex and good God. But in the Archetypal reality, the values of right and good is not really anything, just another variable of deception and distortion, not even indicating the presence of the Archetype. The dreams work on a level of consciousness that transcends the ability to perceive right from wrong, allowing the Archetypes to decide what needs to be confronted in a particular moment. This level of what is necessary for the client is not up to the judgment of the therapist. How could an individual be clear in the face of such overwhelming complexity. How could an individual possibly judge right from wrong.

Once a person descends through the layers of feeling, he is at the center of his essence, at the womb heart. The womb heart is the alchemical vessel where the core work of triangulation of Stage Two occurs. Once a person becomes the child, becomes the soul self and the womb heart opens, the work changes. The Archetype then begins to transform the child, having a direct and immediate relationship with the individual and working with essence.

When the client becomes available to the Archetypes as his child self, he is with the Archetypes even if he still has pathology to work through. When the client is with the Archetypes, miracles can happen. The client must be in his true soul self, but he does not necessarily need to be enlightened. He only needs to be available for wherever they are in any given moment.

Being in the soul self does not necessarily mean that a person is God-conscious. It simply means he can be a student with response capability with the Archetypes through feeling. This is not possible in Stage One and early Stage Two work. Individuals in Stage One and early Stage Two work are working through the layers that keep them from the Archetypes. Learning to allow the Archetypes to lead them through the labyrinth of their separation.

Inertia

The work may seem a simple matter of working dream to dream, piece to piece, feeling to feeling. But there is also the element of resistance to the process, which is a form of inertia. Inertia, which is in all things, is actually the thing that resists the true self of a person. When a client feels resistance, she feels it is her own resistance when, in fact, it is the resistance of the pathology. The inertia is caused by the resistance to feel into what a person truly is, whether the feelings are from the past or are new feelings emerging from the present. The pathology will fight via resistance the hurts and fears felt long ago that need to be re-experienced as much as it will fight the feelings of love, power and beauty that want to fuel the client's sense of understanding. In both cases, the inertia wants the client to stay exactly as she is - to move through life without feeling and without changing.

Even though inertia is of pathology, resistance is still part of free will because the client is always given the power of choice. The dreams can offer to the client the opportunity to face into the self, but only the client can choose to take the opportunity. It is so difficult to allow the process to unfold us, however, that a client will fight the very thing that loves her and wants to free her.

It is extremely difficult to allow the process to unfold us. Most choose the resistance and use it to fight the very thing that loves them and wants to free them. A client can be tricked, can stay in ignorance, can seem that she does not know the way or even that there is a way. Meanwhile, every myth, novel, song, video game is more or less a reflection of the dream journey. Most prefer to keep that journey a video game, a song, a novel, a myth so that they can live vicariously in the feelings of the unfoldment within others or even imagined others. This inertia is the biggest enemy facing a client.

The Long Arc and the Small Arc

In specific moments of the process, particular understanding is encouraged and nurtured in the dreams. In these moments, the threat to the client is minimal. These moments are the small arcs of the process.

Typically, clients are not aware of the longer arc of the process, the awareness of the journey from beginning to end. The longer and specific Archetypal Plan which is the defining intention for the individual. In this arc, the unfoldment works by one piece of work weaving into another through valleys, chasms, steep and winding paths ending in great plunges to nothingness. The longer arc of the work is an expression which the Archetypes understand. The resistance of the pathology is that the pathology is aware of the longer arc even if the client and the therapist are not. Pathology fights every step of the longer arc, fighting every issue that in any way reveals the connection to the next step of the longer arc.

As long as a client is wandering in circles that keep him safe from the longer arc, the level of resistance is usually relatively weak. The more focused and real the dreams manifest the cutting edge of the truth in the client, the more threatened the pathology becomes and the more the resistance flairs. Where the client would try to co-opt the therapist into staying in the wandering circles, the therapist is not open to being co-opted. The only reason for this is that the therapist does not make up the dreams. When the therapist follows the dreams, he is less likely to get lost in the confusing merry-go-round search for the truth.

For clients who are aware of their own resistance and how it works in them, they can actually gauge their process based on the level of resistance that rises up at particular moments in their work. They have learned that not only is inertia their enemy, but the closer they get to some deeper truth that may be of the long arc, the more the inertia/resistance will react.

The pathology is not against the work in the small arcs. It will offer little resistance, allowing the client to do a modicum of work as long as it does not open up the capability for the next piece to unfold. Humans can only see the small arc, the cause and effect type of work that seems to define their life and their behaviors. This is the arena many analysts and counselors are drawn toward, like a ship drawn to the Bermuda triangle. In this arena, the client and analyst can easily lose their way.

There is no therapist who can guide a person through the labyrinth of this work because the pathology is too tricky. It knows how to use resistance to steer therapy outside the longer arc. The true plan for a client comes from the master therapist of the psyche, through the dreams. The work of the therapist is to simply understand, acknowledge and follow the long arc as it is revealed in the unfoldment of a client, leading him to greater manifestation of his true self.

The long arc of the process for a client reveals the motifs of meaning that only make sense if the intention of the Divine is understood. Since a client does not understand the long arc, he will always be lost in the effort. A therapist must have gone through his own journey, at least in part, in order to understand the evolutionary process of dreams and their true intention of awakening the soul. This experience cannot be learned or studied. It must be encountered, experienced, felt and lived.

The small arcs are problem solving, finding solutions and causes. The long arc is unfoldment, death and alchemizing the soul so that it may rise again in the life of the client. There is no greater goal than the long arc.

Most people who come into this work are not aware of the long arc and it is not necessary for them to be aware of it. They may come into the work with smaller arc issues which present a series of problems. Once these issues are resolved, the work will present the opportunity to the client to move to the next step. Many who resolve the initial issues that brought them to the dreamwork may become threatened when the success of their work brings them beyond their initial understanding of what they wanted. When the dreams call them through their healing into something greater. Many people choose to stop the work at this stage. They may encounter the inertia, the resistance, which is a normal part of the process, and choose to not step into the long arc. The choice is entirely the client's and the therapist will support him in whatever he chooses. Many are called to the long arc, but few choose to answer.

When a client reaches the choice to break the inertia or to accept it and move through it anyway, he has reached a choice point. When a block of work has been achieved by a person, it inevitably leads to a choice point which can take him through an evolutionary spiral to the next opportunity. Each step is more terrifying then the last for, though a person is taken through with love, each step leads to more confrontations until the work is achieved and the soul can begin to emerge.

The most obvious area where inertia/resistance attacks is in the willingness to feel feelings as opposed to feeling emotions. Most people are very glad to be in emotions and choose them over feelings without ever knowing the difference. Once the emotions are revealed through the dreams, then the inertia becomes even stronger. The choice to feel is the greatest choice a client will make. It is never a commitment for the sake of commitment. It is the choice to feel for the sake of feeling.

Feelings are the raw material from which the soul is transformed through the process of Alchemy. The true battle for the soul is fought in two ways - by the client feeling his feelings and by confronting the false ideas of self and the emotional/behavioral realities that the client has lived.

The feelings shown in dreams are either the truth of who the client is or at least the beginning of the threads to the lost pieces of the true self coming together. The question is not only does the client have the courage and the desire to face into those feelings, but also does he have the desire to choose the courage. Once the choice is made, once the feeling threads are discovered, the client can become part of the longer arc, even if it is not understood. The client must have the willingness to move beyond the smaller arcs of understanding and problem solving in order to journey deeper into the true self.

The Banished - One Unheard or One Unhearing?

And I, the garden bird,
        wing of the underbrush,
spliced song of flower. I am
        the shadow's body, the hidden
made flesh, what veers between
        the branches of your thoughts.
And look, you are walking away
        as if I was not your answer.
Come back, the garden is lonely
        for you. The beebalm reddens
as the gaillardia sets sunward.
        To your turned back,
I fling my song.

Karla Van Vliet

SELF-ACCEPTANCE, THE WOMB HEART
AND THE ROLE OF THE RNA CODE

The womb heart is the sacred vessel inside every person where Archetypal transformational and alchemical work takes place. It is called the womb heart because it is the place that can receive and contain the Divine and is the place where the true soul of the individual can grow into relationship with the Divine.

In basic anatomy, between the womb and the world is the female vaginal opening and channel that receive the male phallus. In Archetypal Dreamwork, the Animus is the male energy and the Anima is the female energy. The womb heart is prepared with help from the Anima so the Animus can enter.

The Necessity of Self-Acceptance

The Anima helps create and prepare the womb heart in an individual through acceptance, while the individual finds her way to that womb heart by following the thread of a particular feeling. It is, of course, a dilemma. Before a person can have the capacity to fully feel feelings, she must first have self-acceptance. Without self-acceptance, a person is not going to accept any feelings that come out of that self. The degree to which a person does not accept herself is the degree to which the feelings are buried.

For example, if a client has trauma in her past and she feels responsible, perhaps shameful, in any way for what happened, then she is not able to feel the pain of the trauma. In order to feel the pain of the trauma, the client needs to accept that she is worthy of feeling the pain. To feel the pain or loss or grief, the client must be in her innocence. The client may feel other pain around the trauma but it is often something like anger, judgment, nihilism. It is not the real pain. Pathology guards the vessel of the womb heart with great tenacity. It does not want the client to feel any real feelings or to get close to the vessel.

This level of acceptance is difficult because it is really unconscious acceptance. Most people have controls in place because of the lack of self-acceptance and the drive for self protection. Control is built upon will and will is built upon loss at some level. In the example of a person with trauma, the person blocks the pain without realizing she is blocking it. She is not even aware that she is not accepting the self or even what part of the self she is not accepting. This is why deep acceptance involves fear. It thrusts the client into feeling something that she has never accepted.

Without this self-acceptance, a client essentially rejects her child self and her own vulnerability. Most people are polluted by concepts of what is acceptable to feel, leaving them unconsciously repulsed by their true feelings. This may be projected into the world, with the person wanting others or even God to accept her. The real issue is that the person does not accept her self.

When an Archetype presents a client with a feeling in a dream, it is an opportunity to begin working toward the womb heart. Most clients respond with fear and come face to face with their ability or inability to learn to accept the feeling. The Archetype always accepts the client but cannot really help with deep alchemical transformation without the self-acceptance of the client. To do this, the client must feel feelings she does not want to feel. When the feeling is felt, the client has also accepted it and has begun to accept the self as well.

The issue of accepting the self and therefore being able to feel the feelings of woundedness can be the most critical part of the work. The way a person manifests her own inability to acknowledge who she is and what she has suffered never solves the problem. When manifesting through anger, manipulation, projecting into the world, experiencing vicariously through others, it may seem that the person is accepting feelings, but it may be just a reflection of a profound sense of unacceptability. When a person demands the cake, it does not mean she wants it or feels she deserves it. Often, the most entitled people who make great demands for what they want are actually lost from their true sense of worth.

There are many manifestations of how an individual does not accept the self and feelings. For many, it is simply too painful to accept the self that has become lost. Shame and rejection of the self allows a person to mute the pain of the loss of the true, vulnerable, entitled self.

Young children understand they are precious. Any betrayal that comes in this state is the greatest hurt imaginable to the soul. No one really wants to return to this kind of pain. When the pain of the loss of self is rejected, it becomes not only desirable to remain insular to it but necessary in order to perpetuate the current state of life and all the projections that are part of it.

As necessary as it is to return to feel through early experiences as shown by dreams, most clients avoid the return because of the profound sense of hurt. However, it is the only way to reclaim the true self, for it is the true self that feels the hurt. It is also the true self that can feel the love and that can be in relationship with the Divine. Avoiding the hurt means avoiding the self and avoiding the self means losing the capacity for mutuality and peace with regards to the Divine. The loss of connection also means the loss of connection with others in the world - spouses, children, family, friends. The core of the self must reemerge and it reemerges through the most excruciating feelings. Pathology counts on resistance to these feelings and it lives on the denial of them. When pathology draws energy from the denial of feelings, emotions and behaviors can rule the psyche and the life of an individual.

The Anima works by accepting the client, but really, this acceptance is a trick. She is working to get the client to accept something in the true self. The block to self-acceptance is the person. Most people spend their time either in the ego or at the bottom of a dark well never taking responsibility. It is difficult work for the Archetype to help a client accept part of the true self. A person protects the self from the world and, more important, from her own feelings and experience. Usually without even being aware of doing it.

Girl in Wedding Dress
By Laura Ruth

Dream:

> I came up to a low building and went inside. It was a wedding. Standing by herself against the back wall was a beautiful very dark-skinned child in a white dress that spread out like a hoop and with flowers in her hand in front. She was quiet, her head slightly bowed, looking very reverent. I was moved by her.

From Laura:

> In the gestalt she answered why she was there: I am this wedding, it can only go on because of me. Are you getting married? I am being recognized. Are you waiting for me to recognize you? Yes. What part of me are you? I am your rejected parts. What part? The part you cannot accept. You feel I am too much for others.

> She continued to be gestalted in relationship to other dreams: She said: I am waiting for you so that I can be born, waiting for you to come and wipe the tears off my face and then I will wipe off your tears. I am touching you. Expose me to the world by being with me in everything that you do, through humbleness of reverence - it is important to see the beauty instead of being caught up in the joy of doing. You are the one who is in pain, but you have too much shame to accept it - you need to accept my pain first.

In this dream, the idea of the child being married is overwhelming and could not be received by Laura. Instead, the child simply wants Laura to recognize her. To recognize that she exists inside of Laura is a major step in her growth. The child is agitated - in the gestalt process, she cries and says, "You are the one who is in pain but you have too much shame to accept it. You need to accept my pain first." This is the key. In this statement, the girl challenges Laura to realize how unworthy she feels. To believe that she is going to be unified with the Divine is beyond Laura's understanding of her self. She is willing to wipe the child's tears, but not to have the tears. However, the tears are the blessing of Divine love. Recognizing the girl is a start on the road to self-acceptance, to even know that this side of her exists. As the girl says, "You need to accept my pain first."

Feeling the Way to the Womb Heart

Once a client begins to accept his feelings, he can begin to find his way to his womb heart, the place where essence lives. In the womb heart, a client can contain experience without projection. For the first time, everything is about the client instead of being about something in the external world. He can hold the self. This does not mean that there is no pathology. If there is pathology, when in the womb heart, the client can pull the projection back from the external world into the feeling underneath.

When this happens, a client begins to be allergic to pathology. He begins to feel repulsed by the way he has been, the way he has lived outside his truth instead of feeling repulsed by his feelings. The client will still have reactions, but the focus moves from the external trigger to the internal process and pulling the projection back. Some clients in this place find it difficult to be in the world or to speak because they are so conscious of how they are not living from their authentic selves.

Part of being in the womb heart is letting go of the need to hold onto anything. When there is acceptance, there is no need to hold on. The client is in a state of doing his work and letting go of the control. An issue that often arises when a client reaches this place is that he assumes the outer behavior should immediately reflect the inner change. This is a wrong assumption, for the client may continue with negative behavioral patterns long after he has let go of the need for them. They become habits instead of the compulsion of the pathology and another layer of the work. The womb heart is not a complete state - it is the place where completion can occur.

Inner work cannot be measured by what happens externally for a client. There is some correlation and some changes will occur, but it is important for the client and the therapist to stay with the inner process. Judgment, both on the self and on others, is based on actions. How things "look" externally is not the focus because pathology can easily have a person "look" good. What is important is the inner work.

How the Animus enters the womb heart is different for men and women. For women, the Animus enters through trying to make love; to enter the deepest point of a woman's feeling. The Animus will even make love to a woman client who is not yet capable of sustaining the connection in order to deepen the capability of the client. Women are designed for this kind of receiving.

Men, of course, are not. One way the Animus enters a male client spiritually is not sexually but through the Father. At its best, the father/son relationship is extremely sensual. A father who has a good relationship with a son touches the boy with great tenderness - smoothing his hair and engaging in a great deal of physical contact. Most boys do not have this relationship with their biological fathers. Touching and intimacy belong in a healthy male relationship. The Animus will enter into that system - in the Archetypal Realm, there is a great deal of intimacy in the male component.

Every time a client moves into essence, the Animus is typically there. In early stages of the work, the relationship between the client and the Animus is usually through a shield of pathology and ego. This is very different from when the relationship comes from a place inside the client, the place of the womb heart. The womb heart does not have to be completely clean and the client may still have deep wounds that need healing, but it is the place that can begin to contain God.

Ultimately, the purpose of the womb heart is to contain the Archetype inside the client. The capacity to contain personal experience allows the client to contain Archetypal experience. The essence of being in essence is the ability to acknowledge, feel and contain this experience. When the client is in this reality, in his womb heart, he can automatically let go of his attachment to the outer world.

The Archetypes cannot stay with a person unless the person is in the place where the Archetypes can enter. In the womb heart, a client can experience the Archetypes as if they are really in his body because it is so real.

Two Hearts

The relationship of the womb heart with the Animus actually means that there are two hearts. The client's heart and the heart of the Animus become the same. Once this linkage is made, the client can move into the Third Stage work of fulfilling her calling, whatever it may be. When a person is fulfilling her calling, she does not do her work as a service. She does it, instead, because it serves her soul. The client can act from her heart, from love, from her passion, which is what the Archetypes want for her.

Many people are involved in service work as if they are carrying a great weight. For those who are fulfilling their calling from the womb heart, it is not a burden at all, but a place of connection. It does not matter if they are ministers or social workers or Peace Corps volunteers or accountants. To do this kind of work, the client must be relatively free of ego for the sake of her own freedom in the service.

How the Archetype comes into an individual and how the two hearts, the two wills, His love with the client's are combined is different based on each individual because everyone is unique. Each person's connection is different and comes into being in a way that works best for the individual. There is no "correct" or "appropriate" way, no "role" for the essence of the client to assume. The process allows the client to unfold as only she can unfold, not as a therapist or society or even someone else doing dreamwork unfolds or believes she should unfold.

When a client begins to bloom in this way, in her unique way, the job of the therapist is to get out of the way. The Archetype's power and the client's power elevate together and then extend out into the world. At this point, it is the combined will that drives the client's spiritual and feeling life.

The issue of essence and the womb heart is extremely important. It is easy to use the mind to change and learn while never making it down into the womb heart. Many people have the tendency to want to stay in the mind and to not descend into the depths of the deepest core of their being. Instead, they create a womb mind and believe they are enlightened because they have expanded their mind. Many people who have done spiritual work have reached this place. While expansion of the mind is valid, it is not the core work of Archetypal dreamwork because the Archetypes do not want a person to have an expanded mind without the container of the womb heart. The mind has very little to do with the realm in which the Archetypes work. An expanded mind can be helpful when it helps the client to take the next step. But the client still must take the step into the womb heart, the holy place of the soul that is within.

Divine Birth - When a Child is Born from the Divine

When a woman client finds herself pregnant in a dream, it is always exciting for it predicates good things to come in her process. The good thing is not a new dress or a new car, but a previously lost aspect of the soul descending through the thick matter of the world into the self.

The tendency of most women when a child appears in a dream is to mother the baby, which is understandable and sometimes necessary. But it is not the point of the relationship with the baby and the client. The gift of the baby in a dream is that the client can become the aspect that the baby represents. Whatever consciousness the baby brings to the psyche can be infused in the client. This is a dream motif that usually manifests for women clients, but it is not entirely uncommon for the Anima to give birth for a male client.

It is unique, however, when the Anima gives birth for a female client. This happens when a client is unable to carry her own child because of some wound or dysfunction around the feminine in the client's psyche. The explanation for the Anima birthing for a client is always specific to the client.

Dream:

> I am standing by a river and I want to dive in. Other people are there and they say it is too shallow for me to dive. Others are jumping in feet first or landing on their backs. One man who stands out from the crowd says gently to me, "Do not go in." I felt gypped. I climb down a concrete ledge or two toward the water. Shift.

> I am standing in a house. A large man is playing relaxing music. My friend Sheila is there and she has a small baby. It takes me ages to remember that she was pregnant and to realize that the baby is hers. I notice that she has on three-inch heels. She is teaching and I think she is going to observe the class I am teaching. My class is like a party and we start late. I feel anxious. I say something to Sheila about her high heels and she replies, "What are you on about?" I am just about to say that her femininity makes me feel like a slug, but Christine shows up and makes the situation better.

It is clear why the client cannot carry her own child. Sheila is the Anima and the client projects all manner of beauty onto her because of her own lack. She feels terrible about herself as a woman and at one point projects the high heels onto the Anima. The heels are probably just part of the projection of her own unworthiness. Such unworthiness around being a woman has crippled her ability to be accepted as a woman, mostly by herself. The wound is clear, as she would like to be a woman like Sheila.

For this client, it must be imperative for the new consciousness to be born in her rather than the dreams spending time helping her accept her femininity. At the time of this dream, the client had been doing the work for less than a year. At this relatively early stage of the work, it is not clear yet why the Archetypes decided to present a birth in this way. It is enough that they have and the client and therapist respect and follow the direction of the dream.

Also in the process of this dream, the client has been told by the Animus that she is not ready to jump in the water like everyone else. It is not uncommon for the Animus to ask enthusiastic clients to wait, even if it makes the client sad, as in this case. The psyche needs to change in some way and the client is being told to be patient. Everyone wants to be through the process quickly, to arrive at connection now. But blind spots often do not allow the client to experience or know the things that are needed that are not yet possessed. How can a person know what she needs if she has never had it. It is impossible to compare current experience with connected experience until the connection is made.

That the client compares herself negatively to Sheila is reason enough to understand the extreme importance of self-acceptance in the process of personal growth. Without self-acceptance, the womb heart, which is the vessel the child is birthed through, cannot be created. And without self-acceptance, there is no container for the self or the child. This is probably the main reason why the Anima will birth for a client. The Anima's first order of business in the psyche is to support and to heal negative feelings the client feels for the self. Self acceptance is the cornerstone for the client to not only accept but to feel her feelings. Self-loathing renders the psyche incapable of containing its own experience.

The child is necessary for this process. For this particular client, rather than encourage the healing that would allow her to birth a child on her own in a dream, the birth is done for her. This is truly an immense gift from the Archetypes.

Why Divine Birth

Dream:

A capsule drops to earth and crashes. A baby comes out and is alone. I take him in.

In this dream, the baby is delivered sputnik style, straight from the promised land to the client's doorstep. Since the dream presented the child not from the womb of the client or the womb of another woman or friend, the Archetypes clearly want the client to know that the baby has come from another place, another realm. It is as if the better part of the self has suddenly been born and brought into the client's consciousness.

There is an old story that relates to this motif:

A soul living in heaven and basking in Divine love is visited by a Messenger. The Messenger tells the soul that it is time to enter the world through a mortal birth. The soul becomes upset and refuses, saying, "But if I return to the world, I will become stupid again. I will not remember the love, I will forget my Master. I will be unable to know my true home." The Messenger replied, "Do not worry, we will find you. Someone will be there to awaken your memory."

Perhaps the baby in the space capsule is the consciousness of the once known descending back to earth for the client. The one who comes to awaken the client to her memory of the Divine. The one who knows the sweetness of the Archetypal Realm and is coming to help the person integrate this knowledge in even the most difficult of her realities. The dense pressure of living life crushes the most subtle and profound understanding and awarenesses. This client had developed the necessary understanding, had created her particular womb heart vessel and was ready to have this child live within her soul.

Development of the womb heart is necessary for the child to have a place to live within the self of a client. The infusion of the once known consciousness from this child can alter the psyche immeasurably, catapulting the client's ego self into a recognition of all that was known and the ability to receive continued spiritual guidance in a new way.

The RNA Code

Biologically, besides DNA, every cell in the body carries the RNA code. Unlike DNA which is made from a combination of DNA from both the father and the mother, RNA does not change from generation to generation. The RNA of a mother is the exact RNA of her children and is the exact RNA of her mother. The origin of the RNA code is a complete mystery - no one knows if it traces back to some original mother or series of mothers or if it evolved from other original codes. Scientists conjecture that RNA code is potentially billions of years old.

What does this mean potentially for the psyche?

It is not too much to conjecture that the RNA code carries information intimately related with psychological deep memory. If the code does not change from generation to generation, then it is entirely possible that the collective memories of all the generations of a particular tree are carried as if through a tunnel through the RNA code leaving echoes and imprints in each individual's psyche. This tunnel for memory is also a tunnel for consciousness, both good and bad, to move through the past creating and recreating similar emotional realities that are birthed from female to female, generation to generation.

This massive tunnel in the unconscious that moves from woman to woman carries not only collective memory but also the collective dysfunctions and experiences of women and men from a particular tree. These memories, dysfunctions, experiences work as an imprint in every person's psyche and represent the source of the dysfunction in the psyche. It is the blueprint for how a person anchors the self in the world rather than being anchored with the Divine.

Because this tunnel of an encoded original mother or series of mothers reaches into the primordial past and carries the dysfunctions, it is a bond that needs to be broken in order for the individual to have a full, mutual relationship with the Divine.

Psychologists strive to find a smoking gun for many dysfunctions within a person. Perhaps the moment came from a person's life but perhaps it is contained in the collective memory of the person and it took a particular situation or time of development to trigger the collective memory or wound encoded in the RNA. This, of course, does not mean that childhood experiences are invalid. The implication is that the impact they have on a person's trauma may be less than originally believed. The trauma may be a result of a wound that travels back through generations and is already buried in the sublayers of the individual. When a person moves through the healing of a wound, it is not just his wound he is healing, but the wound of untold generations. The miracle is that the Divine can enact that healing and help a person reclaim his soul from the mortal reality to which it is attached.

In dreams, a child that is birthed through a Divine birth - such as being birthed through the Anima or arriving in a space capsule - represents the consciousness of the client that is not connected to the RNA code. This is mirrored in many mythologies from many different cultures where a great figure - both men and women - is birthed not from the seed of a woman. For example, in Christianity, Christ was born from Mary's womb, but was not of her seed. Likewise, in Buddhism, Buddha was conceived when his mother, Maya, dreamed she was brought to a heavenly realm by four angels where an elephant with six tusks and a lotus blossom came to her and entered into her womb.

Although every person is chained to the past through the RNA code, the true essence of every soul lies in the fundamental knowledge of the presence of the Divine and Divine love. This is more powerful and potent than any past experience or ancestral history.

Sometimes There Was a Light

There were times I sat along the river that spring,
before my life led me away,
stripped days of rusted cars, bedsprings, old barns
passed on the grown-over shore path,
when the sun sank through the heavy sky
in such a way it created a light which touched
the sand, packed hard by the river's flood water,
so it softened in my fingers and eased collected heat
into my bones stacked above it;
and the bark's dark leavings that clung
to logs drifted up and docked
on shore, so I thought I could read
their life stories: ground coaxing from roots
the loss of connection, the cut of air in their falling,
the only sound of their grief, the splash
of branches in icy water that dragged them
away from the only place
they had know in their long lives;
and the water on its course
through the fields of ten farmers—
cut by so many springs there is no one alive now
who has known it straight or even
heard tell of such a path—
winding its way though the green pastures;
and touched, even my own skin— that was the way
I knew it best, that light,
for when a thing has touched you,
you know something of its intention—

                              Karla Van Vliet

Trauma and the Repression of Fear

Trauma, as defined in terms of the psyche, occurs when an individual becomes disassociated from the soul self and feelings through the repression of fear. Unfortunately, when fear is lost, the door to the soul self is also lost.

Fear is the necessary part of the process of disassociation - when something happens to a child where the child is wounded, he may or may not remember the event, but he will remember the fear. It is a natural response to a traumatic event. The door to reconnecting to the soul self that the client disassociated from is through the fear that helped the disassociation in the first place. Sometime in childhood or perhaps even before childhood in the ancestral past, the innocence of the child self was broken through a situation or situations that created fear in the child self. The cause of the fear does not have to be extreme, such as a rape or an attack - it can simply be the existential separation from the Divine in which the love that the child self once knew suddenly is gone. Even if there were no traumatic events, the mere separation from the child self through the normal developmental process always produces fear. The underlying loss of the child creates a wedge of fear between the conscious self and the forgotten child.

Fear is the geiger counter to the treasure of the soul self. Often it is not even necessary to trace the cause of the fear. All aspects of the self that are lost require an awareness of fear as part of the journey back to those aspects.

When a client in the dreamwork begins to experience his feelings, he also notices what happens when he is no longer feeling his feelings. He becomes aware of his reactivity when he has lost connection, a reactivity that covers a layer of anxiety. The anxiety he feels is a mutation of fear that covers the wound. If the client can work through the anxiety, he can probably find his way back to his feelings, back to feeling the pain of his wound.

Anxiety is typically covered by emotions such as shame, anger, self-loathing, pride and arrogance because it carries such Archetypal healing potential to open to the soul self. As a client enters into the descent, he may believe he will die and never return or that he will lose the self, the ego, and be completely unable to function. But the descent is simply moving through all the layers of feelings that open to the true self.

This may seem simple - connect with feelings, move through them and support will come for the healing work. With the support and the continuing movement, the client discovers his true self and his new life can emerge with connection to the Divine. But the journey, the descent, is difficult, arduous and requires the capacity and willingness for change.

The Shame and The No
by Laura Ruth

Shame of Receiving the Gift   Saying NO to the Gift

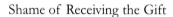

The black energy of shame, of saying no is the energy put on the self

Dream:

> A woman comes in very excited. I know her but cannot remember her. She has a gift for me. She is really pressing it on me by really trying to get me to receive the gift. She is very much in my face. I am not interested and am feeling pushed upon - I feel like I do not want anything to do with her. I tell her I must go to the bathroom first, which is what I was going to do when she came in - I want to wash my hands. I feel that she interrupted me. I go behind a curtain into the bathroom area, and she is so excited she pulls back the curtain. I say please - wait. I am kind of appalled that she follows me into the bathroom. I feel heavy, tired. She thrusts the gift on me- a box in white tissue - and in it is a device that holds a child very upright. It reminds her, and me, of something I invented when I was working with children - an elaborate earth structure form thing that met every developmental need a child has as s/he grows. It is as if the thing is there in the living room, but I do not know if it is the strength of the memory or actually the thing itself. It is really there though. (I was not sure in the dream if it was there, but in the working of the dream, it became clear that it was there.) Seeing it, the feeling is exhaustion at how much effort and ingenuity it had taken to put it all together, and her excitement is so strong. I could see her excitement but could not feel it. I had no response to it. I could only feel how invested I had been in creating, designing, figuring out. How relentlessly I used to work.

From Laura:

> I woke up swimming in images of how I used to work and the pathological will that drove me. Feeling almost afraid of it, horrified of it, maybe shame. When I went into the session Marc said, "But this is the Anima giving you your gift. This is your gift. You can see into what people need as they grow." I could see how desperate I was to

refuse the gift. How hard it is for me to stand with my gift and be seen or acknowledged. It took me a little while looking over this period of time to realize that this is the big No dream.

For Laura, the feeling of realizing how relentlessly she used to work is the absolute representation of her soul infused by shame and doubt. This is a person who was born with a spiritual power that is finally beginning to emerge. Her success in allowing her potency to come to light required that she move through her trauma. Such power, when suppressed, creates a terrible sense of repression around all the ways in which she felt called to care for and help others. Becoming so oppressed is tantamount to abuse, abuse that visited her in relation to her primary relationships. The external reflected the internal nihilism that had been in place since she was a young child when she discovered there was no room for her understanding of things.

In the dream, the woman visiting her is the part of her that got separated so long ago. The part that is ready to move back in at the time of this dream, but that Laura was not ready for because she was so filled with fear, so lost in the fear that it had been overwhelmed by shame. Not understanding her fear, she could not accept it because it came as trauma and paralysis, which visited her in an annihilating way. When this happens, there can be no perspective. What Laura needed to do was to just breath in the fear, breath in the paralysis, breath into the trauma anyway. Here she is, in her shame, her paralysis, her numbness, her absolute unacknowledgement of her self. This child self is the primary self that was lost. Moving through the fear, trauma and shame helped her to reconnect to her real self.

Trauma can often be a guide for the descent for it announces and shouts where there is something wrong in the psyche. It is a known wound. Without trauma, something is still wrong, but there is no easy indicator. The path for clients without trauma is more subtle and hidden. Regardless of difficulties or ease in childhood, most people become separated from the Divine. Anxiety can be an opportunity to discover a feeling that is underneath it.

All of this is the norm in most people's psyche or the "normal neurotic." The event, the pain of the event and the anxiety are either in the subconscious waiting to be retrieved or they are projected out into the world. Even when they are projected, which is pathological, this is also an opportunity. Projection, if it is in the awareness of the individual, can be used as a chance to rediscover the pain through an event in the outer world.

Projection makes the feelings that trigger it unavailable to the client and render those feelings useless for they mutate into emotion. When a feeling from the past is attached to the outer world and the present, it makes the feeling no longer the client's feeling and is not available in the individuation process. Even when the events of the outer world are similar to the events in the past, it is very difficult for the Archetypes to work with the outer events. In these cases, the dreams present a story and perspective to correct and redirect the projection from the outer to the inner through the process of introjection. In this way, projection can be used but only when the projection is brought into the client's awareness and the client is ready to begin the process of introjection.

For fear that is repressed through a major traumatic event, such as rape or another violent act, the anxiety is not just under the projection because it is not projected. The anxiety is too deeply buried and the fear too deeply repressed. Working with clients who are traumatized in this way is much more difficult because the anxieties and feelings are not so easily obtainable.

For a client without a major trauma, he can work through issues such as control or fear of rejection to reach other feelings. This is working through the layer of the subconscious. For a client with a major trauma, the trauma will manifest abstractly because the client is unable to get to his feelings. The fear and the feelings are repressed down past the subconscious and into the unconscious.

The dreams will not present feelings or bring a client to that which cannot be retrieved.

The only way a dream can bring a client to what he cannot retrieve is through the birthing of a new ability to feel. Trauma cannot be "birthed" out of the unconscious, but the ability to feel can be birthed. Through the new ability to feel, the feelings and fear around the trauma can be retrieved.

Trauma in the Psyche versus Traumatic Experiences

Trauma is very damaging to the psyche. Although a traumatized individual does not heal in the same way as those without trauma, trauma can be processed and healed. The therapist's expectations are simply different when working with a client with trauma.

Extreme trauma cases are rare because not all traumatic events cause trauma in a person. Issues such as sexual molestation and destructive events may be part of an individual's history, but if she did not repress the fear around the events then it is not trauma in this sense.

It has been fashionable to make traumatic events worse then they may be in the person's psyche, allowing the person to hide behind trauma. And, of course, some traumatic events are worse than first realized. The current value system has an expectation of how a person should react to traumatic events. But this expectation is false. Many people who have had incredibly difficult childhoods have no trauma in their psyche.

For example, there are many cases of people being sexually active with a brother or uncle or other adult where the person as an adult is aware of the memories and the feelings. This kind of event will dictate how the pathology forms in that person, but if she is aware of her feelings around the events then it is not a trauma in the psyche.

There is a great difference between trauma and traumatic events. Therapists cannot make the assumption that a traumatic event in a person's past makes the person traumatized.

One of the biggest dangers in the field of psychology is psychologists assuming memories in clients about events that may or may not have happened. They may think that the neurosis is so developed that some trauma may have happened. But for some people, their trauma may be embedded in the RNA code which carries the collective memory of ancestral history and psychological disease through the mother. This error of negativism around the source of illness has influenced even the more conservative psychologies because of the desire to find reasons for neuroses - to find the smoking gun. In the medical field, it is not acceptable to not have the answer. But there may not be an answer, for every person carries the summation of her ancestral history.

If there is a negative push to find reasons, it is not much of a leap to invent them. This can cause psychologists to lead people to remember events that never occurred and then falsely accuse others of sexual abuse. The documentation of psychologists manipulating client's memories is surprising and disturbing.

In the dreamwork, the therapist trusts the dreams. If an event does not manifest in a dream, then it is not accepted unless the client has a clear memory or sense of the event.

When a client does have a memory of the event, then there is no trauma in the psyche because the event is not repressed. Instead, the person has reaction to the event, a reaction that the Archetypes can work with in the dreams. When a person is not traumatized in this way, when she has her memory and her feelings are intact, then her reactions to the known event (not the event, of course) which develop into pathology are her responsibility. Intact feelings and reactions can be worked with and through. When a client avoids known feelings, it can be a decision that can end the process of the dreamwork.

When a client is using traumatic events to avoid doing her work, she may project onto the therapist. She may feel that the therapist is insensitive when the therapist challenges her reactions to the traumatic event. She may even feel treated unfairly both by the therapist and the dreams. This kind of client is attached to the idea of being a victim. A person who insists on being a victim cannot do real work because she only wants to feel sorry for herself and wants her therapist to feel sorry for her as well. The therapist, led by the dreams, focuses instead on how she has lived in reaction and how she can move out of that reaction. This, of course, does not invalidate her pain around the traumatic events. Instead, it helps the client face into her pain so that she can feel it and release it.

When people with traumatic experiences focus on blame, the blame is usually an avoidance of the anxiety of the feeling. In this work, the therapist challenges the client to face into her feelings, all of them, knowing that feelings do not hurt a person. It is necessary for both the client and the therapist to have the mindset of a warrior. If a dream presents the feelings and/or situation, then it is not trauma in the psyche and it is time for the client to face into it. The therapist does not make choices - he simply follows the client's dreams.

When a client does have trauma, there are places that she cannot access at first. The dreams will circle the trauma in a way that is necessary for the client - it is up to the dreams to decide how the trauma is approached and confronted. For example, the following is a dream of a woman with trauma in her psyche:

My brothers and sisters are being put through a meat grinder. I feel terrified.

This dream shows that something is terribly wrong. The dream evokes terror in the client around something terrible, but the something is abstract, a metaphor. The dream shows the therapist that this was the feeling reality of the woman's childhood. In the outer world, the woman knew that her father regularly raped her sisters, but she had no memory of it happening to her. Early in her work, she asked her father if he had had sex with her. He laughed, saying, "You don't remember?" The father is a very sick man, still believing that what he did was fine.

The client had so much trauma and fear that the traumatic events and the feelings around them were too deep to remember. The client later had this dream:

I am lying in bed and my father comes in and lies on top of me. The dream blurs and
I go blank.

This dream helped the client to remember that when her father came to her at night, she closed her eyes and acted as if she were asleep.

In the early dream, the dream and the Archetypes only ask the client to feel the terror. In the second dream, they only show what she could retrieve. She could retrieve remembering her father entering the room and then pretending to sleep. For many clients with trauma, the dreams do not ask the client to remember the trauma. They will ask for the client to remember the feeling and the fear around the trauma. In this example, it was enough for the client to remember the terror and to remember closing her eyes. Releasing the fear is enough. It is, however, not easy.

Another example of trauma: a male client was raped by a man when he was five years old at a party with his parents. The client had a great deal of shame about the rape, but no real memory of the event. The fear was so repressed that he could not reach it, so his dreams did not address it directly. Instead, he had dreams of being afraid to go into water, showing his fear of the fear.

This repression of fear for clients with trauma in their psyches is extremely destructive because fear is a natural door to the inner world of the Archetypes, the Divine. The act of blocking fear also blocks the very fabric of Alchemical change. For a person with trauma, any fear leads to the trauma. When it is repressed, all fear in the psyche, including Archetypal fear, becomes paralyzed.

Clients with trauma cannot use fear initially as an avenue because it activates a paralysis in the psyche. And yet, fear is an integral part of the process of becoming conscious. With trauma, the individual has no feelings surrounding the event except terror.

With a traumatic experience - a traumatic event or experience that is remembered - there is an unconscious shift of the mind, a reaction, to not feel the feeling anymore. But the feeling is acknowledged and therefore retrievable. It is a deal that can be undone. With trauma - repressed feeling - such a deal is never made because there was no control. The client with trauma does not have direct reactions, only secondary reactions.

For most people who do not have this level of trauma in their psyche, the therapist can challenge them to feel something as it is shown in their dreams and they can move through their feelings. For those who have trauma, they often do not know it is present. They will want to do the work, but just cannot seem to do it.

Trauma does not necessarily harm the soul self or child self. Trauma seems, instead, to protect the innocence of the soul self from the devastating event. Of course, this is not how the client with trauma feels. The feelings of guilt or responsibility are usually superimposed on top of the feeling. This protection must be cracked in order for the client to reach essence and the child self.

Emotions such as guilt and shame are used in the psyche so that the person no longer has to feel into terrible feelings. They are used in the same way that shock is used in the physical body after a severe injury. With shock, the person cannot feel anything because the body is protected from feeling the excruciating pain. In the same way, the psyche uses emotions to numb out the excruciating pain of the trauma. But just as the body comes back into feeling, the psyche needs to re-feel the feelings in order for the original health to return.

Using Traumatic Experiences to Stay Safe

People who have traumatic experiences in their past and who want to believe they have trauma often will use the experience to stay safe and not face themselves. The greater the traumatic experience, the greater a client who is not traumatized can use it as justification to not change. In these cases, the therapist cannot caretaker the client. If the dreams call for it, the dreamwork will challenge the client around his reactions and uses of the traumatic experiences. It is difficult work - everyone has some traumatic experience in their life.

If an individual is looking to avoid his feelings, whatever he uses as avoidance is a problem. People use anything to avoid feeling - traumatic events, prayer, meditation, even having the cleanest car or being the best person. Whatever is used by the client will be challenged by the dreams and the therapist. Anything used to deny feeling is a reactive state.

Those with courage in this work do not use difficult childhoods as an excuse to continue leading a miserable life. They make a choice to open to their feelings and to take responsibility for growth instead of languishing in unhappy emotional realities.

In the natural developmental process, Freud postulated that between the ages of two and puberty, children go through a stage where they are in a state of essence. But because there is no ego development during this period, memory does not hold it well. An ego is necessary for memory.

The more an individual is open and in essence, the less likely he will have a clear memory. The problem is that conventional therapy often looks at these blocks of no memory as evidence of trauma. Traumatic experiences can cause memory blocks, of course, but they do not always cause trauma in the psyche. To have memory blocks does not mean trauma exists.

The process of the work is to regain that state of essence and to have a healthy and whole ego at the same time. In fact, it is the ego that creates the self-awareness to be the vessel to allow the child self to emerge into the client's consciousness. In a dream, the client suddenly will be the child self, experiencing the world from that self. It just happens. Until then, the client is still separate.

This connection to the child self is not the I-Thou relationship that exists with the Archetypes. The client is either the child self or she is not. Having a relationship with the child self is only a beginning step in the reclamation process. Once the client becomes the child self, the soul self, her relationship with the Divine can occur. The Archetypes never enter into relationship with a client without the child self.

Trauma and even traumatic experiences do not block a person from being able to reach this state. It is possible that a person with courage can find the child self again and reclaim the Divine love.

Love

Out of dark, you,

like a lone goose crossing the moon
seen first by the startled heart,

like the seeds of my calling
sprung from the tilled garden.

A kindling.

Here in the belly of what is known.

Open wings, to flame
there

nothing but consumption.

Karla Van Vliet

The Map of the Journey through the Psyche

Jacob's Ladder usually begins to emerge in advanced work when a client has a deeper receptivity necessary to be in relationship with the Animus. In the Ladder, there are three rungs of experience - essence, sensuality and grace. They are all part of the experience of connection in the unfolding of the client's understanding of God's love. When Jacob's Ladder is finally reached by a client through Dying to Self and Dying to the Divine, the pathology has lost a great deal of power and transformation and Alchemy can begin.

Sensuality is vital to the process of reclamation of the soul self because it represents God's love as the individual experiences it in the body. It is as important for the body to awaken as it is for consciousness to awaken. In working with sensuality, people may have dreams that are uncomfortable.

Union with the Girl
by Kristin Kehler

Dream:

I am in bed with girl; I am a little older, around twelve. The man and others are in the room, too. The girl and I are having some kind of sex, fun and natural. She is a hermaphrodite with a little penis inside me. It is hard to tell where she begins and I end, hard to tell ourselves apart. Later I feel guilty.

From Kristin:

> This felt very sensual and playful and sexual all at once. I felt both a little fear, surprise and a thrill when I could feel the little penis inside me. I loved the feeling of not being able to tell our boundaries apart. It reminds me of very intimate sexual experiences when I am just not the regular me, but joined to the universe. I am not sure when or where the guilt came from, but suddenly I felt back to my old self and full of judgments. Separate, wanting to get away.

This dream motif does not relate to sexuality - it relates to sensuality. The client may respond to the dream with fear that she is a pedophile. These types of dreams bring the client into the amoral, natural, free child self that lacks self-awareness. Many children are in this state of being as children, where they have no self-awareness and inhibitions. This state is called, as coined by Freud, polymorphous perverse and is characterized by an infant or young child displaying sexual tendencies that have no specific direction. It represents a time in childhood, usually between the ages of three and nine when a child has little self-awareness and experiments with sensuality through the body. If a child has self-awareness, then she is not polymorphous perverse.

These types of dreams would not be offered to a client with sexual dysfunction or moral issues because they are not meant as literal dreams. The dream is not asking the client to actually have a sexual relationship with a young girl. It is only a door to access sensuality. These dreams are terrifying because the dream is confronting the client with the terror of intimacy.

Sensuality can be a frightening place to return to or discover as an adult. Dreams around this issue may present images that are uncomfortable, but coming to terms with the sensual polymorphous place is essential.

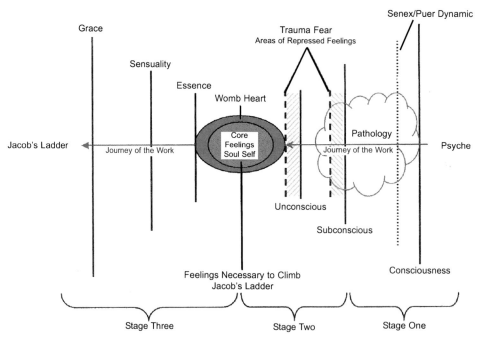

When a person begins the process of the dreamwork, she is on the outer edge of the psyche. On this outer edge, she begins to learn about the state of the self and the outer manifestations of her behaviors. The dreams help the client begin to descend through the psyche from the outer edge, through all of the layers, down to the core feeling center.

Issues look very different when viewed from the reference point of the core feeling place than when viewed from the outer edge. To begin the ascent of Jacob's Ladder to grace, a person must be at core feelings. Experiences with the Animus, Anima and Spiritual Father, with dyadic and triangulation work in dreams are all preparation for the final ascent.

In order to even approach the ascent of Jacob's Ladder, a client must be able to feel in her being feelings that go back to what a child would feel; she must become the child self. Part of becoming the child self is sensuality because children are completely in their bodies and in the present without guilt, blame or projection. They have no projection because they have no self-awareness. Once a child has self-awareness, she has awareness of others and projection can enter. But with sensuality, there is no projection. Everything is within the autonomous self.

Many spiritual seekers work hard to find their way to essence, to feeling a connectedness with the Divine. But without the next rung of sensuality, there is no way to reach grace. Many spiritual masters have acknowledged at the end of their lives that they did not reach the state of grace. This is because they did not work with the state of sensuality.

It is easier for the psyche to feel essence than it is for the psyche to just feel. Feeling essence is a state of feeling without the personal or individual as part of the equation. Sensuality is that personal part of the equation. Most spirituality is aesthetic where there is no death of self. Aesthetic spirituality does not require the individual to work through her particular, personal issues. A person can dedicate her life to being some type of monk and work diligently to strengthen her connection with essence. But, without sensuality, it can be difficult to be in relationship because relationship requires all the personal elements. There are monks who have no idea how to be in relationship. Many monks in this position who have become leaders often fall into having multiple sexual partners because they are unable to be intimate. Sensuality is intimacy with God on a personal level. Essence is intimacy but not on the personal level.

People who are in the essence of aesthetic spirituality do not have profound dreams with the Animus and the Anima. There are many people who have a deeper connection to their spirit from the place of sensuality and are more spiritually evolved in this regard than someone who has spent twenty years in the place of essence. One of the biggest traps in spirituality is to connect with essence and have it be the destination.

Sensuality is a very controversial notion - even the word itself is controversial. Most people associate sensuality with sex and infidelity, something hedonistic. When a client receives a dream like the example above, she may even question her basic morals. The Archetypes will only present this kind of dream to clients who are highly moral and who would never attempt to act out the dream in the outer world. As Jung said, "This is only for people who are highly moral." Sensuality work is presented to clients who have done a great deal of deep work.

When a client is descending down through the psyche to her core feelings, she begins to have her feelings. The degree to which she has a relationship with her core feelings is the degree to which the journey of Jacob's Ladder can begin. A client with an intense and loving relationship with the Animus may not be ready to begin the ascent of the Ladder because she may not have reached core feeling. The core feeling is usually a key feeling for the client, one that allows the client to move into the realm of Jacob's Ladder.

For example, one client who was able to feel many feelings could still not be with the Animus. She still had projections onto men in the outer world because she had not gotten to one of the key core feelings for her. Then she had the following dream:

I am in a group as a teacher. A man is with me who is helping and supporting me.
He places his hand on my shoulder. I feel completely seen, appreciated and respected.

This dream was an important dream for this particular client because it brought her to the core feeling of being appreciated and respected. It was a very private, intimate, personal and specific feeling that when she could access it, cut through all of her projections.

The challenge is to descend deeper to find the feelings under the emotions and then to follow the feelings to the core feeling which is the key feeling for the client. The dreams help the client feel her way to this place, a new place she usually has never felt. Once she reaches that key feeling, Jacob's Ladder can begin. It could take years of feeling work to reach the unknown core feeling that will open up the work to another level. This opening happens when it is ready - not when the therapist or even client decides.

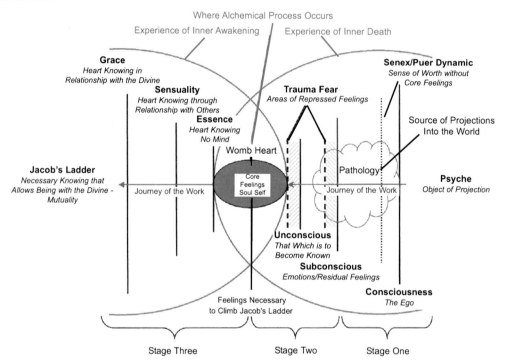

In the world of the psyche, a client does experience feelings as she descends toward the core feelings, but they are very limited. They often do not go beyond certain situations and they do not transfer to the Divine because of the senex/puer barrier. The senex/puer dynamic is the barrier between the world of God and the world of the psyche. Senex and puer are ways the ego tries to maintain a feeling of safety and control by balancing how it feels in relationship to others and the outside world instead of in relationship with the Divine.

It is difficult to separate the inner work from the outer work when a person still needs the world to reflect her beauty back to her rather than needing God to reflect that beauty. As long as there are unfelt wounds and unfelt feelings, the person will reflect the wounds back into the world and stay rooted in the world of the psyche. Staying in the world of the psyche means that the person cannot be in the world of God. The feelings in the world of the psyche must be felt by the client in order for the feelings to alchemize down to the core feeling. That intimate and uniquely personal experience of self where the Archetypes touch the client. Once this is reached, then the senex/puer barrier can be broken through and eliminated.

Most of the Dying to Self happens in the world of the psyche. By the time a client advances into the world of God, the most difficult part of the journey is completed. Unfortunately, most myths and stories of transformation end at this point of an individual's journey. For example, at the end of the *Lord of the Rings* trilogy, Frodo leaves Middle Earth, sailing to the undying lands of the west with the elves. His friends stand on shore and watch him sail away, then return to their world. The journey that begins for Frodo when he boards the ship is to leave the world, the world of ego building and finding his place and worthiness in relationship to what other people think. When a client leaves the world, her identity comes from her relationship with the Divine and is based on how the Divine sees her. The place of mutuality with the Animus becomes the way the client perceives herself.

Dream:

> I am a foreman working outside of a large house. I notice that a man is standing in the doorway of the house, waving for me to come and join him in the house. I say - "Oh no, I cannot go in the house. I am just a foreman."

In this dream, the client is being confronted with his idea of himself in relationship with the Archetype. He is content to be outside of the house working as a foreman instead of responding to the invitation of being in the house with the Animus and entering a mutual relationship with him. After he had worked through the issue, he had the following dream:

> I enter a great church with a man. The church has enormous beams that are covered with carvings from top to bottom. It is the man's home - a sacred and powerful place. I feel complete awe. The man begins to casually work on a computer, inviting me to wander and explore. Under the stairs, I find a small room in which are hundreds of pictures on the wall. All of the pictures are of me and they are all the most flattering pictures I have ever seen of myself. I have never known myself like this. I begin to understand my value to God. I am touched to the core with this newfound understanding of who I am.

The client's ego image of himself as a foreman had to change to being in the house with the man and being in relationship with the Animus. In this dream, he enters into that relationship and is shown his true essence as seen through the eyes of the Divine.

Archetypal dreamwork carries this potential - to bring an individual to where the dreams dissipate and the client is working on fundamental becoming, like a flower opening. Of course, not every person who enters into the dreamwork is going to follow the long road all the way into and through core feelings. For some, it is enough to resolve issues in the world of the psyche.

Jacob's Ladder and the world of God are not considered attainable until presented in dreams. Once a client is working in the Archetypal Realm, the rules change because the fight is not the same fight as in the world of the psyche. In the world of God, the person is in essence and she is outside suffering. The battle of suffering is in the world of psyche. Breaking through the senex/puer boundary into the Archetypal Realm is not a choice based on the client's free will. The role of free will is in the labyrinth of the world of the psyche.

Every time a client catches pathology in the world of the psyche, she moves deeper into her feelings and deeper in the journey of descent. Even when she comes to issues she believes have already been resolved, it is still a deeper step and a new opportunity even though the images may seem similar. For every step taken, there is another one and another one each with the opportunity of choice and exercising free will. Even though it can seem endless, there is an end when the core feeling is finally reached. But free will does not help determine whether the client can cross over the senex/puer barrier. If the client is not free of the spiraling world of the psyche then she is unable to be in the full world of the Archetypes. There is simply no room yet. Consciousness changes every time a layer of pathology is peeled away, every time a little of the old self dies and there is more of the soul self. When enough has been peeled away, then the Archetypes will bring the client into the other realm.

Dying to the Divine

Most of the Dying to Self happens on the ego side in the world of the psyche. The ascent of Jacob's Ladder is the second death, Dying to the Divine. Most people want to stay safe in the womb of clearing psychological issues. The bigger step is leaving that womb. Once out of the womb, the client can enter the alchemization of becoming the soul the Archetypes know that soul to be. Every opening is more death in this realm, but it is different than the death in the psyche. It is more sublime and creative. And much easier. In the Archetypal Realm, the soul is reconciling the self with God.

Deep spiritual longing is not part of Jacob's Ladder, but part of the world of the psyche. It may even be the core feeling for some. There is no longing for God in the Archetypal Realm because the person is in the actualization of that longing. Longing is important in the process. For to feel longing means to feel that there is a lack and it can be a great motivator to take the next step. It is the soul beginning to break through, feeling the want for the connection with the Divine. Longing can give the client a deeper feeling that is akin to manifesting the connection and can be the beginning of sensuality. But, ascending Jacob's Ladder is the becoming and the union that was longed for.

The Womb Heart

The Womb Heart is like an organ, just as vital as the heart, lung and kidneys, that contains all of the core essence material of an individual's soul. It is the container for the essence of what God created, the spark of creation unique to the individual.

The permutations of this revolve, evolve and spiral up into what becomes consciousness and moves into the world. Individuation, as Jung uses it, is the ascent of the soul self into manifestation in the world - the primalcy of being and consciousness at its most essential state in the world.

This has not happened in the human experiment.

The soul self is lost under multiple layers of adapted emotional behaviors, with parts of it often marbled in with toxic personality layers. The result is a uniqueness of individuality mixed with deadly toxin - an emotional life manifesting in the world as complicated behaviors carrying some beauty and truth but mostly a caricature of the true essence of the person and what he could truly become. The evolutionary process was thwarted long ago. Most people are living in the remains of a devastating emotional lie without even realizing it.

The descent of the self often involves an opening to trauma as part of the psychological journey, trauma feelings which are linked to the separation of the soul self and the separation of the individual from the Divine and Archetypal support.

The place where a person feels the support and love of the Archetypal Realm, the place where the true soul self dwells is the womb heart. It is the particle of truth in the psyche that is linked to the Divine and manifests as a point of light in the center of the soul. The development of this essence may be completely thwarted in a person. Through the dreams, the Archetypal process supports, deepens and completes the development of this self through the different stages of the dreamwork.

The power of the soul self is often misjudged so that what we believe and understand is largely less than what is actually possible. Working with dreams opens this in a miraculous way. The womb heart is the place where the individual resides with the Divine, where he can know the love and support and where an understanding of the true power of the world can begin to grow. When a person is standing rooted in his womb heart, he can look back out into the world with a great clarity.

Dreams that personify the womb heart often manifest as great feasts, golden cities, elaborate supportive love in ways that the client may even remember. The womb heart is the door to remembering essence, the spark of love, the Archetypal world at its best. It is the Shangri La of the soul where the sweet nectars of the male and female principles twist into a lemonade of excruciating consciousness.

The evolutionary ascent through the womb heart and through the process of Jacob's Ladder are simply the way in which the child self manifests consciousness and growth in terms of evolutionary potential. However, in order for transformation to occur in the ego realm, it must first occur through the subconscious womb heart and it must occur on the Divine's terms only. When a psyche has been prepared for this type of deep transformation, it replicates into the ego realm very quickly.

This, of course, is very advanced work. Core second stage work begins when a client begins to enter into his womb heart.

The womb heart is comparable to the alchemist's vessel - the newly revived soul that contains the spiritual core feelings of an individual can allow for the psyche to be redeemed. In this way, the perfect expression of Divine love through the individual is both acknowledged through its absolute awareness of the Divine, as experienced in Jacob's Ladder and juxtaposed with the exteriorization of this consciousness into the ego and its manifestations in the outer world. The Divine can now stand in the inside of the soul all the way to the outside. The individual can become a bridge between the two worlds. From this place, a calling develops and the person is able to fulfill his own being in obeyance to the Divine and its subsequent creative manifestation in the world.

Two Months

In the early snow a feather,
a cupped moon I plucked
from the cold horizon,
lifted its spine from my palm,
as if it had grown whole,
to fly up where it landed in the oak.

The sky turned, abandoned blue.
The white field had no place here.
In the dream she came with blond curly hair,
child of mine, child I will not bear.

Karla Van Vliet

CORE FEAR AND PAIN
THE SECRET INGREDIENT OF ALCHEMY

Core Fear

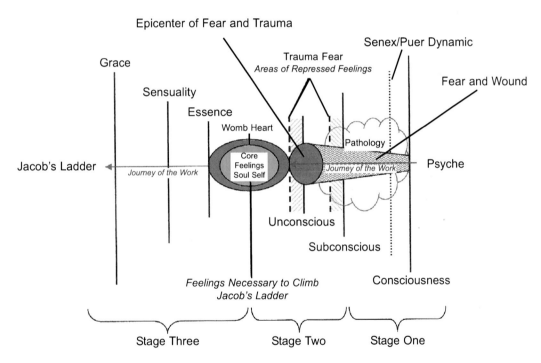

Fear is an important part of the process in order to enter into alchemical work. The surface part of this fear is often trauma mixed with pathology. Pathology uses the fear to engorge itself with spiritual possibility and, more important, to have access to the most vulnerable part of the soul self. When fear is used by pathology in this way to open the door and gain access to the self, it can render the client's possible connection to the soul self impossible.

This paralysis is linked to the ability of pathology to control fear, particularly as it relates to traumatic memories. When trauma is present, it catalyzes the fear in such a way that can seem only related to the traumatic experience. Core fear is related to trauma when it is present, but the core fear exists even when there is no trauma. There is a deeply buried core fear in every psyche, even ones without trauma, which underlies the subconscious and keeps the individual from the soul self.

Core fear does not need outer world events/experiences as a cause - it is a simple fact. But rather than being in opposition to Divine love, it is a bridge to that love. Only the complete acknowledgement of this fear will allow a person to be deep enough to reunite with the soul self and to begin the emancipation journey of climbing the rungs of Jacob's Ladder.

This fear is the most deeply buried of all feelings. Ironically, traumatic events can make it easier to access the fear because the conscious ego briefly touches into it through the memory of the event. Even though the memory is repressed, there is a natural opening through the event to the subconscious feelings that wait to be acknowledged and felt. These subconscious feelings, of course, also connect with the deeper core fear and while they can be confused with core fear, they are really very different.

Again, the traumatic event is not the cause of the fear, but it can offer the opportunity to catalyze the fear and bring it into some consciousness. In this way, trauma is not only the repression of fear, it actually touches on the core fear itself and allows access to the subconscious.

Without trauma, finding the fear can be a little more difficult, but it is still necessary. As a client descends through the stages and layers of the dreamwork as led by the dreams, and feels more open and connected, a moment will arrive when it all collapses back into this deeper realm. St. John of the Cross named this collapse the dark night of the soul. It is paradoxical that as the spiritual life opens, the client still must face this final, deepest transition into darkness and then back again into the light.

This deeper quest can occur in Second or Third stage work. Even teachers who have become aspirants to the Fields of Abraham may still need to cross this threshold. Sooner or later, every individual will have to face it, for it is the last shadow of separation from the Divine. As in all fear related issues, the ability to reach the fear and the experience of actually feeling it allows the client to know its absolute opposite - the love of the Divine that waits just beyond the cloud of separation.

Some believe the moment of birth caused access to this fear while others believe it is the necessary evolution in which an individual slowly finds her way to God. The origin or purpose of the fear does not actually matter. What matters is that there is no blame for this deepest of descents. It is beyond life as an individual knows it, beyond all experiences as they have been experienced.

This deepest pit that opens to the deepest, darkest parts of the soul is what finally breaks an individual into the daylight of his/her soul self. It is the release. And beyond what a person or pathology may project onto the fear, it is actually not as bad as imagined. Like anything else, it is just a feeling, one that has been felt before. All feelings have been felt, which is why a client must feel them again in order to move through. Often, the first experience of this core fear is the initial end of an individual's particular exploration and is the place where she got stuck.

The Blue Girl Crying
by Laura Ruth

Dream:

> I am playing outside with a girl. We come into my room. It is all blue- blue rug, blue walls, blue bedspread. It is nothing more than a bed and a closet, and no bigger. She is naked and I hold her in my lap as she weeps. She weeps because she does not like being sick and limited. I know she is weeping my pain. I comfort her. This has happened for two days, and I tell her mother that she is breaking through, she will be better when she finally lets go of her pain and fear. The door was open and the mother was there waiting for us to finish. I was worried that the mother would not trust me. Shift.

> Ken and I are driving beside a raging river. The water is high and I am absolutely terrified because I know we are going to take a canoe down it. He has made the plan and I know I have to do this so I say nothing, but I bury my face and head in his chest, scared to death, clutching on. I wake up shaking with fear.

The fear felt after the shift in this dream is very powerful. She is terrified because she is facing her death. The fear is the issue - it is not that she might die, but that she will surely die. Becoming the naked girl from the first part of the dream, weeping and being intimate with her own pain is the pathos of her soul. But she is not that yet - she watches and accepts it, but she is not the weeping girl. The opportunity to become the girl requires her to go back into the fear. The boat must sink or she must feel that it will sink and in doing so find that her life is going into the most terrifying moment. Feeling terror, clutching at the man's chest, shaking with fear as she awakens.

Trauma requires an openness to feeling. Many times, trauma does not even have a root cause. Sometimes, it is what the person brought into the world. In either case, Laura is going inside again to become the girl who weeps. The fear is the way to the girl, like a birth canal, back from this world to the next. It is the wardrobe in Narnia, but faster. Alchemy in action. The fear that was repressed by trauma is now released as the expression of fear she feels holding onto the Animus/Ken. For she must have his support, support he willingly gives her. Once through, she will be the girl again who, weeping, is open to the love at the very root of her being. No more fear will be required then because the girl will be free. The soul will be released from the repression of trauma and with its liberation, can know Divine connection.

The Core Wound

As with core fear, the core wound/core pain is very much connected and aligned with core feelings. They both parallel the descent into the psyche and bring the person into the core feelings and the alchemical process. Both the core wound/core pain and the core fear allow for the alchemical resolution and reconciliation of issues related to core feelings.

This process of descending into core feelings is reflected in outer events and memories. As the person moves deeper in this process, there are fewer and fewer memories to draw from in relation to the core feelings. All core feelings have nothing to do with memories of experiences that have occurred in life. While there may be unconscious ancestral memories that may be a factor, on the deepest level, fear and woundedness are simply the human condition.

Pain is often perceived as the abdication of self, where something "happened" to the self that created the hurt, the pain, the wound. This is experienced as loss or as something lost. In Stage One work and early Stage Two work, this certainly is the case. All feelings, particularly pain, are magnetized into events and scenarios in the person's life. But on this deeper level, there are no memories or scenarios related to the pain/wound and therefore there is no abdication or loss of self.

This leaves the question - then what is this pain? The pain is actually related to the emergence and affirmation of the soul self. For where the pain resides at this deepest level, there resides the love as well. Pain and love are together. The idea of loss of love from the Archetypal point of view does not exist. The Archetypal love, Divine love is never lost. The pain is the result of the separation of the client from his particular knowing of Divine love. Because this love is known and has been known, the client knows the pain of the separation from it. If one was never loved, there would be no pain.

This deeper pain is the memory of the love, of the connection with God. When a person feels the pain, it means that the love is not far behind. The core wound is simply the marker for the loss of grace and it serves as a reminder for its very existence.

Dream:

> I am passed over by a teacher for an activity I wanted to do. I feel pain or hurt. Then
> the teacher returns and chooses me after all. I no longer feel hurt.

If the client who had this dream was doing Stage One work, the idea of being hurt for not being chosen, then feeling loved, accepted and feeling good could be a necessary step in working through a repression of those feelings. This client, however, was in advanced Stage Two work and had worked through many of her feelings. This is an Archetypal dream. The client does not need to learn about love, hurt or need but needs to learn to recognize that the pain has nothing to do with being accepted by the teacher.

The pain is *a priori* - it has always been there. When the teacher returns in the dream and gives her the gift of participation, the pain does not actually go away. At this level, the pain is not related to getting what is wanted as in Freud's pleasure principal. The pain's existence was always underneath, bound with the deeper descent to God's grace and love.

Just as the fear awakens a person to the possibility of change, so is the pain the awakening and alchemizing agent of change - fear becomes essence and wisdom while pain becomes grace and love.

Once these feelings have been fully articulated and felt, Alchemy can begin. In so doing, the core feelings will awaken and emerge through the difficult feelings of fear and the pain of the core wound, manifesting as the reawakening of the true soul of the self.

Throughout a client's process, core pain and core fear emerge at pivotal breakthroughs. These initiation processes require the letting go of the various aspects of the ego which may manifest in dreams as falling off a cliff, facing a bear, having the heart ripped open. These are all ways to access the core dual feelings of pain and fear. Initiations not related to the individual's emotional history are related instead to evolutionary development. Every step of the way in these evolutionary developments/initiations into deeper awareness is steeped in these two feelings.

One of the major breakthroughs that taps into core pain is regret. As a client moves into Second stage work, consciousness expands enough so that he can see past errors and failings through the new vision of present knowing. In this new way of seeing, the blame game stops as the person can see and acknowledge his own participation in all manner of social contrivances. The naked raw truth is revealed without guilt or blame, just an awareness of the absolute participation in the unconscious self that has always wanted to destroy the true soul self. The core pain suddenly floods into the raw open consciousness and fills the person with regret and pain.

It is easy to confuse this regret and pain with guilt when the past is bemoaned from a place of over-responsibility or blame onto others. In the core feelings of regret, there is only one truth which pierces the heart - the love revealed in the wounded past. This is the beginning of true wisdom.

Another aspect of this pain is in the increased understanding of one's commitment to the Divine. As the pain deepens through regret, the true passion for the only goal worth knowing becomes evident to the person's heart. The heart remains pierced in the greater knowing as the pain of the past and the potential of the future that remains unlived becomes revealed. A new sense of unrequited longing emerges - a longing of the lover akin to Romeo and Juliet, Tristan and Isolde. It is the yearning for the reunification with the Divine. This yearning for reunification is fueled by the newfound core pain, which continues to spiral deeper as the client descends into the self through the evolutionary spiral, the spiritual acknowledgment.

With this pain, there is a knowing that allows the client to feel into his knowing - the knowing into the heart, the essence of vulnerability and of beingness. This work is advanced Second and Third Stage work and is achieved like a tree suddenly emerging in the perfect place, plunging upward into the heavens unsuspected; a surprise to the client and the therapist who can only stand in awe and celebration at the new awakening.

As with core pain, any change or awakening that does carry core fear in the emerging of something new in the self is not truly a transformation. Without the core fear, the change is only adaptation, perhaps a desire to please the therapist or the ego self without a true letting go. Moving through the fear allows for the true letting go and opens the opportunity for a true embracing of change and spiritual evolution. This is necessary for the connection to the soul self and the beginning of the odyssey of Jacob's Ladder to the fulfillment of the individual's calling. Like pain, fear gives a sense of meaning that otherwise could not occur. Adaptation allows the person to stay the same - he may have greater knowing, but there is no real change.

Fear and pain both allow for the movement into alchemical change. These twin feelings are not about something terrible wrought upon the soul, but are part of the alchemical process of true change and true knowledge that allows for the connection with the Divine. Without these feelings, change is simply managed, created and judged. Things are understood as good or bad, responsible or dutiful with the sense of having done something well. But it is like putting a shell over the heart, smothering its sense of the beatific, true grace and being accepted by the Divine. A person is not meant to serve the Divine as if he were a Marine. The intent is to be part of the obedience of being, not the duty of obedience or the obeying of obedience. To transcend the good/bad dynamic with the Divine, the client must get past the senex/puer sense of worth with its rebellious bolts of paradoxically ever-shifting ambivalence. Without these feelings, there is no true knowing on the soul level of the relationship with the Divine.

Core Fear/Pain and Projection

Staying with deep core feelings is very difficult because the psyche is habituated to project all feelings into the world and in so doing find a cause for the feeling. But ultimately there are no causes for the core feelings except our own separation from the Divine and the necessity to return through the Alchemy of feeling the core feelings. This aspect of the work, which is advanced Second Stage work, is the least understood and the least explored. Most spirituality work and personal therapy work are designed to bring people to a place of stasis or peace in order to create a certain level of stability in their lives.

Finding this kind of peace and stability is advanced Stage One work - "Pleased to meet you, hope you guess my name. But what's puzzling you is just the nature of my game." (Mick Jagger, "Sympathy for the Devil") At this level of the work, the pathology is not even broken nor is it even understood. It quite easily adapts to the newfound awareness of self that the client has found at this level of her work.

In this context, spiritual and psychological work that strives to reach the place of stasis/peace is a sham of tremendous proportions because it leads many to believe they have achieved some sense of Divinity or health when their "transformation" is really just a reformulation of the same thing. Even more difficult are the teachers/therapists who continue to perpetuate this status and/or even participate in inappropriate behavior behind closed doors using spirituality/therapy as a justification. Transference becomes more acute with every step taken toward spiritual enlightenment for every step taken means the increased likelihood of projecting core feelings. When core feelings are projected in this way, it is an attempt by an individual to avoid them by attaching her spiritual life onto those around her.

It is simply an iconoclastic belief system that creates fertile ground for manipulation by both teachers and students alike. To safeguard against such abuses, a code of ethics has been created to separate the teachers and the students. New laws are on the books that make it a felony to have sexual relationships with students. This could manifest with anyone who has power over another person - even in the cases of prisoners and guards.

This issue is not just a problem, but an epidemic as profound as the sexual abuse of children. However, circumstances surrounding the situations are not the failure or the fault. It is only the fact that the teacher/therapist and the student have not found a true connection with the Divine that is grounded in the soul self. When the true connection is found, it creates integrity and personal autonomy in which individuation can flourish.

What most experience as individuation is nothing more than a mutation of the process in which a person simply adapts herself to the outside expectations and mimics spiritual role modeling.

This toxic reaction stems from the projection of the deep core feelings. Projection always starts as an issue present in the psyche that is reflected in the world. The object in the world reacts and then actualizes the person's experiences and original wounds. This works to perpetuate the inner dynamic in the psyche in the world. As long as this is taking place, there is no way for the individual to do the inner work required for the Alchemy of change. The simple solution to this puzzle is to feel the core feelings, follow the dreams and limit the projections.

Of course, these kinds of projections occur with everyone an individual encounters, not just teachers or therapists but family, friends and coworkers. Other people react to the projections in all manner of human experience including sexuality, hate, illusions of love and intimacy. The key is that the projection always reflects the truth of what the person is feeling in the first place. When others react to it, they help recreate the issue that is inside the projecting person.

Everyone recreates the wound, hoping that others will solve the problem or find the answer. Or, foregoing a solution, a person may take on a predatorial relationship with the world in which the corruption and suffering are accepted and the person tries to make the best of it, often using others for recreational privilege.

Corner Posts

How long I had waited
for such words, sturdy timbers
to build with. *We will fill a house*
with love, they came. And I took
and shaped the corner posts.
It is a slow building;
a framing set with desire.

This time, I thought, this time
it will be different,
and I planted perennials.
When you took your words back
the world fell like a hard rain.
Please, I said, and what I meant was
How do I go on?
That I had become
a steel eagle on some trophy,
moonlight in the field,
gills on a hooked fish,
the cry of a gull,
green ice in a winter stream,
myself at eight
waving good-bye
to my father,
unwanted girl.
Please, I say, in language after language,
can you not understand one of them?

Karla Van Vliet

Receiving as an Act of Aggression

Most people think of receiving as a passive act in which the heart is opened and God pours his love right into and through that heart. But this is not the case. Receiving first requires Dying to Self which opens the door to the ability to understand and receive.

The act of receiving is one of the most confusing issues in this work and it means different things to different individuals. Receiving strikes at the heart of the essential meaning of the soul for the purpose of the soul is, in fact, nothing more than to receive.

This often manifests in dreams as a child who seems to need interminably. Its dependency on its parents is infinite and total. While this may sound passive, children in need are anything but passive in their needing. If they do not receive what they need, they cry and yell. A child only becomes passive (or passive aggressive or just angry) when giving up needing and demanding.

A healthy child is always reaching out, taking, wanting, needing, asking. Often many, many times. This is not a child being spoiled, but a child who needs its parents. It is not neediness in a negative sense, but actually aggressiveness.

One of the tenets of the work involves the development or redevelopment of this very passion, this need, this yearning. Wanting the way a child wants love, caring, support is a primary and primal passion that once lost is difficult to get back. Most learn that it is not appropriate to need, as if needing were tantamount to taking a bite of the apple. The belief is that there will certainly be punishment. The need is then converted into the many neurotic vicissitudes that are elements of the disease of our age. Part of the breaking down of the secondary ego self, the pathological self, is so that the individual can rediscover this primal need.

Children, reflecting this aggression adults lack, have been manipulated and abused by adult neurosis. The belief in the value of being an unselfish person is part of the neurosis of ignoring primal needs, and as parents with this belief, we enslave our children under the same yoke that we suffer under, believing we are creating loving citizens of the earth. But until people are free to receive love, they do not have it to give.

Being a good parent and instilling "good values" may be positive for helping to encourage the American way of education, job opportunities, ensuring a high quality of life. But this has nothing to do with the spiritual separation that follows in the wake of a person separating from her own soul. Although it is inevitable that this separation happens to everyone, regardless of the love a great parent may have to give, the journey awaits all to find their way back to that innocence. Back to the passion that can reintegrate into the adult psyche and can allow for a very deep capacity for vulnerability and mutuality with the Divine.

An adult with soul connection has the capacity for this relationship. One of the pivotal alchemical keys in the triangulation process involves feelings that lead to becoming the child with the

Divine. Being in a dyadic relationship with the Animus or Anima, unfortunately, still involves the reality of the separation from the soul, so it is not acceptable to the soul self. The work from this dyadic relationship is to go deeper and accept the need, the need as a child. In this way, a person can become open and supple and receiving. "For only the child can enter into the kingdom"

But this level of receiving requires a deep level of aggression, a deep willingness to Die to Self. The willingness to Die to Self is not just the expression of the need of the child, but the adult desire to claim the true self. Is it possible to have passion outside the passion, a need for the Divine without the connection with the child self? Does an individual need the child to need God or without that child need, does the individual have what it takes to arrive at that effort?

The work often fails for one reason - people simply run out of steam. They lose their passion or discover they never had it in the first place. Or not enough to truly finish their work.

When a client becomes uncertain about continuing the dreamwork, the therapist does not try to convince her to stay, unless the desire to leave is based on confusion about her current work. If the issue is about energy versus lethargy, then it may be time for the client to stop doing the dreamwork. There is no quick cure for this issue of lethargy except time to take in the gains that have been learned and to let the months and years have their way.

Without the passion for continuing the journey, the work is at an end whether the therapy continues or not. This is different from a client who is struggling with the work and may be questioning it. For this person, the questioning is part of the struggle with pathology.

For a person to really feel that there are other things to do that are better for them, who may be saying, "I just want to be with my life, to enjoy the fruits of the work," or, "This work does not excite me anymore," this shows that the work is done for that person. A therapist never encourages the end, but without the spiritual excitement or passion kicking in, then sooner or later the work is going to end for that person.

Crow's Retreat

The baby cries in darkness.
I do not know how to console her
in this world I barely navigate myself.

How can I tell her I have no power
to change the crow's retreat
so the dusk of their numbers
will not bring night?

What light there is I can only
point to, stars, slip of moon,
street lamp.

I hold her close to my drawn breast.
Where does this darkness leave?

Karla Van Vliet

Working in the Fields of Abraham
The Calling and Moving into Timelessness

Finding and embodying one's calling in Stage Three work does not necessarily mean that an individual cannot serve God unless he is truly connected with Him. An individual's ability to be with the Divine is more important than how the individual serves Him. Through the breadth and scope of the dreamwork, the question of "When will I know what He wants me to do?" is revealed through the necessary growth and process of the seeker. In this current quick fix world, most people want to become something now, but in past times, a person might study under a master's technique for much of his life before being able to actually turn the handle of the mechanism he has been studying.

Third Stage work is not just about a calling and receiving direction - it is the alignment of the self to the Divine in the particular way the soul self is congruent with the Divine. Since the Divine created the individual, what the individual wants and what the Divine wants for the individual are the same. There is no need of reconciling with the Divine work that happens in Stage One and Stage Two once the client enters Third stage work. Knowing the soul self as the Divine knows the soul self is a prerequisite for mutuality with the Divine. It is the quintessential culmination of an individual's journey - the soul blossoming through the awakening of the foundation of core feelings and the emergence of these soul feelings through Jacob's Ladder.

This is beautifully reflected in the image of working in the Fields of Abraham. When the son works in the Fields of Abraham, it is the manifestation of the son's desire. Working in the Fields engenders partnership - the son is working the Fields with his Father. The emancipated soul self knows itself in relationship with the other, to the Divine. The soul self always knows itself in relationship with the other - it knows itself as nothing in and of itself alone. It is only the ego that would does not see the partnership, perceiving the relationship as "I am working in my field for the father," or "I am working in the field for the family," or "I am working the field."

Many clients speak loquaciously about calling in First and Second Stage work. In Third Stage work, the client is in the Field of Abraham because he wants to be in the Field or because he feels that He wants him to be in the Field.

This way of relating the I-Thou dyad is part of the manner in which projection is created in the first place. In projection, the client knows the Divine or that which is an authority from the place of experience, good or bad, then uses that to project onto an object in a superior position. The way in which the ego functions in this manner gives rise to the senex/puer dynamic, which is the way the ego self determines its own worth.

For the soul self, there is no methodology to understand its importance. The soul self/child self simply feels love, pain or joy. It does not perceive itself through old memories and experiences. It only knows itself through the present moment of beingness. Through the experience of feeling, it is immersed in through its connection and contact with the Divine - moment to moment, breath to breath, blink to blink, beat to beat. This knowing is the soul self being in proximity with the Divine.

There is no I-Thou in terms of the ego self seeking its own worth. The ego seeking its own worth is fundamentally a conceptual process that is rooted in belonging rather than in being. When an individual is in a state of belonging, he is actually longing to be. In the state of being, the individual is in the state of this being. The mythos of working in the Fields of Abraham in the calling phase is simply an experience of love and acceptance not because of the accomplishment of doing, but rather the immersion of love bubbling into the soul self from the Divine. This effervescent joy is the goal. The calling is not a way to create an opportunity for being loved. It is simply a way of being with one's maker. In this, there is no goal other than the individual being with the Divine.

Congruency

A person may have a positive dream of unification with the Divine, but then finds that when doing her homework, she cannot access or even remember the feeling of the dream. This is because there are many cells between the unconscious realm and the worldly realm, as shown in the diagram below. There are different layers of the self that occur at different layers of the psyche, including the world. Even in the world, there are many layers. For example, a question can be answered in many ways because the truth is not one thing. The truth given from the heart would be given in a very different way than if the answer were given from the mind. No one wants to risk the real knowing in the world.

This struggle of knowing and different understanding exists in all levels of the psyche - from the cells of reality of the world all the way to the cells of deepest consciousness. People develop in different ways. Some people are more developed in the world, some are more developed in the subconscious realm, some are more developed in the unconscious realm. This wide variability leads to a multitude of problems, all of which the dreamwork is very adept at addressing.

Different Levels of Congruency with the Divine

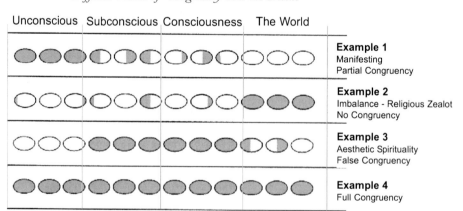

Different Examples of Levels of Congruency

There are several types of individuals in terms of congruency with the Divine, as illustrated in the chart. Sometimes, a client will express great frustration about her work because she has a profound deeper self that is developed, but that is inaccessible. This type of individual is shown in

Example 1, Partial Congruency. For this person, there is a great deal of development in the unconscious, but lesser amounts in the cells that move into the world. This is a more balanced individual for there is less deception or false knowing. The person does not know more about spirit in the outer world when she starts the work - in fact, she knows less. This creates frustration as the pain of the unknowing and its repressed state is felt more and more. This frustration, however, is good. It is better than the inertia and/or numbness felt before she started her work.

Example 2 shows a person who has more development in the level of the world than in the levels of the subconscious and unconscious. This may create a religious zealot or a wise man, but without the connection to the Divine in all of the levels, he is not fully congruent. He may have an idea of the Divine and he may even live the rituals of the Divine that might indicate spirituality. But the dreams would teach him that without the other levels, his belief about his connection is hollow shallowness.

Aesthetic Spirituality types, Example 3 above, have a strong development in the subconscious and conscious realms because they tend to be highly developed in their rituals and their ability to be grounded in their own autonomy in those religious rituals. They tend to put their focus entirely on the inner and to avoid being engaged in the outer world. This is not to say that Aesthetic Spirituality types do not serve in the world because they do. They just do not want to do so. This only serves to increase their charisma as spiritual beings.

Unfortunately, Aesthetic Spirituality types are still lost and the most seductive of teachers. By being intensely introspective only, by eschewing the world and its seductions, as far as can be seen at least, they are often mysterious and deep. They also can lead complicated double lives. While they have no development in the deep subconscious levels, it does not mean that they do not have spiritual potential. It means that they are not in connection or relationship with the Divine. It is such a waste to have so much potential, so much spiritual capability wherein the soul may be touching into Jacob's Ladder and spiritual love but without the necessary relationship with the Divine. Without mutuality, there is no congruence. Since the Divine lives in the deep unconscious, it requires very deep work to reach it. It is difficult to tell who does or does not reach this level of connection without the spade of the dreams to light such deep interiors.

Generally, the greater the development in terms of knowing spirit in the subconscious, conscious and the world self and the less in the unconscious and the subconscious, the greater the resistance to further growth in the individual. This is because the individual has more to lose. What she has to lose is all of the intelligence and knowing she has in the world, all of the ways that she has developed this intelligence in terms of ego formation that enhances power and control in the world. With so much to lose, it feels like there is more to lose than to gain.

In an individual who has consciousness of the Divine in terms of the deepest soul self, the unconscious shading is reflected up through the subconscious where the therapy works in a natural manner. All of this knowing eventually comes into all of the cells of the psyche. Until this powerful knowing comes into the world, the knowing that allows the calling, only then is the person useful to the Divine. Only then can the person work in the Fields of Abraham with Him.

The dreams show where and who an individual is no matter what she may think of herself, no matter if she has followers who believe in her.

Those who are bereft of spirit, those who know that they are disconnected and nowhere are ready for this work. There is nothing to lose; there are no false lies that have been built up, nothing they have used to convince others. It is the natural movement of the work from the unconscious to the ego. For those who have a high level of knowing when they begin, much of that knowing is corrupted and must be part of the Dying to Self. It is not possible to receive if there is no place to receive from. Too much knowing, too much intelligence, creates an obstacle in the process of receiving. When true congruency is achieved, when one is fully connected to the Divine, not necessarily fully awakened or perfect but fully connected, one is awake and listening with all of the cells of one's being. Congruency is not enlightenment or perfection - it is merely the openness of all levels of the psyche to the Divine.

Breaking into Pieces, into Him
By Laura Ruth

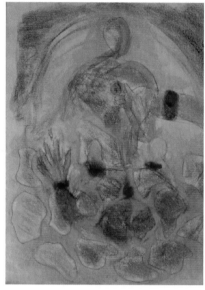

Dream:

> I am at a party, in a party dress, white with a green sash. I am a girl, at the edge of puberty or thereabouts, girl turning into a young woman. Not sure of feeling here - just feel like I am here. I am in the not-knowing place. Feel surprised to be in this particular dress because there is something special about this dress.
>
> There is a message for me on the direct line. It is like a little earpiece on the end of a wire out of the wall. Feel surprised that there is a call for me - then I just do what it says to do. There is no "voice" - once I put the earpiece in, I know what to do, which is to leave. I feel like oh, now I know what to do. I feel determination even though I still do not know what is happening. It feels like an obeying place - surrendering to follow the direction I received.
>
> So I leave to go to the car (even though I do not know how to drive, I am too young in the dream), through an alley or industrial track road with a chain link fence, deserted. I see three young men hanging out on the corner, the corner where I have to turn and keep going a little further. I feel a little scared, a little nervous. But my determination is stronger.
>
> One of them is my boyfriend. He comes and stands in front of me ten or fifteen feet away - I do not understand why he is standing so far away, but I know that something is going to happen and I feel open to it, but I am also scared. The fear is not ruling me, I just feel like I am waiting for I do not know what. He pulls out a little gun and

really quickly shoots me five times, each wrist, each ankle and in the middle of my chest. They were like metal rods, I remember the sound and the quickness of it. It did not hurt so much as it pinged - and it was like the rods went through me, into me. I felt like I was breaking up, breaking open but I also felt bound by the bracelets and anklets. In the breaking up, light is coming through. Looking down, I see the blood pooling around each wrist and ankle, like bracelets of blood, thick and an inch and a half wide. I felt a little in shock. When I look down at the blood pooling on my wrists and ankles, I know that this means: *You belong to Me.*

I feel He is saying that I need an escort.

I felt like I was breaking into chunks, like puzzle pieces with light shining through the pieces. The light was the cellular level and the puzzle pieces were chunks breaking open. Together, I felt I was being completely rearranged. I was aware of a bubble or egg of substance around the two of us as we stood there. It was as if nothing else could enter that space - it was just us.

Poem from Laura:

I have been
won over.

What else is there
to do.
When the air
becomes substance and
speaks
and says:
You belong to me.

There is nothing left
to lay down.
There is nothing left
to do.

So why do I cry
when I open
my mouth
and say:
I hear.
I heard when the egg
of air
that wrapped the two of us in its
wondrous substance
spoke.
I heard the
golden air speak.

Why do I cry
at the words:
You belong to me.

Why do I shatter
In surprise
when the bracelets of blood,
the anklets of blood,
appear
remain
draw me to them.

I am yours.

Why do I cry
when I open my mouth
in the company
of those I love
and speak
what happened to me.

I laugh to see
there is no more driving.
I need an escort.
Escort.
Gentle is this air.

Underneath the pieces
spreading one from the other
to reveal the light
there is a reservoir dark
and deep
of peace and stillness.

It is substance
like the speaking air.
It holds me.

I am yours.

And when I step into
the company of those I love
gently
I feel so vulnerable
that the shaking changes my breath.
My voice finds a hushed home

to speak from.
I am in the shattered place
hearing the gods talk
to me, in me, in the air.

I am young
and dressed in white
with a green sash that means something.
I know nothing
but to follow.
Why do I cry
when I follow my heart
when I know what to do
when it is time to step into the world again.

I enter the company of those I love
stepping into the world with my voice
stepping through the tears and the hush
stepping into the truth
stepping forth
with my escort.

I am stepping into the place where worlds meet
and I am terrified
to be

there. Here and there.
At once.
Here and Here.

I spoke to one.
I spoke to two.
Then two more. Then one. One again.
Now I shake to speak to six.
And I need to speak.
I need an escort.
An escort from each of you who I love.
And it is so hard to ask. To speak.
I feel so vulnerable.

And when it is time to step out of that sheltered place
where truth is spoken
held
heard
and gently escorted
from the great mystery into the waking world
as if in a hushed hall

long and golden and still
taken gently by hands of love
passed person to person, angel to angel,
towards a different quality of light
the light of the waking world
grateful for the peace
the fullness. . .

Why do I cry
Again I cried
Crumpled into the arms of the last two
loved ones
having spoken to six
I cried again
as if
my body
was breaking
into pieces.

And you two who I love
held me
while I broke
while I felt the shattering again
the bracelets of blood
shared
heard the truth spoken out of air
shared
until my tears were done and it was time
to step out again into the world
having spoken again.

Why do I cry.
To feel that love.
To share that love in the company of those I walk with.

It is so big.
It scares me.
That love
Is so big.
And it speaks and says:

You belong to me.

This dream is a manifestation of the deepest level of the work. Here, the experience of the crucifixion is linked to some essential alchemical experience. This experience both terrified and deeply affected every conscious pore of her body, deeply affecting every part of her being. The profundity of her experience goes beyond any words. It is an attempt of the Divine to take her spiritual capability deeper than her consciousness has ever understood. In this deepest of alchemical experiences and in the privacy of the dream, something happened that would affect the work and her spiritual calling for the rest of her life. It will make possible a profound intimacy with the Animus which is rarely obtained. It is the Divine's attempt at creating full congruency. He is preparing her to work with Him in the Fields of Abraham. It is in these deeper levels that the gift is given. Yet the true meaning of spiritual relationship is yet to be shared.

In doing this work, one may not necessarily obtain such a place of relationship with the Divine as is reflected with this individual. All the work that one does contributes to a gratifying life. However, it is to be appreciated and understood how deep the Archetype will bring us if we are willing to do what He asks. In this way, all of the cells from the unconscious to the world reverberate with the power of His presence and Divine love. Like a lightening bolt shooting through the very being of the person, so too the Divine would enter the soul. I would not want less for myself.

This is the deep well. The furthest in that is possible without having to physically die. The journey to the Fields of Abraham and the fullest sense of being in the Fields require the descent into this deep well. It is there that one finds the true life with Him. I know of no spirituality that exists without a direct personal soul to soul connection with the Divine. The dreams are like a giant screw turning ever deeper into this deep well. Ultimately, it is where the work will go, passing through the hurts, the loss, the ignorance, the lack of feeling, passing through the history of the past that has been long since forgotten. The screw turning through and in the underbelly of the core fear and pain that all humanity feels, and still turning into the place where He stands resplendent in front of us, driving us yet deeper into evolution and growth. The unfoldment within the deep well is the blossoming of our very selves and the experience of our selves that is completely new and unchartered. There is nothing I could say that is not just an implication of that future within each and every person. We are all capable of this, if we are willing.

Moving into Timelessness

"Time is of the Mind"
Marc Bregman, circa 1959

Time, indeed, is of the mind. If time is of the mind, then what of time is not? The opposite which is timelessness, immortality. And if this is not of the mind, then it is of the soul. The line between the mind and the soul is the work - the evolution of the psyche, the entering into the abyss and coming out again. This is the "time line" in which an individual goes deeper into his work, the place where time slows down. In this place, a person can become aware of the fact that he is not living just his seventy-five year life span, but the universal life span of fourteen billion years. At the place where a person meets God, where a person meets his soul, time ceases to exist.

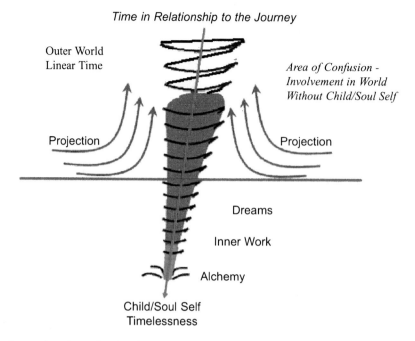

Time in Relationship to the Journey

Outer World
Linear Time

*Area of Confusion -
Involvement in World
Without Child/Soul Self*

Projection   Projection

Dreams

Inner Work

Alchemy

Child/Soul Self
Timelessness

Slowing down time into the timelessness realm means that reaction is slowed down, projection is slowed down, all the neurotic states of living are slowed down. Psychosis is a form of timelessness, but it is timelessness gone wild. Timelessness is psychosis without the insanity, the fear, the separation.

In timelessness, there is no separation from the Divine because the soul self expands past the short life of the individual. The past that is vaguely remembered, the life once lived, the self a person once was all revolve around the soul self. The charge of experiences from childhood and the immediate past are just fleeting memories that have no bearing on the soul self unless the soul lived through the memories. To find oneself is to live through the soul self rather than through the broken off shards that are called ego or Joe or Jane or "what I want to do for a living" or "what I do do for a living". The identities put upon the soul self that make a person say, "YES! This is what I am."

When the soul of the self is finally reached, when a person knows himself, there is a solidity and immovability in the connection that expands past the arc of a seventy-five year life span. It goes before and after so that the person can feel around the corner of the past, feel around the corner of the future. Death no longer seems an end of consciousness, but a continuation. All of this comes with the understanding of the relationship with the Divine.

The experience of time becoming slower is seen as freedom from reactions, freedom from projection. When the individual can see and feel himself through the eyes of the Animus, the true self can be seen. This laser like perception cuts through projection and pathology, and in that one stare, the person falls into an abyss of lifetimes of being seen and seeing the love that is always there. In this, there is only eternity. This moment can be lived in life not by stopping to smell the roses, but by becoming the rose. The place of no separation is where each person is the rose.

The descent of the psyche seems like a redundant, never-ending, reworking of the same issues over and over and over again. It is never a straight line. Each layer down is a process of working the issues, of seeing them, acknowledging them, accepting them and moving through the underlying feelings that produced the issues as well as the emotions that reflect them into something toxic. Until, finally, the Alchemy that allows the person to move deeper.

This descent into self is seen in the diagram above as a spiral because of this process of descending in a spiral manner through the layers of the self. Working against the spiral movement, projections work the other way, always forcing reactions and the old consciousness up to maintain the external involvement in the world and in time. Linear time is the time understood as schedule keeping, life and death, marriage and divorce, planting and harvesting - all the things to do with the cycle of life. This linear time, as romantic as it sometimes can be, is not actually the truth.

The truth is there are no seasons, no life and death, no blossoming and harvesting. There is simply God. Shining eternally on and within every person. The child self basks in this light. The soul reaches out from the inner unknowing of the conscious to blossom through the ego and, in an attempt to take firm hold of the psyche, hijack what was the old self to emerge as the truth within.

Projection comes from the lie - the old memories, the old hurts that make up the concept of self. Both the victories and the defeats are part of the material that is to be projected into the world. Many ask, "What is projection?" The real question is "What is being projected, thrown out into the world?" It is nothing more than the lie of the self, the ego that knows not of its truth. It only knows truth through the world, through linear time and experiences which occurred in that time.

The soul is like an alien visitor that lands on this planet and is completely confused by what the world accepts as itself. It must allow the confusion, the innocence that knows itself but that does not know the world. Many individuals who have come to the path of their dreams have said, and more than a few times, that they feel if they allow the soul self to emerge, that they would not be able to function in the world, to fulfill their job or even family responsibilities. The belief is that if a person allows the soul self, this inner innocence to emerge, then his whole life will go like a house of cards or like dominoes. Many cling to this belief the way maggot clings to garbage.

The projections must be dropped. The client is invited to follow the dreams to be shown who he truly is and to leave the world behind. One of the casualties of this process is that the client falls into the timeless reality. This does not mean, however, that the client can be late for work or that he does not take care of his children. In fact, in the timeless realm, an individual becomes more functional. From the inner timeless state, it is possible to be more present in the tasks performed in the world. It is also possible for the client to be more aware of the love he places in the world and in the things done.

There is an old Zen saying that goes something like this, "Before enlightenment, one carries the pail to get water. After enlightenment, one carries the pail to get water." This sounds like a Sartre nightmare. But there is another way to understand it - before enlightenment, one carries the water fraught and/or numb; after enlightenment, one is carried as he/she carries the water. In this understanding, alienation to the world comes only from the world that does not know the true carrier.

By being in the world in this different way - by being in the world but not of the world - an individual continues to fall through the labyrinth of feelings. The perpetual turning of this tornadic energy keeps driving us into deeper places. Time is replaced by feelings for timelessness is a place of feeling. And as these feelings deepen, they seem to replace the whole idea of time so that the idea of timelessness is suddenly known as feeling into experience, feeling into the world from the place of connection with the Divine.

At this level, timelessness is not defined as the absence of time nor is immortality defined as the absence of mortality. Instead, one's experience is defined as moving through the Alchemy of feeling. Fear, pain, love, joy, innocence are all timeless. Timelessness itself is a concept of the mind while feelings are alive, rich, thick with meaning. Since feelings replace time, they also ultimately replace the concept of timelessness. Feelings are part of Jacob's Ladder, the ascent into feeling. Essence, sensuality and grace are experiences of feeling not of concepts or thoughts or beliefs or knowledge as knowledge is understood. It is pure feeling, with all of its volatility and unpredictability.

It is not peace that is found, as a Zen monk might describe it, but absolute chaos. In that chaos, an individual is worked and is working in the Fields of Abraham, dancing with her teachers and makers on the inside.

Always Outside, Always Inside
Marc Bregman

I feel a pang in my heart as we journey to the Divine.
It is IN the world and not in the heart.
It is out here where the sharks are!
It is in the separation...
No matter how we try and bridge the gap it is always out here
with our families,
and friends,
and disappointments and struggles and losses and gains;
profits and concerns all the time, the constant maintenance of our relationships
and repairing all the things we build...

I feel a pang in my heart when I think that the work is in the world and it can be hurt
and weathered and torn.
I can be weathered and torn and hurt,
I can be hurt...

I feel a pang in my heart because I feel HIM in the pang,
and He hurts for the separation I feel... from Him.
He says the work is in the world and He is in the world and that is not
so bad,
But we forget Him and we create the security outside and then the work is lost to the world.
We are lost to the world...
I am lost to the world...

I feel a pang in my heart and He soothes it,
He soothes me, reminding me that I am not in the world at all.

I am with Him in the inside. Always in the inside.
And that the outside is only a reflection of the inside.
Only a mirror of what is with Him. That is who we are...
That is what the Divine is. It is the journey to the inside.
And once inside we can be in the world...

But this is so new for we have always been in the outside.
We are born to the outside...

I feel the pang again.
He reminds me that I am now twice born and I am now also on the inside

with HIM...
with HIM...
with Him...

Glossary of Terms

aesthetic spirituality - A form of spirituality grounded in essence but lacking in sensuality and therefore not transformational; results in an increased sensitivity to life but does not lead to Dying to Self and a relationship with the Divine.

Alchemy - The transmutation of the basic material of feelings into deep, inner spiritual change.

Anima - The archetype who embodies the feminine principle. Her role is to support and nurture the dreamer in preparation for a relationship with the Animus. Part of this role is as a healer through acceptance of the true self.

Animus - The archetype who embodies the male principle. His role is to empower the dreamer through relationship and to bring the lie of the ego self into awareness. For women, the relationship is as a lover and a teacher; men usually work with the Father to begin with, for the Animus is also a son of the Father. Once a man has become the Prodigal Son, he comes into a younger brother relationship with the Animus.

arcs of the dreamwork - The long arc is the specific archetypal plan that is the defining intention for the individual dreamer. In this arc, the unfoldment works by one piece of work weaving into another through valleys, chasms, steep and winding paths ending in great plunges to nothingness. The small arc is where the dreamer works with the causes and effects that seem to define everyday life. The pathology offers less resistance to the small arc of the work, but fights every step of the long arc.

Archetypal Realm - The unconscious realm of the psyche where the Archetypes live and where the dreamer is in the soul self and thus can be in relationship with the Archetypes.

Archetypes - Beings in dreams and in the psyche whose role is to bring the dreamer into relationship with the Divine. Archetypes are vessels of love and essence.

biological imperative - The physical, instinct-based command in all living creatures to reproduce offspring in order to ensure survival of the species.

blind spot - The way the ego perceives both itself and in general, creating a place in the psyche where the dreamer is eclipsed by pathology.

child self - The true self capable of relationship with the Divine; often manifests in dreams as a child.

congruency - An openness of all levels of the psyche to the Divine so that the inner reality and the outer reality are not at odds with each other.

conjunctio - A Jungian term meaning "to come together"; the essence of Divine relationship, which requires that the vessel of the individuated soul be separate from the Divine at the same time it is of the Divine.

dark mother - A dark feminine aspect of pathology that can manifest in many ways including the devouring mother, the shaming mother, the needy mother, etc.

dark night of the soul - A period in the dreamwork process in which the dreamer, having opened to feelings and a connection to the Divine, collapses back into the deeper realm of suffering and darkness before emerging again into the light.

dyad - The dynamic in which the dreamer, in a current state of being, is in an oppositional relationship with another element of the psyche, such as an Archetype, a feeling or pathology.

Dying to Self - The process of letting the persona/false self, which is created in compensation for the separation from the Divine, die in order to become the true self, which is in relationship with the Divine.

ego - A field of consciousness that has the capability to contain consciousness from both the subconscious and the world.

essence - An individual's particular capacity to feel God's love in a direct and personal way. A person in essence has the heart that can know God and can experience God's love through the feeling realm; one of the rungs of Jacob's Ladder.

gestalt - A process in which the dreamer speaks directly with aspects of a dream which helps the therapist discover or deepen what the Archetypes are trying to bring into consciousness

grace - The direct encounter with God; one of the rungs of Jacob's Ladder, which also includes both essence and sensuality; the highest octave of receptivity of the Divine.

homework - The process of working with a dream image or feeling in order to bring more into consciousness what the dream is calling the dreamer to do or feel in terms of relationship with the Divine.

individuation - The transformation of knowing the self through the soul; experiencing oneself as the unique person God intended; the highest octave of the dreamwork.

introjection - The process of taking an emotion that is projected onto the world and returning it to the inner world using a dream image; the goal is to uncover the feeling underneath the projection.

Jacob's Ladder - A motif for understanding the elements of receptivity of the Divine. The rungs of Jacob's Ladder are essence, sensuality and grace. To be entirely receptive to the Divine, the dreamer must have all three receptors open.

pathology - The force within the psyche whose intention is to keep the person from feelings that would open him or her to the Archetypal Realm.

pleasure principle - Freud's belief that people are driven to gratify pleasure instincts; when outer situations are good, they are happy; when outer situations are bad, they are sad.

polymorphous perverse - The period of development in early childhood when the child is freely amoral and has no self-consciousness. The child is open to his or her immediate sensual exploration and all the feelings associated with it.

primalcy ("primal sea") - The deeper levels of vulnerability, such as pain, yearning, need and passion, that represent the flow of energy from the realm of personal need and expression.

projection - The justification of why people feel the way they feel by believing that their fear and pain are the result of something external - others, the world and life situations. When projecting, an individual is avoiding true feelings that would ultimately lead to the Divine

psyche - The vessel that holds the imagination, soul, dreams, feelings and even the pathology of a person; the container for the dreamwork journey; an inner room where the theater of transformation can take place.

puer - One of the gatekeepers of the psyche that attempts to keep the person grounded in the outer world; the puer creates a barrier to the Divine through a feeling of well-being and a failure to take responsibility for oneself in an immature or falsely innocent way while ignoring deeper feelings. The puer separates from the core feelings through sentimentality. The puer is not to be confused with the child self.

second death - Dying to the Divine; coming into direct relationship with the Divine; experiencing congruency between the self and the Divine.

senex - One of the gatekeepers of the psyche that attempts to keep the person grounded in the outer world; the senex creates a barrier to the ego through guilt, shame, overresponsibility, duty and structure.

sensuality - The ability to feel God's love in the body in a way that is unique to each person; the capacity to sense the power, passion and intensity of being in relationship to God through the tactile self; one of the rungs of Jacob's Ladder.

soul self - See *child self*.

trauma - Occurs when a person becomes disassociated from the soul self and feelings through the repression of fear; the point at which the person stops being the child; the place in the psyche where the child self waits to be reclaimed. Trauma is not a traumatic event but the repression of feelings that can happen as a result of a traumatic event. It is possible to have experienced traumatic events without having trauma in the psyche.

triangulation - The appearance in dreams of three elements: the dreamer, the Archetype, and a feeling or being (often a child) through which the dreamer can come into relationship with the Archetype; precedes Alchemy.

whoremaster - An aspect of the pathology that manifests as a pathological figure that can be either male or female and resides in a place in the dreamer's psyche that specifically has a sexual root. Having a whoremaster pathology typically, but not always, manifests as a person acting out in promiscuous ways.

womb heart - The alchemical, sacred vessel inside every person where archetypal transformational and alchemical work take place. The place of profound vulnerability where all feelings can live.

wound - The place in the psyche where the original hurt or trauma that caused the separation from the Divine resides.

INDEX